MACHINES

AND

MORALITY:
the 1850s

*"Lower Manhattan from New Jersey, 1845-50," a gouache by
Nicolino V. Calyo.*

MACHINES

AND

MORALITY:
the 1850s

BY ROBERT SOBEL

Illustrated

THOMAS Y. CROWELL COMPANY

NEW YORK · ESTABLISHED 1834

Designed by Judith Woracek Barry

Manufactured in the United States of America

ISBN 0-690-00266-1

Library of Congress Cataloging in Publication Data

Sobel, Robert
  Machines and morality: the 1850s.

  Bibliography: p.
    1. United States—Economic conditions—To 1865;
2. United States—Industries. 3. United States—
Social conditions—To 1865. I. Title.
HC105.6.S65 1974   309.1'73'06   73-14729
ISBN 0-690-00266-1

1 2 3 4 5 6 7 8 9 10

The Origins of Interventionism
The Big Board: A History of the New York Stock Market
Panic on Wall Street: A History of America's Financial Disasters
The Great Bull Market: Wall Street in the 1920s
The Curbstone Brokers: The Origins of the American Stock Exchange
Amex: A History of the American Stock Exchange
The Age of Giant Corporations
For Want of a Nail

Conquest and Conscience: the 1840s

FOREWORD

Machines and Morality: the 1850s is the second in a retrospective series, commissioned by Dun & Bradstreet Companies, Inc., and published by a distinguished subsidiary, Thomas Y. Crowell Company, Inc., that focuses on the significant socioeconomic events and trends of past decades and their effect on business. The first book in the series, *Conquest and Conscience: the 1840s*, also written by Dr. Robert Sobel, was published a year ago.

The richness of America's historical landscape is itself justification for renewed exploration. Yet the significant purpose of this series is to delineate the decade-by-decade progression of American business—within the broader framework of social and political events, combining to shape a proud though occasionally flawed heritage.

Although we are often told that history does not repeat itself, the frequent remarkable parallels between past and present tempt us to believe otherwise. History, to be sure, cannot repeat itself, just as no moment, nor any other measure of time can pass more than once. However, the nation's past mistakes can be repeated; its successes can be redoubled; and in times of crisis, its spirit can be revitalized. And as history recounts the greatness and failings of our forbears, it can—it should—afford a better understanding of ourselves, and our own capabilities.

In the current era, the decade of the 1970s, American business is greatly concerned with reaffirming its place in society, and reassessing its responsibilities to society. Business is frequently held accountable for the nation's ills, although the cause and effect relationships are often obscure. Yet management must face the present challenges put to it. In these endeavors, Dun & Bradstreet is hopeful that some insight will be gained from these historical presentations of business in society.

Chairman of the Board and
Chief Executive Officer

CONTENTS

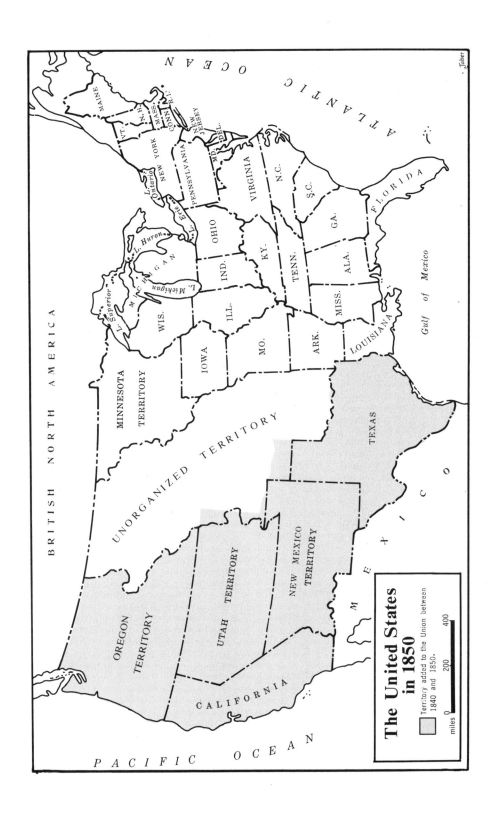

The United States in 1850

Territory added to the Union between 1840 and 1850.

miles 0 200 400

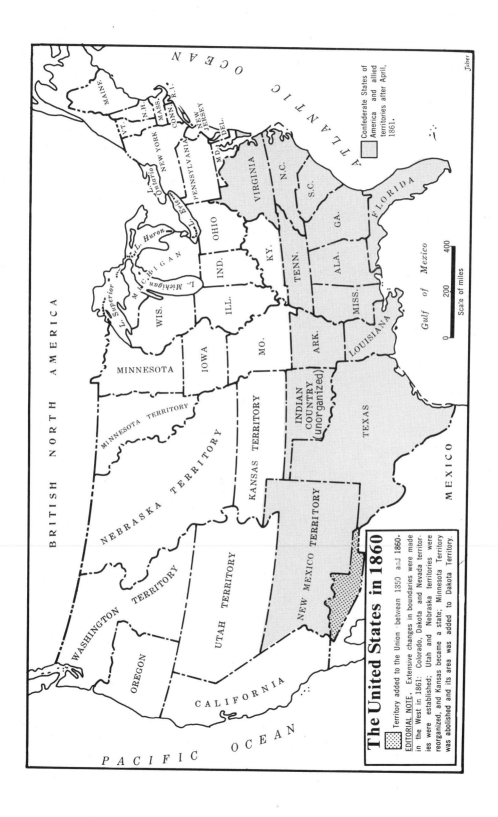

The United States in 1860

Territory added to the Union between 1850 and 1860.

EDITORIAL NOTE. Extensive changes in boundaries were made in the West in 1861: Colorado, Dakota and Nevada territories were established; Utah and Nebraska territories were reorganized, and Kansas became a state; Minnesota Territory was abolished and its area was added to Dakota Territory.

Confederate States of America and allied territories after April, 1861.

MACHINES
AND
MORALITY:
the 1850s

INTRODUCTION

January 5, Saturday. Another New Year, and the beginning of a new decade. Thus far I have found it a dreary period enough. Were I possessed of a reasonable, average good sense, I should be of good courage, dismiss all my forebodings, and look forward to the happiness which more or less is mixed up with the other ingredients in twelve months of every man's life, and not to the inevitable cares and the possible sorrows that are only made heavier and more bitter by anticipating them—and I should think more of the things to be *done* than of the things to be enjoyed or suffered. But I'm not commonly very rational on the subject of borrowing trouble, and for the past week I've been in a particularly uncomfortable and unreasonable state of mind.

SO WROTE GEORGE TEMPLETON STRONG, A THIRTY-three-year-old Wall Street lawyer, in the first week of 1850. Strong was concerned over the state of the city, where urban crime was on the rise. He worried about the nation, where the men of compromise were being challenged by others who stood for moral causes. The business climate troubled Strong, for although the depression of the early 1840s had passed, he feared a new one was on the way, due in large part to weaknesses in the nation's financial structure.

Strong had experienced a personal tragedy the year before; his wife had lost her first baby and almost her own life. He had also suffered through several minor illnesses of his own. Such problems weighed on his mind in January, 1850. Nonetheless, he was of good cheer. Life was good, in the main, and would get better. His wife was better, and they planned to have other children. His parents, though aged, were in good health, and Strong's business career was doing well.

Though hardly typical, George Strong's attitude reflected those of many on the eve of the 1850s—problems and hope, interwoven.

The decade would bring great change to the country in the form of an economic transformation from an agrarian nation to a budding industrial one. Towns would blossom into cities and small railroads become major carriers, while the newspaper industry would become more powerful than Strong or anyone else could have imagined in 1850. There would be a business collapse, then a swift recovery. The insurance industry would enter into a growth phase, while the business of credit, already important in the 1840s, was to become even more so in the following decade, a vital handmaiden of the new industrial order.

George Strong would prosper, even as the nation appeared to march toward a major confrontation. Machines and mo-

2

rality—these would be the two major concerns of Americans in the 1850s. Machines helped lead the nation into a new period of material well-being. Morality presented Americans with a paradox that seemed insoluble. It was a decade, then, of success and frustration, accomplishment and failure.

All of these were shared by Strong, though on a minor scale. And on the last day of 1859, the now forty-three-year-old lawyer looked back and thought of what the past decade had meant to him. Peace had given way to talk of war, conciliation to threats of conflict. But as he had been in 1850, Strong was more concerned with what the years had meant to him personally. Writing in his diary, he said:

> December 31. This year and this decade will soon be among the shadows of past times. It seems scarce possible ten years have passed since we went out of the forties. They have been ten years of change. Two more have been given me—the two little men whose portraits Ellie and I have just been admiring: God protect them both—and two more have been taken away, my mother and father, since December 31, 1849.

1 / CONFIDENT AMERICA

IT HAD NOT BEEN AN EXTRAORDINARY NEW YEAR'S EVE by any measure. The upper classes in New York and Boston, St. Louis and Chicago, New Orleans and Philadelphia, met in small parties on Monday evening, December 31, 1849, and talked and toasted the night through. At the stroke of twelve many raised their glasses to the memory of George Washington and the health of Zachary Taylor, the hero of the Mexican War and president of the United States. The saloons and dives were packed with members of the lower class, seemingly intent on drinking themselves to insensibility on cheap gin. It snowed that night in Boston and Chicago, and the next day both cities reported the deaths by freezing of several mendicants who overdid their celebrating. Meanwhile, on the small farms of New England, the larger ones of Pennsylvania and New York, the plantations of the South, and the many family holdings that surrounded them, families and whole towns gathered for the celebration. Farmers in log, plank, and sod hovels in Indiana, Illinois, and Missouri welcomed the New Year by continuing their every-day-and-night work of trying to keep their farms together. A newspaper in Chicago spoke of the benefits of the land, the promise of the new decade. Its words were echoed by similar journals in other parts of the country. Of course, it was not the start of a decade—that would come in 1851. But Americans like to celebrate, and even then were addicted to the practice of measuring their progress against the scale of ten-year intervals.

Few peoples in the history of the world have believed so much in progress and its inevitability as Americans, and those of the 1850s were no exception. The celebrants that evening might have reflected on the successes of the previous decade —recovery from a severe depression, a successful war against Mexico, the extension of the nation to the Pacific and the addition of new states, the discovery of California gold that marked the beginning of a new era of prosperity and, what was more important, the promise of more to come. Reflective Americans might have noted that ten years earlier there had been prophecies of dire events, and that none of these had taken place. There had not been a sectional war between slave and free areas, as the abolitionists had predicted. Nor had there been a class conflict between wealthy and poor, native-born and immigrant, as some political factions had desired and worked for. Several religious sects had predicted the world would come to an end in the 1840s; although they had relatively few adherents, other Americans, noting civil dissension and riots, might have been forgiven doubts as to the continued existence of the United States as a political entity. Both the world and the nation survived into the 1850s.

The 1840s had been a hectic time, one of protest and violence. Abolitionism, women's rights, utopian socialism, and temperance attracted followers. Mystical religious and semi-religious sects, phrenologists, rappers and dunkers, and other bizarre individuals and groups came to the fore and received more attention than perhaps they deserved. It had been a decade of fads and fancies, with P. T. Barnum as good a symbol as any. The nation's destiny, which older Americans believed had been ordained in heaven and established on earth by the founding fathers, seemed clouded in such times. But America survived these strains, overcoming or absorbing several protest movements and defeating or deferring others. The nation seemed reinvigorated by the effort.

Americans who had been alive during the Revolution—and there were many in 1850—could reflect on the progress the nation had made in its short history. In 1790 the United States had a population of some 3.9 million and a land area of 864,000 square miles. The 1850 census showed that there were 23.3 million Americans living on 2.9 million square miles. Of this number, only 17.3 million were native-born whites, while an additional 2.2 million were foreign-born. The rest—3.8 million—were Negroes, of whose number all but 400,000 were slaves. The slave and foreign-born populations formed majorities in some parts of the country, although each was far from the other.

One of every seven residents of the Northeast was born in Europe; in 1850 the South's white population was 5.6 million, its slaves, 3.2 million. Few immigrants were drawn to the slave states, since there was relatively little demand for their labor. Thus, the population increase in the South was due primarily to the birthrate. In 1850 there were 892 white children under the age of five for every thousand white women between the ages of 20 and 44; the figure for slaves was 1,087. In more than one-third of the southern counties there were more slaves than whites; the birthrate clearly indicated that the number of such counties would grow rapidly in the next decade.

The increased immigration to the United States in the 1850s was caused by the desire for greater economic opportunity and political freedom. Almost every part of the old continent had been wracked by revolutionary forces in 1848. The Young Ireland movement led an insurrection in Tipperary which failed, resulting in further repression in that land. In May the Frankfurt Assembly met to deliberate the possibilities of liberal German unification, and this too ended in disaster. Revolution in France led to the fall of King Louis Philippe and the establishment of a shaky republic. Nationalist movements in Austria-Hungary were ruthlessly suppressed by the government. Generally speaking, the losers in all these civil wars were drawn to the United States, among them idealistic and ambitious Irish peasants and middle-class German farmers and businessmen.

Europe sent 308,000 immigrants to America in 1850, a record high which would be broken the following year, when transatlantic fares were as low as $10. More than half of them came from Ireland, while another 78,000 arrived from the Germanys. Then, in 1851, another 221,000 Irish came to America, most to settle in large eastern cities, but some to journey to western farmlands. Eastern newspapers carried sto-

ries of the "Irish invasion," and demands for immigration restriction, loud in the early 1840s, were heard once again. But
1851 was to be the peak year for Irish immigration; during
the 1850s the end of the potato famine and improved agricultural conditions at home, hopes for independence, and the
lure of other foreign ports would lead to fewer and fewer settlers each year. By 1854 only 101,000 Irish came to America.
In contrast, German immigration increased sharply, reaching
a high point of 215,000 of a total of 405,000 immigrants in
1854. Wealthier than the Irish, the Germans were able to
move westward shortly after arriving in America. While
New York and Boston were rapidly becoming Irish enclaves,
Cincinnati and St. Louis were to be German-American in
character.

These demographic forces changed the population structure of the nation in the 1850s. Some 5.6 million more native-born Americans inhabited the United States by 1860,
approximately half of whom were second-generation Americans. The foreign-born population increased by 2 million in
this decade; the number of foreign-born Americans was almost double its 1850 figure. In this same period the nation
added approximately 400,000 Negroes to its slave population,
almost all in the South. By 1860 there were 7 million whites
in that region, and 4.1 million Negroes.

Virginia led all southern states in population in 1850,
with 1.1 million inhabitants, while Georgia, with 906,000,
was in second place; but neither state grew rapidly in the
1850s. At the other extreme was Texas, whose population
tripled; in 1860 it had 604,000 people. Florida, Mississippi, Alabama, and Arkansas showed impressive growth, but only the
last of these doubled its population in the 1850s. As for the

other southern states, they tended to stagnate. South Carolina had 668,000 inhabitants in 1850, and 704,000 ten years later.

New York's population rose from 3.1 million to 3.9 million in this decade, a population increase greater than that of the combined South Atlantic states except Florida. Massachusetts increased by 236,000 to a total of 1.2 million; it added more citizens than did any southern state except Texas. By 1860 Pennsylvania had more inhabitants than the combined populations of Virginia, Georgia, and Texas.

The Northwest experienced an even more rapid growth. In 1850 Ohio had slightly fewer than 2 million inhabitants. Some 400,000 were added in the next decade, and Ohio became the third largest state in the nation in 1860. In the same period Illinois went from 851,000 to 1.7 million, while Michigan and Wisconsin doubled in size. Minnesota, with only 6,000 people in 1850, had 172,000 in 1860. And in the Far West, California's 1850 total of 93,000 swelled to 380,000 by 1860, and Oregon's 12,000 to 52,000.

In 1810 32 percent of the American people lived in the South; by 1850 the figure was 27 percent, and in 1860, 26 percent. The Northeast showed a still sharper decline, from 55 percent in 1810 to 40 percent in 1850 and then to 37 percent in 1860. The West, with only 13 percent in 1810, rose to 33 percent in 1850 and 37 percent in 1860.

These figures offered a message that was clear enough: the balance of American political and economic power was rapidly shifting westward. The nation's future would be determined west of the Appalachians, and within a generation or two, west of the Mississippi. The Irish in the Northeast, the Germans in the Midwest, the Negroes in the South all seemed to threaten the old native-born power structures. These figures, more than any speech made by any political leader or any bill passed by Congress, would determine the future political and economic life of the nation.

Despite the many reasons for rejoicing, the national mood was somewhat somber on New Year's Day, 1850. For one thing there was the serious cholera epidemic that had swept the South late in 1849, and was now on its way to the Midwest and Northeast. Not until spring would its ravages end, leaving hundreds of thousands dead. Southerners blamed the epidemic on the North, which in turn noted that the first cases appeared in New Orleans. Anti-Catholic elements in the large cities and the Midwest believed it no accident that the cholera had come with the rise in German and Irish immigration. In early 1850 the Supreme Order of the Star Spangled Banner was organized, to fight Catholicism and immigration throughout the nation and demand a closing of the ports to newcomers.

Social reform was still in the air in early 1850. The abolitionists still predicted ultimate victory. Crusaders for women's rights received more publicity than before, as Mrs. Amelia Bloomer began wearing what seemed to be trousers in public. The first Women's Rights Convention, held in Seneca Falls, New York, near the home of Mrs. Elizabeth Cady Stanton, took place in October, and some fearful men thought they smelled revolution in the air. Then there was the talk of a revolution in morals, which was evinced by the popularity of Nathaniel Hawthorne's new novel, *The Scarlet Letter*, an underground best seller. Such events might well have convinced middle-aged and elderly Americans that the world in which they had been raised was on the verge of great change.

For many Americans change meant the West, and the Far

A Currier lithograph, dated 1851, celebrating Amelia Bloomer's recent fashion innovation.

West in particular was in the midst of change in 1849. This vast land, running from the old Louisiana Purchase to the Pacific, remained unorganized for the most part. Already one part of the new lands, California, had provided America with the valuable golden dividend. But California also created problems. Violating laws and the Constitution itself, California had declared itself a state, written a constitution, and held elections, and now demanded Congress recognize it and admit its senators and representatives to their seats.

12

California's rapid growth also raised the issue of a transcontinental railroad, which the older sections agreed should be constructed as soon as possible. But they disagreed as to its eastern terminal. Some spoke out for New Orleans, others for Chicago, while a third group favored St. Louis. One of these cities seemed destined to receive the congressional boon, but which would it be? Illinois, Missouri, or Mississippi would become the key to the West, and the West, as always, was the key to the nation's destiny. New Orleans or St. Louis would assure a southern destiny, and all that implied, while a Chicago terminal would indicate the West would be dominated by, settled by, and vote with the old North in all matters of importance. These included the tariff, internal improvements, the banking system, foreign policy, further national expansion—indeed, all matters of national concern, including the unspoken but unsettled question of slavery, which haunted the nation in the 1850s as it had during the previous decade. Upon their resolution rested the future of southern cotton and midwestern wheat, the future of American industry and the growth of its transportation network, especially the railroads. Unless and until these residual problems were solved, the nation would know no peace. And while the parties were taking place throughout the nation, and the 23 million Americans of that day and night met to celebrate or think of the past and future, the issue was being debated and discussed in Washington's drawing rooms and chambers, in the rooming houses where most congressmen lived, and in the cold streets and frozen-mud avenues of the capital.

If the nation's political leaders succeeded in finding a compromise on several remaining issues of the 1840s, one that would satisfy, pacify, or neutralize the leading factions in the capital, then it would appear America could face a decade of peace and prosperity. If they failed, it might mean civil war in the first year of that decade.

The political atmosphere of 1850 was confused and clouded. Ten years earlier politics had been relatively simple. At that time there were two loosely organized coalitions of state and local parties known as the Democrats and the Whigs. The Democrats generally opposed a national bank, favored lower tariffs, found support among immigrants and southern planters, frowned on a national program of internal improvements, and were suspicious of men of commerce. Their hero was Andrew Jackson, and they followed his protégé, Martin Van Buren. The Whigs accepted the rudiments of Henry Clay's old American System, which included plans for internal improvements, a national bank, higher tariffs, and measures favoring the emerging business class. Both the Democrats and Whigs were national, with clubs in all parts of the country. They were ideological enough to have cores and generalized philosophies, yet nebulous and pragmatic so that local Whigs and Democrats could take stands opposed to those of national candidates. In 1840 neither coalition took much of a stand on slavery, in part to avoid the issue, but even more because at the time, it was not believed a major source of political contention.

This changed in the 1840s, and as both parties twisted and turned to meet and avoid the problem, a third political grouping appeared. It went under several names, but after the Mexican War was best known as the Free Soilers. The new grouping drew from both of the old parties—from the Whiggish Adams clan of Massachusetts and the Democratic

Van Burens of New York. It was strong among midwestern farmers, had support in parts of the commercial world, and indeed seemed a growing force in all parts of the nation save the South. In the presidential election of 1848 Whig Zachary Taylor received 1,360,000 popular votes and 163 electoral votes, while Democrat Lewis Cass of Michigan's totals were 1,220,000 and 127. Running on the Free Soil ticket, Van Buren received 291,000 popular votes, 120,000 of which came from New York. Had Van Buren not been on the ballot, most of his votes would have gone to Cass, who then would have captured New York's 36 electoral votes and with them, the presidency. The Free Soilers provided the balance of power in 1848, and promised to do even better in 1852.

The Free Soilers also ran congressional candidates in 1848, and while most were defeated, 12 did manage to win election to the House of Representatives. The new House, which met in December, 1849, also contained 112 Democrats and 105 Whigs. As had been the case in the electoral college, the Free Soilers provided the balance of power in the new legislature.

Immediately they began to bargain for power with the two major parties' leaders. It appeared that whichever party the Free Soilers favored would organize the House and select its speaker. Then the coalition could pass the kind of legislation it wanted to resolve the outstanding issues, including that of the western territories, the tariff, and bank policy, and perhaps even the matter of a railroad. The nation's future too seemed in balance. By 1849 the Democrats had become a basically southern party with a strong but secondary northern contingent, while the Whigs were strongest in the North, and their southern adherents were swiftly drifting into Democratic ranks. It was North vs. South, Whig vs.

Democrat in December, 1849, with 12 Free Soilers deciding the destiny of Congress, and perhaps the nation.

The key issue at the caucus that December was the West, and its immediate symbol, the Wilmot Proviso. This measure had been introduced as an amendment to an appropriations bill three years before by David Wilmot, a Pennsylvania Democrat. The Proviso stated that slavery would not be permitted in any of the territory obtained from Mexico as a result of the war.

The Proviso was defeated in 1846, but remained an issue in December, 1849. Wilmot was still in Congress then, a nominal Democrat, but one who had risen to power in the Free Soil movement in his home state. As expected, Wilmot was the Free Soil candidate for the speakership. He knew he couldn't win the contest, but given his leverage, Wilmot hoped to influence either the Whig or Democrat candidate to accept the Proviso in return for Free Soil votes.

Howell Cobb of Georgia, a slaveholder and former governor of his state, as well as a one-time speaker of the House and solicitor general, was the Democratic nominee for the post. A gigantic, hearty, and well-liked politician, Cobb was also shrewd enough to realize in 1846 that the Wilmot Proviso would be an issue for many years to come. So he refused to take a firm stand on the matter, alienating some supporters in his own state but adding to his power in the national party. The Whig nominee, Robert Winthrop, was, like Cobb, a former speaker of the House, a protégé of Daniel Webster's, and at the age of forty believed a rising power in the nation. Winthrop had not been as circumspect as Cobb. He was known as being sympathetic to the Proviso, although he shrank at the idea of sectional controversy over the slavery issue. Because of this, southern Whigs refused to accept him, and Robert Toombs and Alexander Stephens, both of Georgia, led six others of their number from the Whig caucus in protest against Winthrop's nomination. But similar walkouts took place at the Democratic caucus, as Cobb continued to play coy on the Proviso issue. As a result, prediction of the outcome was impossible as the House began casting ballots for the speakership.

The balloting went on for more than three weeks and sixty-three ballots before Cobb won the office. During this period congressmen insulted one another, challenges were hurled across the floor, and there were talks of duels in the grassy knolls that surrounded the Capitol. Cobb was safely installed as speaker just before the Christmas recess. While the rest of the country celebrated the holiday, Whigs, Democrats, and Free Soilers caucused in Washington rooming houses, planning strategy for the first order of business: the admission of California as a state, with a constitution that forbade slavery.

The debate on the measure was considered of vital importance for the nation's future, since it involved tacit approval or disapproval of the Wilmot Proviso. It would also prove a major testing ground for northern and southern representatives, most of whom expected it to cap the discontent on the subject that had been felt since the Mexican War. Finally, it would be a curious case of a "generation gap" in Washington, with the great statesmen of the nation's "second generation" —men like Daniel Webster, Henry Clay, John C. Calhoun, and Thomas Hart Benton—having their "last hurrah" before leaving the stage of national politics, while a new generation, yet unknown and untested, prepared to take their places.

One of them was forty-nine-year-old Senator William Seward of New York, a Whig, who said he would accept nothing less than the immediate acceptance of the California consitution as a prelude to passage of the Wilmot Proviso. Toombs of Georgia, then forty, replied that California "had been purchased by the common blood and treasure of the whole people," and if the state were to be admitted without slavery, it would "fix a national degradation upon half the states of this Confederacy." If such came to pass, Toombs concluded, "I am for disunion." Winthrop, the defeated candidate for the speakership, wondered whether a disruption of the Union would be such a tragedy. "I would say let us separate peaceably, as Maine did from Massachusetts, Kentucky from Virginia, and so on." But he was an exception. Seward and Toombs led small but growing cadres of young representatives and senators, each of which was prepared for war if the other won on the California issue.

The old men of Congress, who had fought one another for decades, who recalled the Revolution and would do all in their power to prevent the destruction of a nation they had literally nursed into being, opposed this drift. Their nominal leader was Henry Clay, then seventy-three, who had returned to the Senate in 1849. Together with sixty-eight-year-old Daniel Webster, he would lead other old Whigs who expected to apply the compromise tactics that had worked well in a previous generation. Clay and Webster hoped to count on the sixty-eight-year-old Thomas Hart Benton, senator from Missouri, whose feud with the southern radicals of his own Democratic Party was the talk of Washington. Benton was foursquare for the Wilmot Proviso, even though many of his constituents disapproved of this stand. In speaking of the anti-Proviso forces, he exclaimed, "I would sooner sit in council with the six thousand dead who have died of cholera in St. Louis than go to convention with such a gang of scamps! Let us have our own party and ticket—no taint of secession and disunion and nullification in it!" Benton was willing to see the destruction of the Democratic Party to save the Proviso, but the Union came before the Proviso in his mind, and throughout this period Benton struggled with his conscience on the matter, in the end reluctantly coming down on the side of compromise.

Clay and Webster were joined by a number of politically ambitious younger men, who hoped to make their reputations as conciliators, inherit the Clay-Webster mantles, and go on from there to the White House. Stephen Douglas, the thirty-seven-year-old Illinois senator, was the most prominent of them. Douglas was a Democrat, but a malleable one, willing to follow Clay's leadership for the time being. He had been born the year Clay was speaker of the House. It was not unreasonable for him to hope that by working with the old man, he could achieve some additional prominence, and perhaps take his place. Douglas was identified with popular sovereignty, which held that the people of each area should decide whether or not they wanted slavery. It was a sensible political solution, but would it work at a time when Americans were coming to view the question as moral, and not political at all? Douglas thought it would; he continued to hold that the issues revolving around slavery were political, not moral, and so could be resolved by "men of reason." For the next decade Douglas would lead the compromise forces: he would indeed succeed Clay in this role. But he must have reflected, in 1850, that Clay had failed in three attempts to win the presidency.

Henry Clay

Henry Clay rose to offer his compromise on January 29. He asked for the admission of California as a free state, but conceded the Mexican Cession would be organized without reference to slavery. Texas would relinquish some of its claims on New Mexico, and in return the federal government would assume that state's public debts, which had been incurred prior to Texas' admission to the Union. The slave trade in the District of Columbia would be ended, but slavery there would be guaranteed unless Maryland accepted its abo-

20

lition, and then only on condition the slaveholders be compensated. Congress would enact a fugitive slave law and assert it had no right to interfere with the slave trade between the states.

It was a bold move. Clay realized no compromise was possible on the California question, so he brought together other issues, wrapped them in a large package, and made certain both North and South received benefits. If a small problem can't be solved, transform it into a large one that can be resolved! It was very much in the Clay tradition. What he had done was to bring together all matters involved in the slavery issue, hoping that with the passage of his package, the matter would be resolved once and for all. So would end the danger to the Union. With this done, he could retire in peace.

Clay went on to say that the South would have to accept the fact that California could not support a slave economy, even if the institution was legal in the state. The North would have to agree not to impose the Wilmot Proviso on the Mexican Cession. Southerners would save face, while northerners could reflect that New Mexico, like California, was not suitable for cotton culture. Clay stressed this point. Turning to Seward and the northern Whigs, he exclaimed, "You have nature on your side." While recognizing the North received more than the South from the omnibus measure, Clay noted the benefits the South derived from the Union. He swore he would throw his weight behind a strict fugitive slave law, one written "by the senator from the South who goes furthest."

Clay was answered by his ancient antagonist, John C. Calhoun, who had led the South longer than Clay had the compromisers. Now sixty-eight years old and near death, he too was preparing to pass leadership to a new generation, and his heirs were men like Toombs, firebrands who would stand for southern interests before all. Calhoun was too weak to read his speech, which was read for him by his old friend, Senator James Mason of Virginia. Under no circumstances would he accept a free California, whose admission would destroy the sectional balance. He went on to recommend a constitutional amendment to assure the South equity with the other sections. (Later on, in a posthumous essay, Calhoun would suggest the election of two presidents, one from the North and the other from the South, each with a veto over all legislation.)

Now Webster rose to respond to Calhoun. He repeated Clay's arguments, but with greater force and oratorical flourishes. "Never did there devolve on any generation of men higher trusts than now devolve upon us for the preservation of this constitution, and the harmony and peace of all who are destined to live under it." Attacked by young northern Whigs as a betrayer of their interests, Webster nonetheless did lead some waverers into his camp.

Senator Jefferson Davis of Mississippi, forty-two years old, responded to Webster. Of all the southern Democrats, he was considered the logical successor to the sick Calhoun. But unlike Calhoun, he was willing to attempt conciliation so long as it did not harm the South's basic interests. He was willing to extend the Missouri Compromise line to the Pacific, with the understanding that slavery would be permitted south of the line. In effect, this would negate California's bid for statehood, but at the same time prepare the way for the admission of new free and slave states. And if it was accepted,

Daniel Webster. The statesman's comments on the importance of credit, made in a Senate speech on March 18, 1834, are recorded on a bronze plaque in the main office of Dun & Bradstreet: "Commercial credit is the creation of modern times and belongs in its highest perfection only to the most enlightened and best governed nations. Credit is the vital air of the system of modern commerce. It has done more —a thousand times more—to enrich nations than all the mines in the world."

Davis, not Douglas, would emerge as the Democrats' bright hope for a future president. It was then, in 1850, that the destinies of these two ambitious Democratic senators were forged. For the next decade they would contest one another for the soul of their party.

23

Davis had difficulty in persuading other southerners to yield an inch on the issue, while northern legislators rallied to oppose Clay and Douglas. Senator Salmon Chase of Ohio (forty-two years old) cried, "All legislative compromises are radically wrong and essentially vicious," while Seward proclaimed there was a "higher law" than the Constitution, one that he would follow even though it destroyed the nation.

The compromises were referred to committee in April. Three months later southern delegates met in Nashville to discuss a common strategy, at a conference called by Calhoun. At the time of the call, Calhoun expected to lead the South out of the Union if the measures passed. In other words, he was preparing the way for a civil war. Given his prestige and political support, it seemed possible he could carry it off.

But Calhoun died on March 31, and his senatorial seat was taken by Franklin Elmore, who died soon after. Then Robert Barnwell, a forty-nine-year-old firebrand, took Elmore's place. These events, combined with continued discussions in Washington, served to moderate the tone of the Nashville debates. Some southern leaders demanded secession, but Davis, who rose to prominence after Calhoun's death, was able to win support for compromise. Thus, the death of an aged leader served to bring moderates to power at the southern caucus. The way to compromise would be difficult, but at least it was now possible.

On May 8, the Senate committee reported two bills to the full body. The first provided for passage of Clay's omnibus measures, while the second was designed to prohibit the slave trade in the District of Columbia. It appeared the Clay-

John C. Calhoun

Douglas forces, with Davis' assent, would succeed. But at this point President Taylor stepped in to smash their hopes.

Zachary Taylor had been elected to the presidency in 1848 without making a promise or commitment. He was a southern slaveholder, a Whig, and a man who knew little of compromise. Taylor was a general, a stubborn man convinced of his own rectitude. Nothing would sway him, not even hopes for the success of his son-in-law—Jefferson Davis. Earlier he had said, "I have given and will give no pledges to either the opponents or supporters of the Proviso." But Taylor had also said he would not veto the Proviso if it passed Congress.

The President did not like Henry Clay, who had contested the nomination with him in 1848. He felt Clay's attempts to compromise were weasel-like, unworthy of a gentleman of principle. In fact, he said Clay lacked principles. Take the California issue. Taylor decided California should come into the Union as a free state if it so desired. Now Clay had encased the California issue with all these other things. Taylor would have nothing of it, and no amount of persuading would be effective. He let it be known that he would veto the Clay measures when they reached his desk.

Clay lacked sufficient votes to override a veto. If the veto held, Taylor's friends among the antislavery Whigs would introduce a substitute measure for California statehood. It might be passed, given the President's support. Then Taylor would sign it into law. This would crush Davis' moderates. The radicals would then dominate the South. The result? Civil War.

Once again, nature intervened to preserve the Union. Taylor died on July 9, and was succeeded by Vice-President Millard Fillmore. The new President aligned himself with the moderates, hoping to win their support for the nomination at the 1852 Whig convention. Fillmore named Webster his secretary of state and let it be known that Clay would be his man at the Capitol. The compromises passed. Fillmore signed them into law in September. And with them, so the moderates hoped, the issues of the 1840s were laid to rest.

Clay would resign in 1852, and died days before his resignation took effect. Webster would also die in 1852. Thomas

Hart Benton would leave Washington in 1854, and four years later die in his Missouri home. Webster's seat would be taken by thirty-nine-year-old Charles Sumner, a Wilmot Proviso Whig with a violent hatred of slavery. Benton's son-in-law, thirty-seven-year-old John Frémont, would become California's first senator, and he learned how the Senate worked by listening to the debates on the 1850 compromise. Benton, who had been Missouri's first senator when he arrived in Washington in 1821, spoke with Frémont and other young congressmen and senators prior to leaving for home. "You have come on the stage too late, sir," he said to one of them. "Not only have our great men passed away, but the great issues have been settled also. The last of these was the National Bank, and that has been overthrown forever. Nothing is left you, sir, but puny sectional questions and petty strifes about slavery and fugitive slave laws, involving no national interest." So it seemed to him in 1854. The Clay compromises of 1850 appeared to have ended the slavery issue once and for all. Now the country could concentrate on more important issues—if ever some of these appeared.

At about that time William Grayson of South Carolina and Samuel Goodrich of Connecticut met in Washington, at a party with several mutual friends. Both men were aged, and each had a deserved reputation as a writer. Grayson and Goodrich knew their country's history; in their time they had conversed with veterans of the Revolution, and had seen some of the men who had molded the nation in its first years. The country was at peace when they met; the Clay compromise had held. But the two men, from different sections of the country, wondered whether America was progressing as it should. After all, look at the quality of the nation's leadership. Was it not true that Calhoun was inferior to Jefferson? And Webster to John Adams? And Henry Clay to Alexander Hamilton? Now the second generation was passing from the scene. What of the third? Douglas, Davis, Seward, and Sumner were hardly the equals of Webster, Clay, and Calhoun. Did this not mean the nation was in decline? Goodrich wondered if this were not the case. But he didn't trust his own conclusions. So he turned to Grayson and asked, "Confine your attention to your own neighborhood as it was in your youth. Compare its condition with that of today, and tell me which you think better, the manners and morals of the older time or the present?"

Later on, Grayson wrote of his answer.

> I compared them with those prevailing in my parish at the time of the conversation, and was compelled to confess that the change for the better was immense. Religion had revived. The churches were filled. Sunday was kept sacred. Schools on that day were established. Temperance prevailed. The riotous sensuality of the old times had disappeared. If immorality existed it was at least deferential enough to conceal itself from the public eye. My experience is that of every man whose memory runs back as far as sixty years, when every public day was a day of drinking, disorder, and fighting throughout the country. I replied to Mr. Goodrich by saying that so far as my own people were concerned, I was obliged to admit that the improvement of the present times over the past was incalculable.

So it was with at least one man, one who was well-traveled and experienced. Grayson was optimistic. The outstanding issues of the past had been settled. The horizon was pleasing, and the skies clear. He was certain the remainder of the 1850s would bring additional progress, which would continue on into the 1860s and beyond. Nor was Grayson alone in this.

He concluded by noting that "He [Goodrich] said that he had put the same question to a great number of persons in every part of the country, and had received the same reply everywhere."

It was in such a spirit that a confident America viewed the first half of the 1850s, after passage and acceptance of the Clay compromises.

2 / A TALE OF THREE CITIES

AMERICA WAS A RURAL NATION IN 1850. SIX OF EVERY seven Americans lived on farms and in small villages with populations below 2,500. And many of those in cities or towns were biding their time, waiting for the proper moment to leave the urban centers for the countryside, which in 1850 meant the West. Cities were places of disease, crowding, crime, and foreigners. Native-born Americans and immigrants who had become "Americanized" seemed to prefer the rural life. "To own one's own land is the national dream, in which all true Americans share," editorialized the New York *Herald* in 1855. Yet the cities were growing, and the 3.5 million Americans who lived in them and in towns became 6.2 million in the decade of the 1850s.

The largest American cities were ocean or Gulf ports, whose greatness derived from their commercial functions.

The nation's farms and forests would send their products to these cities, for shipment abroad, with Europe the prime destination. Imports, also from Europe, would arrive at other docks, to be processed by merchants before being broken down and taken into the interior for sale and distribution. The large, old American cities existed to serve interior America. Of course, they had lives of their own as well, and they functioned as intellectual, political, and artistic centers for the nation. But their major activity was commerce. Without this, they would have shriveled, and some even died.

New York had long been the largest American city. It grew in the 1850s, passing the million mark in population at the end of the decade, the first American city to do so. The city was the acknowledged business capital of the nation by that time. Other cities—Boston, Philadelphia, and New Orleans in particular—boasted of their centers of learning and high tone, but had to concede that in terms of pure economic power, New York was unsurpassed. Yet fewer than 10 percent of New York's workers were engaged in manufacturing; the rest were in commerce and supportive activities, such as banking and insurance. Of the big cities, only Philadelphia, with a population of fewer than 600,000 in 1860, had as much as 15 percent of the adult population engaged in manufacturing, while Boston, with fewer than 180,000 people, was at the same level as New York.

All these northeastern ports were diversified compared with New Orleans, the largest American city south of Baltimore and the fifth largest in the nation, with slightly under 170,000 population in 1860. In 1860, only 3 percent of the city's adult working population was engaged in manufactur-

A daguerreotype by William and Frederick Langenheim of the Merchant's Exchange in Philadelphia.

ing. The rest were employed in trade, in what was one of the most booming commercial centers in the nation.

Louisianans would concede that New York's reign as the leading import city of America would go unchallenged. Ever since it had bested Philadelphia in the early nineteenth century, New York had been the prime port of call in North America for cargo ships bound from Europe. New Orleans, situated near the mouth of the Mississippi River on the Gulf of Mexico, was too far out of the way to attract many of these ships, especially those with cargoes destined for the Northeast and the upper Midwest. The Hudson River and the Erie Canal gave New York advantages over New Orleans which in 1850 could not be overcome. But leading citizens of the Gulf port observed America's star of empire was moving westward, and at a rapid pace. During George Washington's administration the United States was a small nation, with only a fringe of settlement on the western side of the Appalachians; the Atlantic Ocean was its most important body of water. The America of Zachary Taylor was quite different. The old Northwest had filled up, as had the Southwest. Texas

An 1855 lithograph of the west side of New York City's Broadway.

THE EDWARD W. C. ARNOLD COLLECTION
LENT BY THE METROPOLITAN MUSEUM OF ART.
PHOTO COURTESY MUSEUM OF THE CITY OF NEW YORK

was a state, and California was knocking at the door of Congress. It was as though a giant hand had lifted the nation at the Atlantic coast and tilted it upward, throwing much of its population across the Appalachians, into the Mississippi Valley, and then beyond the Missouri to the West Coast.

The Atlantic would remain an important body of water for America, but to Louisianans of 1850, the Mississippi seemed the key to the nation's destiny. Together with its many tributaries, the river drained half the continent, entering the Gulf of Mexico just below New Orleans which was the hand that held the key to the entire valley. Then there was the Gulf itself, a prime area for American exploitation. Cuba, rich in agricultural goods, would send its sugar and tobacco to America via New Orleans. And who was to say that within a decade or so Cuba would not be more important for the nation's commerce than England? Or perhaps enter the Union as a new state? Pierre Soulé of Louisiana, minister to Spain in the mid-1850s, thought Cuba should be annexed, and convinced the State Department to make the attempt. Soulé was authorized to offer Spain up to $130 million for the island —a large sum of money at the time—while other Louisianans were willing to foment a revolution on the island, after which the rebels would "ask" for annexation, as had been the case with Texas a generation before. In 1854 Soulé met with minister to England James Buchanan and minister to France John Mason at Ostend in Belgium to plan for the eventual annexation of the island. The three agreed the United States should offer money for Cuba, but use other means if need be to make it part of the nation. The Ostend Manifesto read that ". . . by every law, human and divine, we shall be justified in wresting it from Spain if we possess the power." The London *Morning*

34

Advertiser remarked that "Jonathan's legs are getting so long that he requires more room," and had little doubt that the "Pearl of the Antilles" would soon fly the American flag.

Once in control of Cuba, the United States would probe more deeply into Latin America, either by force or commerce. William Walker, also of Louisiana, spoke of this often, and in 1855 he led an expeditionary force into Nicaragua, making himself dictator of the country for two years before being forced to leave. Walker dreamed of a Central American federation, allied to the United States by bonds of commerce, with New Orleans emerging as the New York of the Caribbean.

Louisianan William Walker, dictator of Nicaragua for two years

Such was the dream of New Orleans' leaders in the 1850s. They were residents of the city of destiny; New York was the citadel of the past. Writing in the *Western Journal* in 1849, a southern newspaperman painted just such a picture of the nation's future. The South would dominate the United States, he believed. But he assured northern readers they would benefit under such leadership.

> [The current of commerce will] flow from the equator in the direction of the poles, carrying the luxuries of the tropics to the inhabitants of colder climes, and returning with the more substantial products of the temperate zones. Thus the bounties of nature will be divided among the inhabitants of every clime; and while, by the agency of commerce the physical comforts of every region will be increased, those prejudices which are so liable to exist between the people of the north and south will be removed, and social intercourse and universal sympathy prevail in their stead.

As might have been expected, most northerners did not relish such a vision. Horace Greeley, publisher of the New York *Tribune*, believed it might be well for New Orleans to want such a future, which would be disastrous for New York or Boston. After all, New Orleans had a large Creole population, whose inhabitants were more akin to Latin Americans than to northerners. Such people could look to Cuba and Nicaragua rather than to England and France. But what of the populations of the Northeast and Northwest? Would these people, who were Anglo-Saxon, Irish, and German for the most part, consent to take second place to Louisianans in such a nation? To a people known as the slickest slave traders in the United States? Would New York bow to New Orleans, the nation's central slave market? Or, as the New York *Courier and Enquirer* put it in 1854, "Does the sane man live

36

who believes that if Cuba was tendered us tomorrow . . . that this people would consent to receive and annex her?"

New Orleans' business leaders might have replied that to reject such a destiny would be to fly in the face of natural tendencies. As early as the 1820s New Orleans had begun its campaign to become the nation's leading export city. The Mississippi Valley was being rapidly filled with newcomers, some from Europe, but most from the older seaboard states. These people farmed the area, and sent their goods down river to New Orleans. Meanwhile, steamship technology was improving all the time, making the water connection all the more useful and necessary. New Orleans' docks expanded in both northern and southern directions. The levees were reinforced, as commerce expanded in good years and bad. Not even depression and war could stop the city's commercial growth. In 1821, as New Orleans closed the gap with New York, the Louisiana *Gazette* poeticized about the bulging warehouses along the banks of the Mississippi, and the wharfs and docks of New Orleans, where goods from all parts of the world were piled high, awaiting transshipment upriver by steamboat or flatboat or to the Europeans by sailing vessels.

> . . . Whale oil and whiskey & rats bane and onions,
> Rye coffee, sperm candles, soil leather & spun yarns,
> Wooden bowls, patent bridles, gigs, harness and teas,
> And a splendid assortment of good white oak cheese.
> Boston rum, bricks, potatoes, tar mustard and flax,
> Clyster, pipes, Dandy cravats and other Nick Nacks,
> Gilt watch chains and seals, not charged at too high rates,
> Swords, pistols, and dirks, for soldiers or pirates,
> Smoked herring and lumber, brogans and goose quills,
> Blank books of all sorts, mackerel cotton cords and corn shellac,
> Domestic straw bonnets and yankee made bellows,
> Brads, bibles, hay, playing cards, ready made clothes. . . .

Scene on New Orleans levee in the cotton season: the wharves and docks loaded with goods from all parts of the world awaiting transport upriver.

DEAN COLLECTION, FREDERIC LEWIS, INC.

Not very good poetry, but a striking example of civic pride.

New Orleans did surpass New York as an export center for some years in the 1840s, and for the next decade the two cities competed strenuously for the prize. At the time it seemed New Orleans might indeed redeem its pledge to capture export domination. In retrospect, however, we realize the battle was destined to be won by New York. New Orleans' had a harbor far inferior to that of New York, reachable from the Gulf only after ships navigated a tortuous ninety-eight-mile channel. Sand bars, delta debris, and currents were always hazards. Europeans didn't like to set sail for New Orleans, a city notorious for its epidemics. Nor did American merchants of the Northeast; not until 1858 would there be a regular sailing schedule from New Orleans to eastern seaboard ports. New Orleans might retain control of the river trade and become a major transshipment port, but it could not compete with New York, Boston, and Philadelphia in the area of foreign trade.

The Mississippi trade was excellent in the 1850s, however, and getting better all the time. In this prosperous period midwestern farmers thrived, and they sent their produce down river to New Orleans, where the wealthy traders and merchants bought and sold their goods and grew wealthy. Steamship dockings at New Orleans' docks rose irregularly in the decade, but rise they did, resulting in a euphoric view of the future at the city's banks and insurance companies. At the same time, New Orleans' financial institutions were small and local, while the New York banks were large in American terms and already international in scope. New Orleans' bills

A daguerreotype by Southworth and Hawes of a paddle-wheel steamer in the Boston harbor, c. 1855.

of exchange often were drawn upon New York banks, and the city's insurance firms reinsured portions of cargoes with their New York correspondents. Finally, by 1851 even the more optimistic New Orleans boosters had to concede the city would not surpass New York in foreign trade. By then the northern city was rapidly outdistancing New Orleans in commerce. In 1851 New Orleans exported $54.4 million worth of goods, against New York's $79.8 million. Imports, never very significant for New Orleans, stood at $13 million, against New York's $144.5 million.

TABLE 1

ARRIVAL OF STEAMBOATS AT NEW ORLEANS, 1850–1860*

Year Ending September 30	Number
1850	2,784
1851	2,918
1852	2,779
1853	3,252
1854	3,076
1855	2,763
1856	2,956
1857	2,745
1858	3,264
1859	3,259
1860	3,566

* Source: F. H. Dixon, *A Traffic History of the Mississippi River System* (Washington, D.C.: 1909), p. 15.

TABLE 2

VALUE OF RECEIPTS OF PRODUCE AT NEW ORLEANS, 1850 and 1860*

Product	1850	1860
Cotton	$41,885,156	$109,389,228
Sugar	12,396,150	18,190,880
Molasses	2,400,000	6,250,335
Tobacco	6,166,400	8,499,325
Other Products	34,049,173	42,881,486
Total	96,898,879	185,211,254

* Source: Dixon, *A Traffic History of the Mississippi*, p. 33.

Talk of a major national role for New Orleans would be heard for the rest of the decade, but it had a hollow ring. The city was one of the most interesting places in the United States. In some ways it was more European than American, with its French flavor, Latin overlay, and Mediterranean-like climate. Once they got over the shock of seeing slave auctions in public squares, foreign visitors found New Orleans much to their liking; they felt more at home there than in the raw hustle and bustle of Manhattan. But geography was working to benefit New York, while the same geography, along with political decisions in Washington, did not favor the gateway to the Mississippi.

The urban struggles between Northeast and South, Atlantic and Mississippi, among the old American cities of the 1850s, saw New York defeat New Orleans. The contest between the newer cities of the interior was closer and more in doubt. St. Louis, which was New Orleans' trading partner on the river, also had ambitions for national greatness. In 1850 they seemed capable of realization. Chicago, too, which occupied a similar position in relation to New York, had national ambitions. The rivalry of these new cities was more intense than that between New York and New Orleans, and in terms of the nation's immediate future, more important.

If New Orleans was Queen of the Mississippi, St. Louis was her consort. An old settlement by American standards, it had been a French bastion in the late colonial era. Then it flew the Spanish, British, and Virginian flags for brief periods, before being returned to France after the Revolution. In 1803, as a result of the Louisiana Purchase, St. Louis became part of the United States. At the time it was a small town of 180 houses, boasting of its first pavement. But even then its value as a commercial center was recognized.

St. Louis is located on a bluff on the western bank of the Mississippi, just below the junctions of the Missouri and Illinois rivers with the Mississippi. The town was, in effect, the dividing point between the upper and lower parts of the

St. Louis docks in 1853.

great river. Only shallow-draft boats could venture far north of the junctures, where the waters could fall to around four feet in dry seasons. As a result of waters spilled into the Mississippi by its great tributaries, the maximum draft at St. Louis was seven feet. So the flatboats and other small craft that plied the upper reaches of the Mississippi, the Illinois, and Missouri, would dock and unload at St. Louis. Their cargoes would be placed on larger boats, and later on steamships, for the trip downriver to New Orleans. Thus, St. Louis was destined to grow with the Midwest and the river trade.

After the War of 1812 settlers had crossed the Appalachians in great numbers. Within a few years they no longer looked eastward to the Atlantic cities as commercial suppliers and customers for their products, but to the Mississippi, the great avenue of American trade. In this period the national destiny seemed to lie in a westward direction, but the immediate commercial future was on the Mississippi. So it was that in 1818 St. Louis became the largest commercial center of the Midwest. By 1831, sixty steamships considered the city their home port; four years later St. Louis boasted of 121 such ships. In 1850, the city had a population of 77,860 and was the sixth largest urban center in the nation, already having defeated its major river rivals, Cincinnati and Louisville. That year St. Louis had a registered steam tonnage of almost 25,000 tons, against Cincinnati's 17,000 and Louisville's 15,000. Three years later the figures were St. Louis, 45,500 tons; Cincinnati, 10,000 tons; and Louisville, 14,000 tons. Was it any wonder, then, that the city's leaders were confident of their future? Nor would they be disappointed with the river's statistics during the 1850s. In 1851, 2,628 steamboats and ships arrived at St. Louis; in 1860 the total was 3,454.

The docks and wharves of St. Louis were no less busy and prosperous than those at New Orleans, understandable since the destinies of the two cities were so intertwined. But the two cities had different flavors and aspects. New Orleans was a Gulf port noted for its strong Creole flavor, a place where businessmen had either to be bilingual in English and French, or to employ translators for one or the other language. St. Louis, like New Orleans a believer in a southern destiny, was midwestern nonetheless, with northern as well as southern businessmen prominent in its affairs. It too was bilingual; its second language was German. German was used in many St. Louis schools, as it was in Cincinnati. Sunday strollers in New

Orleans might relax at a cafe and imbibe sazaracs and brandies; in St. Louis people went to a *bierstube* for long draughts of homemade brew.

The German influence could not be found to any great extent in the business leadership of St. Louis, however, which was predominantly eastern American and, to a small degree, southern. Ambitious pioneers who crossed the Appalachians in the 1820s could rise rapidly in the St. Louis commercial aristocracy; Germans who crossed the ocean two decades later either were blocked from business power or didn't seek it, preferring instead to run the city's shops or purchase large farms on the outskirts. Thomas Allen, a major force in St. Louis' commerce and banking, was born in Pittsfield, Massachusetts. John O'Fallon, who made what by the city's standards was a fortune in land speculation and trade, was a Kentuckian by birth. James Lucas, also a trader, came from Pennsylvania, as did others of the commercial aristocracy. They joined with the few French families who led the city in pre-Louisiana Purchase days, such as the Chouteaus, to dominate not only St. Louis commerce, but social and intellectual life as well. These men had familial links with the Northeast, commercial relations with the South, political treaties with the nearby Indians, and worked well with the German immigrants. The different strains provided an interesting mix that gave St. Louis a flavor unique in the nation. Little wonder, then, that foreign visitors, coming upriver from New Orleans, would remark that St. Louis was no less cosmopolitan than her southern partner, as businesslike as New York, and combined the flavor of Hamburg or Bremen with that of a frontier village.

46

The northern and western parts of the city gave such an impression. But the life of St. Louis was at the docks, and these were southern and western in appearance. An Illinois newspaperman in the city in 1855 offers this account of what he saw:

> The business streets are almost blockaded with boxes, barrels, bales and packages, much coming in, much, also, going out. It is interesting also, to see the wide scope of country supplied from this market. We saw boxes directed to Kentucky, all parts of Illinois and Missouri, Kansas, Iowa, Minnesota, and Wisconsin—a more extensive market than any other city in the world supplies; and when it is recollected that the country is yet new, and not one per cent of its natural resources developed, some idea may be formed of the vast importance of our Western trade.

And that trade would be drawn to St. Louis by the arterial network of the Mississippi River system. Who could deny that these waterways would mold the destiny of the central part of North America, and that this heartland would dominate the nation, or that in time America would be the greatest power on earth? Following such logic, St. Louis fully expected a world role awaited her within the life span of some of the young men working at the docks. Such was the view, at least, of the Missouri *Republican* in 1855, which urged the city's leaders to make ready for this destiny.

> Scarcely an hour during [1854] but some gallant steamer ploughed the waves of the Mississippi, bringing from the North, as far as St. Paul—from the West, beyond the Yellow Stone—from the South, almost to the Gulf, and from the Ohio to the very confluence of the Allegheny and Monongahela, the products of the richest and most extensively improved country in the world. The levee was stored from day to day with the staples of each section. The sugars of the South lay mingled with the cereals of the North, and the manufactures of civilization con-

trasted with the peltries of the Indians. Perhaps in no other mart of the Union are the genius, enterprise and diversified interests of the nation better represented.

The leaders of St. Louis, in the areas of both business and journalism, seemed wedded to the Mississippi at that time. They maintained close contacts with counterparts in New Orleans, but in the mid-1850s tended to show signs of condescension toward their correspondents at the Gulf port, who spoke of the potential of the Caribbean. Let New Orleans take the Caribbean, St. Louis seemed to be saying. Given our position in the Union and location on the river, we can dominate the globe. This, at least, seemed to be the view of some St. Louis leaders, who somewhat smugly waited for their city's destiny to unfold. After all, Cincinnati and Louisville had conceded defeat. What other rival city was left?

Chicago. Unlike St. Louis, it was not a city in 1840, or, for that matter, even a well-developed town. Instead, it appeared an overgrown village, squalid and undisciplined, without any special character to distinguish it from any of a dozen other growing urban centers of the Midwest, or those along the southern coast of the Great Lakes. The opening of the Erie Canal in 1825 had provided an Atlantic access to the Lakes cities; it seemed that one of several ports—Chicago, Detroit, Cleveland, and Buffalo among them—would occupy a position in relation to New York that St. Louis did to New Orleans. Such a city would become a gathering point for products of the area, which would be sent by lake and canal to Manhattan, and from there to the rest of the world. Goods unloaded in New York and Albany would be shipped to the Lakes city for distribution throughout the upper Midwest.

Chicago was well situated for victory in such a struggle.

It was located at the southern end of Lake Michigan, that great body of water that pointed like a finger into the heart of the Midwest. Chicago had a fine harbor, while the Chicago River, though hardly comparable to the Hudson, not to say the Mississippi or the Missouri, provided it with access to the interior. Capitalizing on such natural gifts, and enhancing them by dredging the harbor, Chicagoans had no doubt of their ability to best their rivals on the Great Lakes. Then, in 1848, the Illinois and Michigan Canal was opened. The waterway connected Chicago with the Illinois River, and thus with the Mississippi. To Chicagoans it seemed the United States had been bisected with a watery divide, with their city at one end, and New Orleans at the other. After that, there was little talk of serious rivalry with Toledo or Cleveland. Chicago was out for bigger game.

The city was still small in 1850, with only 30,000 people. Still, it was the largest Lake city in the Midwest, and one of the fastest growing in the nation. Only ten years earlier Chicago's population had been less than 4,500. Extrapolating this growth would be easy enough, or at least this was the thought of the city's boosters. Within this century, they claimed, Chicago would become larger than New York, and emerge as the most powerful urban center in the world. St. Louis looked to the south and New Orleans, and to the promise of the West. Chicago seemed to be seeking growth in all directions, but recognized that its first task would be to seize domination of the Midwest from St. Louis.

Chicago lacked the sophistication of New Orleans and the overlay of culture that could be found in St. Louis. Both of these cities had old families and established ways. Such was not the situation in Chicago, where everything seemed new, raw, and growing. Even its name was fairly new; some of its older residents remembered when it was called Fort Dearborn. And there was some debate as to what Chicago meant in the Indian tongue from which it had been derived. Some claimed it meant "playful waters," while others said it was an Indian term for "destitute." Most noted that a wild, garlic-like plant was called "Gitchi-ka-go" by the Indians—"a thing great and strong." That, to them, was Chicago.

The city wasn't even incorporated until 1833, and when the announcement was made, few stopped to celebrate; Chicagoans were too busy working. "Chicago is a pretty good place," said one commentator at the time, but "only for men that are in business for making money." He thought it "a miserable place for loafers." The loafers could go to St. Louis, or remain in New York or Boston. Chicagoans of the early 1850s were among the greatest boosters of their day. They not only delighted in bragging of their city's virtues, but seemed to take positive joy in learning of immigrant riots in Boston and New York, the cholera epidemics of New Orleans and St. Louis, the paralyzing snows of St. Paul and Milwaukee, and civil difficulties in Buffalo and Detroit. Chicagoans relished jokes and stories told at the expense of other cities, or ones that reflected on their own vitality. There was the one about a plan to buy out St. Louis and turn that city into a "south addition" for Chicago when the Windy City reached that far south in a decade or so. When a New York newspaper reported that wolves were to be found in Chicago's streets, a Chicago paper responded that "Chicago was growing so fast that the wild animals just couldn't keep out of the way." "Our streets present an animated picture," wrote the Chicago *Daily Journal* in 1849.

> Thronged with laden wagons, filled with busy people, vocal with the rattling of wheels, the rush of steam, the clank of machinery and many voices, goods gaily flaunting from awning posts and store doors, docks piled with boxes, bales, and bundles of merchandise, warehouses like so many heart ventricles receiving the grain on one side, and with a single pulsation, pouring it out on the other into waiting vessels and steamers to be borne away on the general circulation, lumber yards heaped with the products of the forest, furnaces and machine shops sending out the exponents of industry and skill. . . . the multitude of strangers whose arrival every packet bugle and locomotive whistle and steamer's bell heralds, all those and more are now pictured upon every observer's eye and swell the diapason of busy life to every listening ear.

As the newspaper indicated, Chicago was a grain and lumber town in the early 1850s. Wheat farmers and lumbermen of the upper Midwest came to look upon it as a natural market for their goods, which would be processed in Chicago's mills, breweries, and lumberyards. Wheat, flour, and lumber were for the most part exported, by lake, canal, and river to New York, and from there would go to Europe. Some of the wood and flour, and all of the beer, would be consumed locally.

Chicago led St. Louis in the wheat trade, handling 1.7 million bushels in 1851 against her rival's 388,000. That same year Chicago shipped 125 million feet of lumber, and St. Louis, 38.8 million. But for most other commodities—pork, lard, salt, and whiskey among them—St. Louis held a commanding position. It was also a larger import center, and Midwesterners purchased their coffee and tobacco from St. Louis merchants.

Views of Chicago in 1858, looking northeast from the dome of the Cook County Courthouse. The first Sherman House is in the foreground.

COURTESY CHICAGO HISTORICAL SOCIETY

53

Chicagoans would boast of their city's growth, while their rivals in St. Louis would respond by pointing to the trade figures. Merchants based in Chicago would travel throughout the Midwest seeking additional business, offering terms rivaling those obtainable in St. Louis. They would contact foreign exporters offering to handle their goods at reasonable rates, often lower than those of St. Louis. Yet Chicago's success was limited, and St. Louis had reason to appear smug in the late 1840s and early 1850s.

There were two reasons for this: trust and transportation.

Trust was vital to the conduct of business, more so then than now, since transportation and communication still left much to be desired. But how could a merchant in one part of the country learn of the reputation and credit-worthiness of his counterparts elsewhere? Or whether a draft drawn on a bank a thousand miles away should be accepted, at a time when bank failures were common occurrences? Word of mouth was one method, but it was uncertain, often biased, and could not be trusted. Past experience was another, but of limited value at a time when so many new businesses were springing up and old ones going bankrupt. A far better method was reliance upon a reputable credit reporter. There were several organizations reporting on credit in the 1850s, but the most respected, and fastest growing, was the Mercantile Agency, founded in New York in 1841.

The Agency relied upon local businessmen and professional people for regular reports on the credit-worthiness of other businessmen and concerns in their locality. These would be sent on to New York, gathered, and offered for a fee to concerned parties throughout the nation. It was through these reports that eastern businessmen could determine whether or not to offer credit to their western counterparts, or decide if they should accept drafts on western banks, which they had never seen in some cases and knew only by their letterheads. Without such a service, business would not only have been difficult, but in some cases, impossible.

The St. Louis merchants long had prized their credit and had earned good reputations. New Orleans and foreign bankers, shippers, and merchants had come to know that Thomas Allen, James Lucas, and especially the Chouteaus would honor their contracts, and such men and firms had little difficulty in obtaining credit in New York, Boston, and Philadelphia. But what of the newer men and companies, organized in the 1850s? These were known mostly by their ratings at the Mercantile Agency. For example, there was the relatively new firm of Livingston and Kinkaid, a trading operation, which sold eastern goods to settlers beyond the Mississippi. In 1853 a Mercantile Agency reporter wrote:

> Livingston & Kinkaid are merchants to Salt Lake, go out from this City with trains of merchandize, fine bus. men, young and active ... been in present business for 5 yrs. Said to have made 150m$. Are considered gd. for all they contract.

And there was W. L. Maddocks, an apothecary (druggist) who purchased his wares from New York and New Orleans. Maddocks's report read: "Been here sevl. yrs ... now pretty good bus. has recently taken a large Stand, honest gd. bus. man, means only moderate, but believed Safe for a few 100$."

Most of the city's beer was consumed locally, as was Chicago's, but even then the St. Louis product was known beyond Missouri. Some was sent to New Orleans, and there was a small but growing demand for some brands on the Atlantic coast. It was important, then, for the leading breweries to guard their reputations, not only for fine beer but for good credit. In a report of 1857 we learn of Joseph Schneider, in business for only two years and eager to expand. Two months before the report was written his operation was destroyed by a fire, and Schneider needed credit to get back into business. The reporter wrote that he "has not done much yet, is energetic and honest, will succeed." Then, a few months later, the reporter wrote, "Married to wealthy lady, and is now proprietor of the *Green Tree Brewery*. Is an energetic, good business man, and cons. him good for contracts." Schneider produced only 3,000 barrels of beer that year. A larger and better known operation, Fritz & Wainwright, turned out more than three times as much. In the credit report on the company in 1858 we read: "Bush, a relative of Fritz, is the head man of this concern. They brew about 10m barrels this year. Own the brewery and cave, and are considered responsible." But Fritz & Wainwright were inferior to Adam Kemp, an "industrious German consid. by some to be worth $100,000, does a v. profitable bus. Consid. perfectly respon."

The Mercantile Agency reports on St. Louis businessmen would seem to indicate that most had good reputations, that the standard for business honor was high for the city at the time, and that easterners might well do a fine business there. The same was true for the city's leading banks. The Boatman's Savings Institution was described as "one of the soundest of our Banking institutions. Cap. stock 400m$. 4000 shares. 100$ each, now dividends declaring, shares now quoted at $575 and 580$ ask. Its deposits are heavier than any other Bank in the city and average a million and three quarters." And even those banks forced to suspend payments in

1837, such as the Merchants', paid back their losses, and liked to boast that their depositors lost nothing in the process.

Chicago's merchants and businessmen of the 1850s had overcome the bad reputations earned during earlier decades. In the 1840s they either lacked the reputations of their St. Louis counterparts or were considered bad credit risks. The same was true for the banks. The St. Louis financial houses were believed conservative by American standards of the day. They would not accept all accounts and were careful in granting loans. In contrast, the Chicago banks were open to marginal individuals and enterprises in the 1830s and often extended credit on meager collateral. The owner of a bill drawn on a questionable country bank might find he could not redeem it in St. Louis, even at a discount. But in Chicago some venturesome bankers, eager for business and willing to take risks to get it, would accept the paper. Prior to the 1837 panic, speculators would take such bills to Chicago, and make modest fortunes in the discount business.

Free-for-all banking practices served to attract business to Chicago—so long as the banks remained open. But the practices also meant that Chicago's banks were more susceptible to failure in bad times. The St. Louis financial and business establishments fared better than did those of Chicago during and after the 1837 panic. Indeed, for a while it seemed Chicago's leaders might seek legislative or judicial action to suspend all debts; such action would have stained their credit for decades. Fortunately, some businessmen and bankers, led by William B. Ogden, were able to block it. In an address to the Chicago business community, Ogden said:

> Do not dishonor yourselves and our city! Remember that many a fortress has been saved by the courage of the garrison in concealing its weakness! Loss of fortune may be repaired but dishonor is

a stumbling block to the confidence of the world! I have suffered loss with you, but I hope have lost nothing but my money!

Ogden prevailed, but several banks and businesses did go
under in the six years following the 1837 panic. Although
Chicago was led by a responsible business class in 1850, memories of the early period were not forgotten. Nor did some of
the old memories die; Chicago businesses often *seemed shakier*
than their St. Louis competitors.

Yet there were exceptions. Jonathan Young Scammon, an
associate of Ogden's, fought hard for stiffer banking laws in
Illinois. Scammon later became president of the Chicago Marine Fire Insurance Company and the Marine Bank, both of
which had excellent reputations. Writing of the bank in
1855, the Mercantile Agency reporter said it was "In every
respect sound and good . . . the best in the City. . . . Our best
houses deposit with them heavily. Its stockholders are among
our best citizens & its directors our most reliable men—very
prosperous." As for Scammon, he "is a lawyer & mgs with
great prudence."

Potter Palmer, who came to Chicago from New York in
1852, quickly established a dominant position in dry goods.
Palmer pioneered in the field, being among the first to permit
customers to take goods home on approval and to allow exchanges if the merchandise was not satisfactory. Yet Palmer
was conservative in his finances. The Mercantile Agency reporter considered him "an excellent businessman and quite
prudent."

Benjamin Carpenter, an Ohio meatpacker who went
bankrupt in 1837, relocated to Chicago, started a new business,
and by 1853 was the largest pork dealer in the city. His reputation was "good." But William F. Mather, a leader in trans-

portation, was viewed as "rather slippery." John S. Wright, a dealer in agricultural implements, was deemed a "speculator," a man "of sanguine disposition & always doing something on a lge scale & generally at a loss."

Some, of course, managed to redeem their reputations. Gurden Hubbard, a pioneer meatpacker, who had survived the 1837 panic, was feared to be on the edge of bankruptcy on several occasions. In 1850 he was "doing considerable bus., partly as agent for other packers and forwarding beef," but was not thought of too highly. Two years later he appears as an insurance agent and his "reputation is fair." Then back to the packing business. Hubbard's credit report showed him "to be a man of considerable means," but one who had not yet paid old debts. "Although many consider him upright, we consider him not trustworthy as we know of mean acts done by him and have no faith in his integrity." The old claims were still not paid in 1856. And Hubbard's credit rating was low as a result.

In spite of this, it would appear, then, that Chicago was developing a responsible business community and financial institutions in the 1850s, but the panic of 1837 and its aftermath were not forgotten in the East. Some of the old distrust lingered. St. Louis' leaders were able to obtain eastern financing for internal improvements during the early 1850s. Yet Scammon and Ogden couldn't interest William Weld, one of the important eastern railroad financiers, in their plan for a revival of the Galena and Chicago Union Railroad in 1850. But the situation was changing, even then. And armed with credit, Chicago would be able to mount its assault against St. Louis for mid-western power.

The second reason for Chicago's apparent inability to attract more of the midwestern trade from St. Louis was the lack of adequate transportation. Most of St. Louis' leaders indicated their confidence in the Mississippi River system, and would consider railroads only where water transportation was not present or could not be constructed. Even then, there was little interest in railroads on the part of the city's commercial aristocrats. The opposite was true in Chicago, which as early as the mid-1840s realized railroads would become vital for its prosperity and growth. Waterways might give St. Louis command of the Gulf of Mexico in time, while the lakes-river-canal system made Chicago the handmaiden of New York. But what of the West? Chicago's leaders believed that that part of the nation would be controlled—and exploited—by the city and men who sent the iron horse into the prairies. Railroads should be constructed to New York, Boston, Philadelphia, and other eastern terminals, they said. In fact, Chicago should become the rail hub of the nation.

The Missouri *Republican* scoffed at the idea that railroads could divert St. Louis trade to Chicago, or any other city for that matter. In 1846 it editorialized:

> It may be properly assumed, that trade, shipping, or business, cannot be diverted to any considerable extent, by mere artificial means from channels which nature, the country, population and their necessities have given it. If St. Louis then, commands at this early day, (early at least in her commercial history), a large commerce, and this, too, without artificial aid or national encouragement, it is but a rational conclusion, that it cannot be diverted, nor can any amount of capital supply the place of rivers which constitute her great highways.

Nonetheless, the Pacific Railway Company received a franchise from the state of Missouri in 1849, and two years later the legislature voted $2 million for construction purposes. St. Louis added another $1 million in 1853, with the understanding that the line would extend as far as Kansas City. This was the first line on the western side of the Mississippi. But construction was slow. By 1860 only 181 miles of track had been laid, and but five of these in 1859.

In contrast, the railroad mania was strong in Chicago. In 1850 the *Daily Democrat* wrote:

> It will thus be seen that we are most favorably situated for the construction of means of intercommunication; and that in this respect the West offers facilities for railroads which are not to be found in the older states. It will be seen also, that of all the places in the West, Chicago is the most favorably placed as the centre of a great net-work of railway communication which will yet be constructed; but which requires the constant care of our citizens to provide that it shall inure to our benefit as to the general prosperity of the country.

Chicago's leaders lobbied for railroads in the legislature, urged private investors to support them, and in general did all possible to insure their construction. The Prairie du Chien; Galena & Chicago; Rock Island; Chicago, Burlington & Quincy, were sent as fingers into Wisconsin, Minnesota, and Iowa in the 1850s, and there were others. In 1850 there was not a single mile of railroad in Chicago; by 1855 the city was the terminus of 2,200 miles, serving an area of 150,000 square miles. And the mileage would double in the next five years.

Even before then, however, Chicago had begun cutting into the St. Louis market. Despite breakdowns, the railroads were more dependable and swifter than water transport. Canal, river, and lake rates were lower per mile than those quoted by the railroads in the 1850s. But the railroads were more dependable, and swifter too. Because of this, net transportation costs by rail were often lower than those by water.

Capitalizing upon this situation, Chicago's aggressive merchants outsold and outmaneuvered their St. Louis competitors. As early as 1854, the Galena [Missouri] *Jeffersonian* conceded that the issue was no longer in doubt:

> Until a year or two past, the business of Western Illinois and Wisconsin, and all of Iowa and Minnesota, was transacted for the most part at St. Louis. Thither went the lead, pork, wheat, corn, wool, and in fact all the products of the mine and farm that this vast country had to spare. To that trade, St. Louis is indebted for her growth and prosperity. She has been frequently warned, however, that her policy in reference to this country would eventually send it elsewhere; but the warnings were unheeded; she remained firm in doing nothing and today her rival, Chicago, from whom she had the most to fear, is in possession of what St. Louis ought long ago to have secured forever. Much of the result is due to the natural advantages of position claimed by Chicago, and the tendency of trade and travel from the West, Eastward; but more to the unaccountable supineness of the St. Louis merchants, who with this change all the while staring them full in the face, have not lifted a finger to ward off the blow. From the Falls of St. Anthony to Burlington, the whole country will be as much dependent hereafter upon Chicago, as the Missouri River country upon St. Louis.

Three years later the British consul in Chicago, Edward Wilkins, wrote that Chicago was indeed the new master of the Midwest. "Chicago may now be considered established as the chief depot for the receipt of domestic and foreign merchandise imported for consumption in the States and Territories west and northwest, and as the granary and primary market for the agricultural products of these regions." Wilkins saw "a great network of railroad . . . growing up, binding all the middle, northern, and western States."

New Orleans remained hopeful of a Gulf and South American future for America, while St. Louis continued to dream of national power, as did the leaders of Chicago. All spoke of the nineteenth century as a prelude to their twen-

A daguerreotype by Alexander Hesler of the Galena levee in Illinois (1852–54).

tieth-century mastery. Some, however, were content with a more limited vision. Chicago's victory over St. Louis and New Orleans meant the Midwest would be tied economically and politically with the Northeast and not the South in any conflict. Such a situation was fraught with significance for men like Stephen Douglas of Illinois, and Jefferson Davis of Mississippi, who already were eyeing one another in rehearsal for sectional conflict in the mid-1850s. To them railroads were not only commercial agents, but the vehicles that might determine the future political climate of America—and which of them would be elected president in 1856 or 1860.

3 / THE ALLIANCE OF RAILS

ON NEW YEAR'S DAY, 1851, THE NATION HAD JUST OVER 9,000 miles of railroad track. Most of the lines were local, centered in the Northeast. Although the railroad's potential was recognized, it was still far from realization. President Zachary Taylor had traveled most of the way from his home in Baton Rouge to Washington in 1847–48 by horse and coach. So did Clay, Webster, and Calhoun, as had Jefferson, Madison, and Washington when they journeyed to New York to participate in the first government under the Constitution in 1788–89. Not until 1848 would the nation's construction companies lay as much as 1,000 miles of track in a single year. And in 1851, only 1,274 miles were set down.

There were over 30,600 miles of railroad track in America in 1861, the result of a railroad boom that was one of the most significant developments of the early 1850s. Construction in 1852 was 2,288 miles, almost double that of the previous year, and in 1854, 3,442 miles were pushed into the countryside, a record that would stand for fifteen years. Then, as a result of overbuilding, depression, and war, construction leveled off and declined. Still, in the mid-1850s few doubted that the railroad was on its way to becoming a major factor in East-West trade and communication, while some were predicting that, in time, the railroad would conquer waterways and roads and perhaps even the great Mississippi itself. When Abraham Lincoln left Washington for his Illinois home in 1849, he traveled west by horse and coach. He would return in 1861 for his inauguration as president on a railroad.

In the early 1850s small lines united to form medium-size operations, new ones were organized that were far more am-

By the end of the 1850s railroad stations such as this one at Framingham, Massachusetts, dotted the eastern half of the nation.

COURTESY AMERICAN ANTIQUARIAN SOCIETY,
WORCESTER, MASSACHUSETTS

65

bitious than would have been dreamed of a decade earlier, and businessmen in New York, Philadelphia, Boston, and Baltimore, who in the 1840s had looked across the Atlantic for trade and profits, turned their attention to the American Midwest and Far West for economic opportunity. Philadelphia pinned its hopes on the Pennsylvania Railroad, four years old in 1850, and in 1852 the line from Philadelphia to Pittsburgh was completed, with the Penn's directors promising that the westward drive would continue. The previous year the Erie Railroad had opened its operations from New York City to Dunkirk, on Lake Erie, which not only challenged the Erie Canal, but opened cheaper and more dependable transport to the entire upper Midwest. Fearful of being bypassed, Maryland bankers and businessmen poured new funds into the Baltimore & Ohio, which entered Wheeling, Virginia, a few months after the Pennsylvania's first trains arrived in Pittsburgh. The news spurred New York's legislators into action. Previously they had urged several local lines to unite for the westward push. Now, in 1853, they chartered the New York Central, which was to be the Empire State's entry in the Atlantic-to-Mississippi contest. Was it too late? The previous year the Atlantic & St. Lawrence, to become the nucleus of the Grand Trunk system, united Portland, Maine, with Montreal, and there was talk of a link with Boston, and then a westward turn across Massachusetts and on to Chicago. New Yorkers were concerned, but not the leaders of Philadelphia, who promptly extended the Pennsylvania into Ohio and Indiana, seeking linkages with the western roads that were driving eastward.

In the spring of 1852 the Michigan Central and Michigan Southern entered Chicago, and these two lines, together with the Pennsylvania, converged on Alton, Illinois. By October, 1853, the rails were joined; now it was possible for a New Yorker or Philadelphian to travel by rail—making several changes along the way—to Chicago. More important as far as Chicago was concerned, it meant that midwestern grain, lumber, and beef, as well as other products of the farms and forests, could be shipped from that city by rail to the eastern seaboard, at low rates and, for the period, efficiently. It seemed a signal of its victory over St. Louis. Then, on February 22, 1854, the Rock Island & Chicago celebrated its drive from the Great Lakes to the Mississippi, uniting these two great bodies of water with twin bands of iron. To many orators this seemed a major demarcation point in the nation's history. Rock Island locomotives that drew morning water from Lake Michigan would replenish their supplies from the Mississippi in the evening. Other connections would follow, as Illinois was crisscrossed by tracks. By 1860 there were eight connections from the river to the state's western border, all with links to eastern lines. Some of these went through Indianapolis, which had glimmering hopes of greatness, and St. Louis had a connection too. But Chicago retained its position as Queen City of the Rails, in the Midwest, at least.

The railroad mania was stoked by bankers and investors, most of whom were New Yorkers or foreigners. Wall Street in particular embraced the growing industry, claiming it would lift the depression from the land and revive the sagging investment scene in New York. During the 1840s the auctions at the New York Stock & Exchange Board had been dominated by canal, bank, and insurance securities, and on a good day 10,000 shares might trade hands. Now that recovery was on its way, American investors nibbled at new railroad bonds and stocks, and by 1852 were taking them in large mouthfuls. Then came the foreigners, especially the English.

After the 1837 panic, when many American firms had gone bankrupt and foreigners had lost tens of millions of dollars on their investments, the English swore never again to return to the American investment scene. The Rothschilds, with branches in all parts of Europe, led the exodus. The head of the Paris office told one American that in the future, his country was off limits for the firm. "You may tell your government that you have seen the man who is at the head of the finance of Europe, and that he has told you that they cannot borrow a dollar, not a dollar." As late as 1850 the Rothschilds held true to this pledge. In that year the Barings, second to none in London, announced the firm would not invest in any American firms, with the possible exception of the Baltimore & Ohio Railroad.

But glowing reports from the California gold fields, coupled with economic recovery in America and the railroad boom, caused this attitude to change. Soon after the Americans had initiated the railroad bull market, the foreigners joined in. American rail securities became the glamour issues of the day, not only in New York, but in London and Paris as well. By 1853 some 26 percent of all American railroad bonds were in the hands of foreigners, most of them English. The Erie, which by 1853 was claiming to be the longest railroad in the world, was controlled by the English, and the Philadelphia & Reading and the Illinois Central conceded that London interests held a majority of their paper. By 1856 there was some $1.5 billion worth of American securities outstanding, of which $800 million were those of railroads. That year foreigners owned, directly or indirectly, $200 million in American stocks and bonds, and almost half this investment was in railroads. By then there were some 720 separate stocks and bonds of railroad companies traded in New York, a greater number than in any category except bank securities. The locomotives of the early 1850s were fueled by wood and coal, but the economic power was derived from dollars and pounds sterling, and these were at hand in plenty on Wall Street and Lombard Street.

It was a large investment for such crude and undependable lines. The roadbeds of this period were not carefully laid, so that within weeks of their completion the rides were rough enough to shake some trains from the tracks. Most rails were of wood topped with metal strips that would disengage from

An 1850s ambrotype of the interior of a railroad shop in South Framingham, Massachusetts.

COURTESY AMERICAN ANTIQUARIAN SOCIETY,
WORCESTER, MASSACHUSETTS

the wood and snake away from the road, causing crashes and breakdowns. By the mid-1850s most lines were replacing these with iron rails, which wore poorly, were expensive, and were either so brittle that they cracked, or so soft that they bent. Each line was free to use whatever gauge track it desired, while there was no standardization among locomotive and car manufacturers. Because of this, passengers and cargoes would have to be unloaded and reloaded at each junction of two lines.

Some railroad companies bravely threw bridges across rivers in their drive westward, but the firms were not as courageous as the passengers who risked their lives on these structures; the bridges broke down or collapsed regularly, causing losses of life and rolling stock, not to speak of cargo and baggage. Other lines used railroad ferries; these were the rule along the Susquehanna. But ferries could sink or collapse, and sometimes did. A passenger going from New York to Chicago in the late 1850s knew he or she was embarking on an adventure. Death could come in any of several ways, and one was through drowning.

If there was not too much water, there could be too little. The locomotives had to stop every twenty miles or so to take on water, usually from nearby stations or streams. If these were empty or dry, someone would be sent on ahead to obtain a supply, which usually came by horse and buggy, with the driver snickering at the balky train and its passengers, who by that time perhaps wished they too had gone west that way. Even the stop was dangerous, for the trains had chancy brakes; if they did work, they gave severe jolts to passengers, as each car whacked sharply against the one in front. One

In May 1858 two New York Central trains tried to pass one another on a double-tracked bridge near Utica, New York; the bridge collapsed under the weight.

passenger, writing of her experience in a New England train of the period, said the passengers were badly damaged during the trip, but the cars suffered more.

> The road was not ballasted for some distance from North Stratford, and the ties were laid on the snow. Snow started to fall just as the train left town. It labored up the heavy grade for a way, then cut off a portion of the train and the crew proceeded with engine and tender, and went on as far as Hobson's Mills, where the water gave out.

Hours later the passengers were "rescued" from their freezing cars by horses and wagons.

A train trip in the 1850s was an event. If not comparable with the astronauts' voyage to the Moon, it was at least as exciting as an auto excursion in 1900 or an airplane ride in 1920. Some trains scheduled regular runs between nearby towns for thrill seekers, who would pay a quarter for the

71

privilege of riding on a train and then bragging of the trip to their friends for weeks. A trip from New York to Buffalo was looked upon as a major undertaking, with the entire family at the station to see the adventurer off, and always someone to ask, "Wouldn't it be wiser to take the night boat to Albany and then go the rest of the way by canal?"

In 1851 Horace Greeley, the noted publisher and editor of the New York *Tribune*, published the famous cry, "Go west, young man, go west!" Two years later Greeley took his paper's advice. He went west, on a lecture tour, and by train. Thinking the trip a news event of some importance, Greeley sent dispatches to his paper. Some dealt with temperance, the subject of his talk, but most were concerned with the railroads, of even greater interest to his readers. Greeley wrote of fouled-up schedules, missed connections, discomforts of travelers, and whatever else he thought his readers might wish to know of long-distance train travel, since so few of them would ever have the opportunity to experience it firsthand. One morning he went to the station to catch his train for the next town.

> I was in ample season but the train that was to start at ten did not actually leave until noon, and then with a body entirely disproportionate to its head. Five cars closely packed with pigs, five ditto with wheat, two ditto with lumber, three or four with live stock and notions returning from the fair, and two or three cattle cars containing passengers, formed entirely too heavy a load for our asthmatic engine which had obviously seen its best days in the service of other roads before that from New Albany to Michigan City was constructed. Still, we went ahead, crossed the Wabash, passed the Tippecanoe Creek Battle ground, ran our engine partly off the track, and got it on again; and by three o'clock had reached Brookston, a station fourteen miles from Lafayette, with a fair prospect of traversing our ninety odd miles by the dawn of Monday morning.

This was not to be. The locomotive broke down several times along the way, and finally stalled, this time for good. The engineer told the passengers that there was a good locomotive forty-three miles up the line. He would go there, bring it back, make the connection, and then take his passengers on their way. The engineer would travel by handcar, of which there were several at the siding.

Unwilling to wait in the cold, dark coach for hours, maybe days, the forty-two-year-old Greeley and several other

Interior of an American railway car in the 1850s (Illustrated London News, 1857)

male passengers offered to go along with the engineer and act as his "pumpers."

> The full moon was bright over the eastern woods as with the north star straight ahead, we bid adieu to the embryo city of Brookston. We were seven of us in the handcar, four propelling by twos, as if turning a heavy, two-handed grindstone ... the car, about equal in size to a wheelbarrow and a half, just managed to hold us and give the propellors working room. To economize space, I sat a good part of the time facing backwards, with my feet dangling over the rear of the car, knocking here and there on a tie or a bridge timber, and often tickled through my boots by the coarse, rank weeds growing up at intervals between the ties and recently stiffened by the October frosts. . . . We made our first five miles in twenty-five minutes, our first ten miles in an hour, but our propellors grew gradually weary. We stopped twice or thrice for oil, water, and perhaps one other liquor, so that we were five hours in making forty-three miles, or from seven o'clock to midnight.

So traveled one of the most influential voices in America in the 1850s, a man who would receive the Democratic nomination for the presidency two decades later. Greeley was not disheartened by the trip, nor did he complain about the breakdowns. He wrote of them because he believed the *Tribune*'s readers would be interested, not because of anything unusual about the train ride. Greeley continued to speak glowingly of the West on his return to New York. In another dispatch he wrote that he saw scarcely a hundred houses during the entire forty-thee miles of the flatcar trip. But "he who passes this way ten years hence will see a different state of things."

If the rolling stock was shabby and the cars shaky, the railroads' finances were on foundations of sand with a superstructure of debt. Armed with state and local subsidies, funds obtained from bond and stock offerings, the railroad managers would begin work on their lines often without much in the way of experience or knowledge. Some of the lines were robbed by their executives and promoters, but the number of wrongdoers in railroading in the 1850s was no greater than that to be found in other arenas of American life. Their failures could more often than not be ascribed to poor business dealings, not unusual in an industry which after all was still in its pioneer stage. Henry Varnum Poor, the great railroad authority of the time, thought most abuses derived from "the inability of stock and bondholders to exercise personal oversight of the expenditure of their money," a good deal of which was wasted.

In this period there was no clear distinction between the roles of the railroad president as executive for the line and as businessman in his own right. Some honored and respected executives saw nothing wrong in accepting favors and even money as "gifts" from their counterparts at other lines. They were unclear as to their obligations to stock and bond holders, and since little accounting of activities was demanded, little was given. Edward L. Baker, president of the Chicago, Burlington & Quincy in the early 1850s, offered to pay part of the salary of the superintendent of the Burlington & Missouri to "protect the interest" of his own line. Edwin Morgan of the Hudson gave free tickets to newspaper editors in return for favors. Other railroad leaders engaged in land schemes, accepted presidencies of companies with which they did business, and offered gifts to legislators in return for votes on measures affecting their firms. Again, none of these activities was considered dishonest at the time, and most of them were public knowledge without embarrassing the individuals involved. George D. Phelps of the Delaware, Lackawanna &

Cartoon comment on rail-road "favors" and "gifts" (Harper's Weekly, *June 12, 1858*)

POLITICAL MARKET.

CONSCIENTIOUS RAIL-ROAD PRESIDENT to DEALER. "Ah! let me see. I think I'll take this bunch of Legislators at $5000 a head. The Senators, at—what price did you say?"
DEALER. "Can't afford 'em less than $10,000 each."
R. R. P. "Well, hand them over. I suppose I'll have to take the lot."
DEALER. "Any thing else to-day. I have a Lot of Editors, at various prices, from a Thousand down to Fifty Cents."
R. R. P. "No, nothing in that way, to-day. But I want a Governor very much indeed, and will stand $50,000 for him. Get me a Wisconsin one, if possible!"

Western, a highly considered leader of his day, spent a good deal of time in other pursuits, profiting at times from his railroad connection. In January, 1855, Phelps submitted his resignation.

> When I first accepted the office of President of the Compy it was with the supposition on my part that all the duties of the office could be discharged in *part* of the business hours of the day. I soon found, however, that the *whole* of my time, and all the energies of my mind and body were no more than adequate to the performance of the services required ... I sustained pecuniary losses quite disproportionate to the aggregate amount of eight thousand dollars received for my services for the past two years ... Your Bye-laws impose upon the President, extraordinary and unusual duties. He must not only examine appraise and report upon every contract made at Scranton, including those for the purchase of wood; but he must also make or superintend the purchasing of all materials ... He is not only required to sign all certificates of stock issued, and all Drafts ... in the payment of debts, but he must countersign every check for any amount of one hundred dollars upwards ... My judgement cannot approve the stringent policy of retrenchments adopted

76

... Should I continue by the devotion of a *part* of my time to the office, I would most cheerfully *give* such services without compensation, but the experience of the past two years convince me that the interests of the stockholders demands the *whole* time and the best energies of the most competent person.

Finally, there was the situation of John Van Schaick Lansing Pruyn, the aristocratic president pro tem of the New York Central and a man of unquestioned integrity, who in 1858 approved the hiring of lobbyists—"respectable persons who would avow their position to look after our interests and to pay them fully for it." Pruyn, only forty-seven at the time, was already tired of the business world. "There is no satisfaction in it," he wrote Erastus Corning, the railroad tycoon. Pruyn yearned for a diplomatic post. "My present position has no pleasure and certainly no profit."

But profit was to be had, even though there appeared little for Pruyn. In large part this was because of the very diversity of railroading, the interconnections between railroad operation, construction, land use, economic development, and politics. Many railroads did not show operating profits for many years, and when they did run in the black, it was only in the best years and then sporadically. However, operating losses could be made up by profits from construction contracts these railroads gave to their own subsidiaries or to construction firms owned by the railroad executives. The railroad might have received land grants from the state or locality, bait to encourage the line either to begin construction or to put out spurs. At the time of the grant the land would be worth very little; although it might be farmed, there would be no way to get produce to markets. The coming of the railroad changed this, making the land more desirable, and causing its price to rise. So the lines "created wealth"; even

Railroads frequently issued ads such as this.

DEAN COLLECTION, FREDERIC LEWIS, INC.

though their operations lost money, still more was to be made through proper land development.

Finally there was the nexus between state and federal politicians on the one hand and local businessmen on the other. This was a time when senators considered their primary duty to be ambassadors from their states to the federal government in Washington. In 1854 New York expected its senators, Hamilton Fish and William Seward, to protect its interests in the area of tariffs, internal improvements, and rivers and harbors bills, against the demands of Charles Sumner and Edward Everett of Massachusetts and James Cooper and Richard Brodhead of Pennsylvania, who were in Washington to obtain

78

benefits for Boston and Philadelphia. Fish was interested in diplomatic problems, while Seward was viewed as a leader in the antislavery crusade and hoped to become president on a platform calling for abolition. These were national concerns, not local, and Fish and Seward were free to pursue them—so long as they remembered they were New Yorkers and provided proper benefits for the people who sent them to the capital for that purpose. In the mid-1850s railroads had joined the list of local concerns, as senators and representatives from Illinois, Missouri, Louisiana and Mississippi, and California jockeyed for position, each trying to obtain passage of railroad legislation favorable to his state.

Railroads were also viewed as building blocks for the American empire, still very much an issue in the aftermath of the Mexican War. As such, they figured prominently in the presidential race of 1852, more so in the Democratic than in the Whig Party.

But there were other issues as well. Political leaders from Louisiana spoke of the need to take Cuba; Missouri and Illinois delegates wanted transportation to the Far West, and were seconded by Californians. The Democrats realized that sectional rivalries were intensifying, and that slavery was becoming more prominent an issue than it had been in the past, and that too was sectional. Yet they hoped that the imperial vision would unite them and the country. In effect, the party wanted another James K. Polk, who eight years earlier had led the country in the Mexican War.

At first it seemed one of three candidates would win the Democratic nomination—Stephen Douglas of Illinois, Lewis Cass of Michigan, or James Buchanan of Pennsylvania. In addition, there was support for William Marcy of New York.

All were interested in the welfare of their states, but more important, these men were compromisers by nature and hoped that through one or another accommodation, state and sectional issues could be resolved at least to the satisfaction of all, if not to their delight. In other words, the leading Democrats were men in the mold of the great Whig, Henry Clay.

None of them was able to secure a two-thirds vote at the convention, and after bitter wrangling the party turned to a dark horse, Franklin Pierce of New Hampshire. He was an undistinguished former congressman and senator who had risen from private to brigadier general in the Mexican War, and at the time of his nomination was practicing law. Pierce supported the Compromise of 1850 and so was, like the others, in the Clay image. He was a northerner with strong southern support. Relatively unknown, he had few enemies; and in 1852, that was an important factor in obtaining the nomination. The convention proceeded to select William King of Alabama as his running mate. The platform endorsed expansionism and manifest destiny. It was, in effect, a southern platform and a southern-approved candidate.

The Whigs held their convention a few weeks later. The party's old heroes, Clay and Webster, had been instrumental in the passage of the 1850 compromise, but unlike the Democrats, the Whigs had a strong and vocal Wilmot Proviso minority. The repeated antislavery statements of the "Conscience Whigs" had led Alexander Stephens and Robert Toombs to leave the party and join the Democrats. Just as the Democrats were rapidly becoming the voice of the South, so the Whigs were showing a decided northern cast. Still, the Whig party searched for unity and victory. They nominated

Franklin Pierce

General Winfield Scott, whose views on the compromise were unknown, in the hope the public would overlook this and remember his record in the Mexican War. The platform "acquiesced in" the compromise "until time and experience shall determine the necessity of further legislation." Thus, the Whigs attempted to straddle the issue.

As had been the case in the 1840s, an antislavery party put forth a platform and nominee. The Free Soil Party nominated John Hale of New Hampshire, and presented a platform condemning slavery in strong terms.

Offered the choice of Pierce and the compromise or Scott and uncertainty, the nation preferred the former. Pierce received 1.6 million popular votes and 254 electoral votes. He ran well in all sections, winning every state but

81

Vermont, Massachusetts, Tennessee, and Kentucky. Scott's electoral total was 42 and his popular vote 1.4 million. Hale received 156,000 votes, and showed strength in New York, Massachusetts, and Ohio; could his votes have been added to those of Scott, they would have switched four states to the Whig column. Still, this wouldn't have been sufficient to deny Pierce the presidency. In this way, the nation indicated its preference for the compromise and its desire to bury the slavery issue.

In his inaugural address Pierce promised to support the compromise and seek annexation of new lands through peaceful means. Nowhere did he mention internal improvements; there was no discussion of railroads. Yet the question was on his mind, even then, since leading Democrats already were pressuring him on the issue.

Pierce was president, but the strong man of his administration was Jefferson Davis, the new secretary of war, while Douglas was the bright star of the Senate. Both men, like the President, were compromisers. Davis was interested in a southern destiny for the nation, with economic power in New Orleans. Douglas of Illinois naturally favored the Northwest-East, with his home city of Chicago achieving further greatness. The party and administration were committed to national growth—but in which direction, and under which section's leadership? That was the question of the day.

As though to indicate his future policies, Pierce authorized the purchase of a small strip of Mexican territory for $10 million. Known as the Gadsden Purchase, it was believed useful for a future railroad that would unite the nation under southern leadership. Such a railroad might well have as its eastern terminus the port of New Orleans. At the same time,

American agents appeared to be involved in Cuba and Lower California, both areas of interest to southern expansionists. If the West was going to determine the nation's future, southerners in the administration wanted their section to settle the region, with the railroad the means of expansion and entry. Thomas Hart Benton of St. Louis and Stephen Douglas of Chicago naturally opposed such plans, even while they favored a western railroad. It was in this atmosphere that the great transportation debate of 1853–54 opened.

Ever since it had achieved statehood, California had lobbied for a railroad, and its proposal, authored by Senator William Gwin, was before Congress in 1853. It called for a federally supported railroad, to run eastward from San Francisco, ending in three different cities—Memphis, New Orleans, and St. Louis. Needless to say, this plan was favored by southerners in the Pierce administration.

There was a second plan, even older than Gwin's, first put forth by Connecticut merchant Asa Whitney in 1844. At the time Whitney tried to interest the federal government in a line from Lake Michigan westward, and after the Mexican War, he favored a terminus in San Francisco or the mouth of the Oregon River. As expected, the Whitney proposal won support from midwestern senators and congressmen, including Douglas.

Benton of Missouri opposed both the Gwin and Whitney plans. He said the nation needed "a great central national highway," and what city was more central than St. Louis? Benton's Missouri constituents were pleased by his remarks.

Finally, there was a fourth proposal, for an Atlantic & Pacific Railroad Company, to be organized in New York with southern backing. The line would receive financial backing from the government to the tune of $30 million. It would run from Memphis through Little Rock, Fulton, and El Paso, and end in San Diego. Branches could be constructed to other cities, from Chicago to New Orleans. All would benefit from the Atlantic & Pacific, but especially the promoters. Cave Johnson, the veteran congressman from Tennessee and postmaster general in Polk's cabinet, wrote of rumors regarding the new line in a letter to his old friend Buchanan.

> Stories are circulating freely in the West that the N.Y. Company, with a capital of one hundred millions, will lobby for the road and distribute stocks among the members [of Congress] and influential agents, and pass it over even a Presidential veto. R. J. W[alker] who is said to have subscribed ten millions is the chief manager in Washington—Law at New York—Foulkes of the Memphis Bank, takes a million, cum multiis aliis, of no more means and less character. There is said to be a provision in their agreement, that *at no time is there a call to be made for more than one-fourth of one per cent*—the work is to be accomplished out of the public land and the surplus money—what a stupendous project! The Yazoo speculation will be thrown into the shade by this stupendous scheme, and the frauds perpetuated in it will be molehills beside the mountain when contrasted with the corruption and frauds which that scheme will introduce into our country; but this is not all, several Presidents, Vice Presidents, ambassadors, and so on are to be made by it, and all the old fogies such as yourself, Cass, etc., are to be thrown overboard.

Then a senator from Pennsylvania, Buchanan still nursed ambitions for the presidency. His Pennsylvania constituents had no plan of their own for a railroad. Philadelphia had long bowed to New York as the capital center. As a Democratic leader, he was urged by many different groups to throw his support one way or another in the struggle over the railroad route. Unable to make a choice and disgusted by open bribery and dealings, Buchanan rose to deliver a broadside against these "leeches," the railroad agents corrupting Congress:

Jefferson Davis

If you defeat them at this session, they will be here in greater force than ever at the commencement of the next. Their importunity will never cease whilst the least hope of success shall remain, and we have learned from our experience that they have both the ability and the will to select shrewd and skillful agents to accomplish their purposes before Congress.

Such cries had no effect. Under the direction of Jefferson Davis, Congress appropriated $150,000 to be used by the War Department to survey the various proposed routes as a prelude to construction of a railroad. Since Davis would supervise the survey, it seemed evident that he would recommend the New Orleans route. Indeed, there were good reasons to support such a choice. A southern railroad would pass through the state of Texas and the organized territory of New Mexico; there were no serious Indian problems in the region; and the land was fairly flat. Advocates of routes to the north had to admit that the northern territories were yet unorganized and had serious Indian troubles. Douglas, still working for a Chicago terminus, moved swiftly to eliminate these arguments. As chairman of the Senate Committee on Territories, he was able to direct the Commissioner of Indian Affairs to begin negotiations to remove the Indians from the northern areas. Then, in January of 1854, he introduced a measure to organize the northern territories, in preparation for eventual statehood.

Always a political realist, Douglas knew the slavery issue was bound to complicate matters. If parts of the new territories were open to slavery, many northerners might object, while the South would demand parity in the admission of new states. Since the entire new territory would be north of the Missouri Compromise line, under its terms it would seem any new states would by necessity be free. This would be unacceptable to the South. If Douglas were to remain popular in Illinois, he would have to fight hard for the railroad, and so needed organization of the northern lands. But Douglas also wanted the presidency, and on the Democratic ticket, at a time when that party was coming increasingly under the control of the South. How could he please his friends in Illinois and at the same time retain his allies in the South? It was a question demanding the sophistication of a Clay for an answer.

Douglas responded to the challenge, and did so in an ingenious manner. First he suggested that the Compromise of 1850 had negated the Missouri Compromise, since the territories acquired as a result of the Mexican War had been allowed to decide for themselves the question of free or slave status. Next, he proposed to divide the new northern territory into two parts, Kansas and Nebraska. Then he introduced a measure to allow the future status of the new territories to be decided by their inhabitants—popular sovereignty. Finally, he convinced southern Democrats that while Nebraska would enter the Union as a free state, Kansas, bounded by the slave state of Missouri to the east, was destined for slavery.

Designed to allow a railroad to be constructed in the West with a terminal at Chicago, the Kansas-Nebraska Act served to reopen the debates of 1850 and revive sectional tensions. This time the divisions were clearer than before, with southern Democrats supporting the measure while northern Democrats joined with Whigs in opposition. Salmon Chase of Ohio and Charles Sumner of Massachusetts attacked the measure as "a gross violation of a sacred pledge; as a criminal betrayal of precious rights; as part and parcel of an atrocious plot to exclude from a vast and unoccupied region immigrants from the Old World and free laborers from our own states and convert it into a dreary region of despotism, inhabited by masters and slaves." Northerners accused Douglas of having introduced the bill in order to gain support for the 1856 presidential nomination. Douglas said little. The South was pleased with the compromise. And his supporters in Chicago were enthusiastic in his favor. The bill passed the Senate by a vote of 37-14 and the House by 113-100. Pierce signed it into law, hoping that, as had been the case in 1850, both sections would learn to accept compromise.

But the President, Davis, and Douglas knew by then that such was not to be the case. In early 1853 railroads had seemed the key to the nation's western destiny, and all hoped the country would be brought together in an alliance of rails. The only difference seemed to be which city and section would dominate this alliance. The Kansas-Nebraska Act, which Douglas hoped would settle the debate in favor of Chicago over New Orleans, proved only a round in the contest. At the same time, it tore open a great wound in Washington, one that would be felt to the rest of the nation even more swiftly than the most rapid railroad locomotive.

4 / THE RISE OF THE FACTORY

PROFESSOR OF POLITICAL ECONOMY AT THE UNIVERSITY
of Louisiana and superintendent of the United States Census
as well as a noted editor and publisher, J.D.B. DeBow was
widely recognized as an authority on the American economy.
In 1852 he published an encyclopedic work on the United
States, much of which was culled from the 1850 census. *The
Industrial Resources, Statistics, Etc., of the United States and
More Particularly of the Southern and Western States* was, as
its title indicated, a view of America from the South, and the
plantation and commercial South in particular. DeBow recognized the need for urban centers as places for the processing and shipment of goods from plantation and farm. They
were necessary, but not particularly desirable. "Though every
nation be, in fact, primarily dependent upon its soil for the
means of support, none can be said to be purely agricultural,"

he wrote, with some regret. "Even where, in a more advanced period, the vast proportion of the people are employed upon the soil, as is the case in the north of Europe, some kinds of manufactures, however rude, will still gradually grow up," he added, as though viewing the spread of a cancer upon the land.

> Manufactures contribute to opulence and luxury, the growth of cities, and their splendors; but the almost incessant concomitant is dense population, and all the evils in the train—poverty, suffering, ignorance and crime. These occur only in the most highly advanced state, and are dependent much, perhaps, upon unwise laws for their intensity. When the manufacturing spirit reaches this point, it becomes a great social and political evil.

Natural or artificial, good or bad, manufacturing, the factory system, urban centers, "and all the evils in the train" grew rapidly in the 1850s. Yet most Americans of 1860, like those of a decade earlier, lived rural existences, and if they were engaged in manufacturing enterprises, it was in those that involved processing of agricultural products.

But farmhands who even then were beginning to make the trek to the rapidly growing factory towns were signaling the rapid growth of the industrial system. So were the immigrants who, instead of setting out for the plains, remained in the port cities to seek employment. In his "Song of the Broad-Axe," written in 1856, Walt Whitman celebrated his America, with special reference to the industrial nation:

The shapes arise!
Shapes of factories, arsenals, foundries, markets,
Shapes of the two-threaded tracks of railroads,
Shapes of the sleepers of bridges, vast frameworks, girders, arches,
Shapes of the fleets of barges, tows, lake and canal craft, river craft. . . .
The tools lying around, the great auger and little auger, the adze, bolt,
    line, square, gouge, and bead-plane. . . .

Interlink'd, food-yielding lands!
Land of coal and iron! land of gold! land of cotton, sugar, rice!
Land of wheat, beef, pork! land of wool and hemp! land of the apple and
    the grape!
See, in my poems, cities, solid, vast, inland, with paved streets, with iron
    and stone edifices, ceaseless vehicles, and commerce. . . .

As Whitman saw it, agrarian and industrial America were working in harmony, to produce a new and better variation of the American Dream. In the 1850s such an amalgam seemed possible. For a while at least the two worlds seemed in balance. The next generations of Americans would think otherwise.

TABLE 3

UNITED STATES MANUFACTURES, 1860*

Item	Cost of Raw Material	Number of Employees	Value of Product	Value Added by Manufacture	Rank by Value Added
Cotton goods	$52,666,701	114,955	$107,337,783	$54,671,082	1
Lumber	51,358,400	75,595	104,928,342	53,569,942	2
Boots and shoes	42,728,174	123,026	91,889,298	49,161,124	3
Flour and meal	208,497,309	27,682	248,580,365	40,083,056	4
Men's clothing	44,149,752	114,800	80,830,555	36,680,803	5
Iron	37,486,056	48,975	73,175,332	35,689,276	6
Machinery	19,444,533	41,223	52,010,376	32,565,843	7
Woolen goods	35,652,701	40,597	60,685,190	25,032,489	8
Carriages, wagons	11,898,282	37,102	35,552,842	23,654,560	9
Leather	44,520,737	22,679	67,306,452	22,785,715	10

* Source: *Eighth Census of the United States, 1860: Manufactures* (Washington, D.C.), pp. 733–42.

Americans of 1860 purchased more domestically produced manufactured goods than had their counterparts of

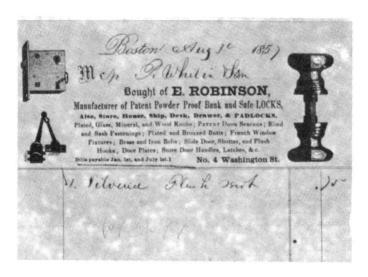

Old bill of sale dated August 30, 1857.

1850. Still, most manufactured goods used in America came from overseas, especially from Great Britain. The United States exported cotton and grain to Europe, and with the money earned by their sale, purchased finished goods. This pattern had been set in the colonial period, and still existed in the 1850s. But it was changing.

As had been the case throughout the previous half century, cotton textiles and lumbering were the leading American industries in this period. Or as the 1860 census put it, "The growth of the culture and manufacture of cotton in the United States constitutes the most striking feature of the industrial history of the last fifty years." American cotton textiles were recognized the world over as offering the best value for their price. Bolts of fabric and large spools of thread were turned out by the tens of thousands each year in the New England factories and mill towns, and from there sent to Boston and New York for shipment to Europe, or for use as trading goods in the Pacific and Asia. More went to the small shops in the cities throughout the nation, where they would be turned into clothing for domestic sale, or for sale in dry goods stores. A. T. Stewart, who opened his Marble Dry-Goods Palace at Broadway and Chambers Street in New York in 1846, boasted he offered more different kinds of cloth, most of it of domestic manufacture, than any other shopkeeper in the nation. The department store idea spread throughout the nation in the 1850s, so that by the late 1850s there were imitations of the Stewart emporium in St. Louis, Chicago, and New Orleans as well as in Boston and Philadelphia. All of these featured low-priced, high-quality American cotton cloth, most of which had been produced in the factories

An 1850 lithograph of Stewart's buildings and Broadway, looking north from below Chambers Street.

THE EDWARD W. C. ARNOLD COLLECTION
LENT BY THE METROPOLITAN MUSEUM OF ART.
PHOTO COURTESY OF MUSEUM OF THE CITY OF NEW YORK

A daguerreotype of a New England mill c. 1855.

of the New England states, with Massachusetts leading the way.

The factory was not new in the 1850s, the first having been established in New England after the War of 1812. Nor were these production centers American in origin, but rather borrowed from Britain. But textile factories developed rapidly in New England, so that by 1850 they produced almost one-fifth of all the cloth in the country (the rest coming from home industry). In 1860 slightly less than half the nation's textiles came from the mill towns.

In its simplest form the factory was a place where management brought together labor and raw materials to produce finished products. It developed when home industry proved inadequate for the task set for it and too costly for the market to bear. But factories did more than that. They encouraged division of labor, standardization, and mechanization. Rather than producing for demand, factory owners turned out their product and then hired salesmen to merchandise it through the region, country, and eventually the world. All of these features were important, for although they first appeared in textiles, they eventually developed in other industries as well.

And each had implications far beyond the expectation of the manufacturers. Division of labor encouraged the development of labor consciousness, and eventually, trade unions. Standardization resulted in uniformity and lower costs, which in turn was translated into greater sales volume, after which the cycle would repeat itself. Mechanization gave impetus to other industries, machine tools and iron in particular, and often resulted in lower labor costs per unit. The need to merchandise products helped create the science of salesmanship, as well as the art of selling, which was quite a different matter. All of these, combined with the rapid development of transportation, fit in well with the national marketing of goods, which in its own way provided a stimulus to almost all branches of business.

Little of this was recognized at the time, but all were present in the early 1850s, and in textiles in particular. From 1850 to 1860 the number of spindles used in American textile mills rose from 4 million to over 6 million, the capital invested in textile factories went from $76 million to $98 million, and the yards of cloth produced from 828 million to 1.2 billion. Furthermore, the cloth produced at the end of the decade was in most instances of higher quality and lower cost than that to be found in 1850. The factory system and all it entailed were present at the beginning of the decade; by its end mechanization and centralization of functions had jelled and matured to the point that most American businessmen recognized it as the way of the future.

The lumber industry grew even faster than did textiles, and mechanized almost as rapidly. In 1850 the nation's 17,-895 mills produced $58.5 million worth of lumber and lumber products; in 1860 there were 20,165 mills in the land, turning out $105 million in wood products.

As had been the case since the earliest settlements, there was no shortage of forests in the nation. But they were being

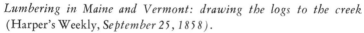

Lumbering in Maine and Vermont: drawing the logs to the creek (Harper's Weekly, *September 25, 1858*).

depleted at an ever increasing rate. Prior to the Revolution, explorers had claimed it was possible for a squirrel to travel from tree to tree, from the Atlantic to the Mississippi, without ever touching ground. This was a more difficult feat by 1860, as increased demand for wood for the construction of ships, factories, and homes took its toll. Maine, for a while the leading lumber state in the Union, was in decline during the 1850s, the result both of forest depletion and the movement of the nation westward. Now western New York and Pennsylvania were prime areas. By 1860 the Saginaw district of Michigan and the Green Bay area of Wisconsin were undergoing heavy lumbering activities. As we have seen, Chicago had emerged as a major center for the sale and distribution of upper Midwest lumber. But most of the mills were in small towns, in or near the great forests, or on bodies of water or railroad sidings, from which the products could be shipped to market. There, as in the textile towns of Massachusetts, the factory system was taking hold. In writing of the lumber mills of Bay City, Michigan, later on, a reporter said:

> The mill, salt-works, and other buildings, cover a very large area. The river-front and slips, from which the lumber, lath, shingles, and salt can be placed on steam and sailing vessels, are a mile and a quarter in extent. The motive-powers of the saw mill and other works are one engine of 760 horse power, and four smaller engines used for various purposes. There are 225 men employed in and about the mill, salt-works and yard.

Significant though the changes in textiles and lumber were in the 1850s, they were slight compared to those in other of the nation's leading industries. Shoe and clothing manufacturing boomed during the decade, and the developments of the shoe industry had major implications for leather. None of the three could have progressed as rapidly as it did were it not for the development of machinery, made of iron, which created additional demands for that metal. Railroading not only affected the carriage and wagon business, which built cars for the carriers, but also helped create a larger market for shoes and clothing, as it did for textiles and lumber. When the decade opened, most manufacturers of consumer goods and machinery produced for local consumption, with a small part of their product sold to jobbers and exporters. By 1850 the lineaments of a national market could be seen, and these would have major implications for American industry.

Foreigners perceived this rapid and important change before it was recognized by Americans. In 1850 only $17 million in American manufactures was exported, the amount more than doubling to $36 million in 1860. Yet in this same period imports of finished manufactures from Europe rose from $95 million to $172 million, approximately half of all imports in both years.

By far the largest share of these imports came from Britain, which in 1850 was recognized as the industrial leader of the world, even as other countries prepared to challenge her. The British were aware of competition, and were particularly interested in the United States. Throughout the early nineteenth century many skilled British workmen emigrated to America, most in search of higher wages, and they used their skills to advantage in helping develop American industry. The higher wages did exist, but still greater productivity in America more than compensated for the higher labor cost. As early as 1831 Nathan Appleton, a major producer of cotton textiles, recognized this, and wrote, "I have no hesitation in asserting that in this particular article . . . we pay a less sum for labor in converting a pound of cotton into a pound of cloth, than is paid in Manchester for the same purpose." British competitors were aware that Massachusetts factories were more fully mechanized than were their own, and feared the Americans would soon seize the lead in some areas of manufacturing. Their descriptions of the early industrial revolution in the United States and the undertones of their arguments sound vaguely reminiscent of contemporary American observations on the Japanese. "Throttle spinning is nearly as cheap in this country as in Britain," remarked one Englishman after a tour of New England's factories, "in consequence of the higher speed at which spinning frames are driven, and the greater quantity of work produced in a given time." Another told a parliamentary commission studying the subject, "I apprehend that the chief part, or a majority, at all events, of the really new inventions, that is, of new ideas altogether, in the carrying out of a certain process by new machinery, or in a new mode, have originated abroad, especially in America." The Americans, he said, had a novel approach to mechanization, one free from the prejudices of the past.

> I should say that most of the American inventions have had their origin in this way: in America we know that labour has hitherto been dear ... parties, not having access to the machine-makers of this country for the supply of their wants, have set themselves about to make a machine in the readiest mode to accomplish that which they required; they have been untrammelled by predilections in favor of a machine already in existence, but having an idea of a mode in which to carry out a process they have at once set their minds and ingenuity to work, and in so doing the most roundabout mode has suggested itself to accomplish the object.

Finally, English visitors were struck by what to them was an obvious American love of machines for their own sake.

"An American's feelings toward a mechanical contrivance is akin to an Englishman's love of an animal," is the way one observer put it. "The great glory of the Americans is in their wondrous contrivances," wrote another, "in their patent remedies for the usually troublous operations of life."

> In their huge hotels all the bell ropes of each house ring on one bell only; but a patent indicator discloses a number, and the whereabouts of the ringer is shown. One fire heats every room, passage, hall, and cupboard, and does it so effectually that the inhabitants are all but stifled. Soda water bottles open themselves without any trouble of wire or strings. Men and women go up and downstairs without motive power of their own. Hot and cold water are laid into all the chambers; though it sometimes happens that the water from both taps is boiling, and that, when once turned on, it cannot be turned off again by any human energy. Everything is done by a wonderful new and patent contrivance. . . .

America served notice on Britain of its technical prowess at the famous Crystal Palace Exposition of 1851, when handicrafts, artifacts, and manufactures from all parts of the world were shown at the great fair, sponsored by Prince Albert and blessed by the Queen. Visitors to London that year wandered through the American exhibit, which though criticized for its randomness and poor selectivity, was impressive for some of its manufactured goods. Colt revolvers won particular praise, with both military and civilians asking for means of placing orders, while *Punch* magazine wrote:

> Oh! Colonel Colt
> A Thunderbolt
> I'd buy—for no small trifle;
> But that can't be,
> And so let me
> Get your revolving rifle!

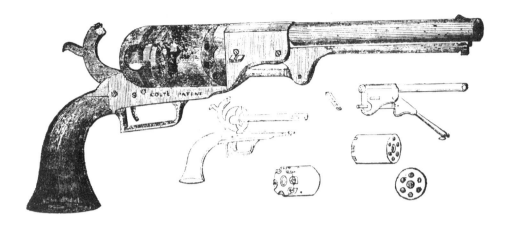

On July 5, 1851, The Illustrated London News *carried this diagram of Colt's revolver, stating that it "is so terribly efficient in its operations as to leave all former inventions of the kind far in the background."*

To which the London *Times* added, "It is beyond all denial that every practical success of the season belongs to the Americans. Their consignments showed poorly at first, but came out well upon trial. Their reaping machine has carried conviction to the heart of British agriculture." The McCormick reaper, which won this applause, was said to be "the most important addition to farming machinery since the threshing machine took the place of the flail." In addition, Charles Goodyear won an award for his India rubber products, Gail Bordon for his "meat biscuit," and Blodgett & Lerow for their sewing machine.

Later that year the "America" won the Cowes Regatta, easily defeating rival British yachts. "No Englishman ever dreamed," said the *Times*, "that any nation could produce a yacht with the least pretensions to match the efforts of

Camper, Ratsey, and other eminent builders." But it did, another indication of the growing superiority of American design and construction.

As far as we know, American clothing and shoes were not sent to London for display in 1851. Visitors to the Crystal Palace were able to view machines used in their fabrication, but not the finished goods themselves. Yet the manufacture of these goods, and the reason for the growth of their industries, was one of the more striking aspects of the industrial scene in the 1850s.

Although the population grew in the 1850s, and during the first half of the decade the nation was prosperous, numbers and wealth were not the reasons for the expansion of the clothing and shoe industries. Rather, their growth was due to two other factors: mechanization and anthropometry.

The science of human measurements—anthropometry—was unknown in 1850. Indeed, the word itself was not in common usage. It was generally assumed that no two bodies were identical, and that clothing would have to be made to order if a proper fit was to be had. During the first half of the century most Americans wore either homemade or tailor-fitted clothes, the former for the poor and middle class, the latter for the wealthy. Of course, ready-made clothing was to be had, sewn by tailors in cities and towns for individuals who hadn't the means for either of the other two varieties. Since the tailor had to guess about measurements, and often the clothing he produced was ill-fitting, the establishments that sold ready-made were called "slop-shops," while the clothes themselves were dubbed "slops." Sailors, workers, and itinerants purchased such clothing, which could easily be spotted by the poor fit.

The same was true for shoes, with dire results for those who had to buy ready-mades. Indeed, in 1850 most ready-made shoes were "straights," constructed so each would fit either foot. The purchase of such shoes was an invitation to orthopedic disaster.

Mechanization of clothing and shoe production gathered steam at this time. One of the more important innovations came in the area of sewing machines. Crude contraptions had been developed as early as the turn of the century, and in the 1830s sewing machines, based on American patents, were used in France. Walter Hunt, G. A. Arrowsmith, and J. J. Greenough patented sewing machines in the 1830s and 1840s, and although some were produced, all either broke down repeatedly or performed inadequately. Elias Howe patented his machine in 1846, and after failing to produce satisfactory protoypes, tried to sell the device in England, where he met with little encouragement. Early in 1850, Allen Wilson of Pittsfield, Pennsylvania, produced a machine, and planned to open a factory for its production. But the Wilson machine was inferior to one produced the previous year by Isaac Singer of New York. Utilizing patents held by others as well as new ones of his own, Singer produced a machine that sold for $40, worked efficiently, and was relatively trouble-free. The sewing machine revolution was on.

Singer and his partners, Edward Clark and George Zieber, produced machines that sold so well others were attracted to the field. Price and quality competition was fierce, as three large firms, Singer, Grover & Baker, and Wheeler & Wilson —took the lead. Then Howe sued them all for infringements of patents. In the end, Howe settled for a generous royalty arrangement, and competition resumed, with Wheeler &

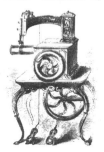
An ad for one of the early Howe sewing machines.

NEW YORK PUBLIC LIBRARY

Wilson emerging as the industry's leader and Singer a close second. Some 130,000 sewing machines were sold in the 1850s, and of these, Wheeler & Wilson accounted for 55,000 and Singer for 40,000. Most were purchased by tailors and men wishing to open clothing factories, and these were attracted to the Wheeler & Wilson model. Singer, Clark, and Zieber also wanted this market, but they set their sights higher: the partners aimed to have a sewing machine in every American home.

103

They began their work in 1852, attempting to convince a skeptical public that almost anyone could operate their device. Clark rented a storefront in New York and placed a woman at a machine in the window, instructing her to sit there and sew. The "exhibition" drew large crowds, who entered the store to watch more closely and ask questions of salesmen and technicians. This represented a new way of salesmanship, as Clark acknowledged. "The business we do is peculiar," he wrote, "and we have adopted our own method of transacting it."

Nor was this Clark's only innovation. In 1856 he announced that anyone who owned an "inferior" machine (meaning any sewing machine that was not a Singer) could trade it in against a new Singer and receive $50 toward the purchase price. Clark sold his machines to clergymen at large discounts, realizing they might recommend them to their parishioners. He offered them to newspaper editors at half price, with the understanding the other half would be paid for by advertising space. Finally, Clark introduced the concept of time purchases into the industry. "A psychological fact, possibly new, which has come to light in this sewing machine business, is that a woman would rather pay $100 for a machine in monthly installments of five dollars than $50 outright, although able to do so." This was Clark's "discovery," as printed in the *Scientific American*. Singer proved a genius at invention and production, and Clark was his equal in sales. Together they laid the foundation for not only a successful company, but a giant industry.

The sewing machine was quickly adapted to the shoe business. To it was added the McKay machine for sewing uppers to soles, with the power derived from George Henry Corliss' reciprocating steam engine, patented in Britain in 1849. Together these made the transition from the shoemaker's shop to the shoe factory even more rapid than that from the tailor to the clothing factory because of the relatively fewer operations needed to produce a shoe, and the smaller number of variations in size. Within a few years large factories were erected in New England and New York, with the industry's center in central Massachusetts. Factories doing $750,000 worth of business annually were not uncommon, while one firm claimed to have sold $1.3 million worth of shoes, produced at its five factories, in a single year.

As was the case with textiles, the clothing and shoe industries underwent a drastic change in sales orientation in the 1850s. Prior to that decade production on *demand* had been the rule. That is to say, most shoes and clothes were made when a customer walked into a shop, indicated his intention to buy, was measured, and later on, picked up the finished product. Given the technology of the sewing machine and related devices, such business techniques were impractical. In order to maximize profits, factories had to turn out goods almost continuously, hoping customers would, like what they saw in the ready-made shops. For the first time American manufacturers of clothing and shoes began to worry about styles not for the individual, but for the masses. This marked the beginning of a subtle but major change in merchandising techniques. Prior to the 1850s, clothing and shoes were *sold*. Beginning in the 1850s and developing rapidly thereafter, such goods increasingly were *advertised*. Selling in the context of 1850 implied a one-to-one relationship between shopkeeper and customer. Advertising, as it developed in the 1850s, was an attempt on the part of a manufacturer (often

Technological innovations such as steam sewing machines brought about dramatic changes in manufacturing, marketing, and advertising (The Illustrated London News, *December 1854*).

rather impersonal) to contact the broad mass of faceless individuals. For the first time, such advertising made its appearance in newspapers, beginning in New York in the early 1850s and proceeding rapidly thereafter. The mass marketing economy was beginning, though as in the case of the national economy, its outlines were barely visible in this decade.

Mass marketing required a better knowledge of the consumer "class" rather than the "individual" consumer. This was where anthropometry came in. Unable to produce what to them must have seemed an infinite number of sizes for the mass market, clothing and shoe manufacturers tried to produce goods in the most popular ones. But what were they? How could such knowledge be discovered? For the most part,

106

on a hit-or-miss basis. Manufacturers of men's suits, for example, would guess as to sizes, send out batches of suits, often with an understanding they would take back those which were not sold, and later on, try to concentrate on the sizes that were purchased—an unscientific method, perhaps, but the only one available at the time.

Not until the early 1860s would anthropometry come into its own as a result of the Civil War. With millions of men in the Union armies, the clothing industry received a giant boost. Now tailors were called upon to produce not one or two, but hundreds and in some cases thousands of uniforms. The information gathered in this period provided the size information and sizing techniques so necessary to the ready-to-wear industries. But in the 1850s, the problem was only perceived, not met.

Most American factories were contructed of wood, stone, brick, or a combination of the three materials. The machines within the factories were often made of wood, although iron- and steel-clad machines were becoming increasingly evident. The agricultural implements that so impressed the visitors at the Crystal Palace were made of iron, steel, and wood. The iron and steel locomotives, which became so popular that the Americans were able to compete successfully with the Europeans for the Russian market, created new demands upon the nation's iron and steel industry. So did the sewing machines that were revolutionizing the clothing and shoe industries.

Much of the nation's iron and steel came from Europe in the pre-Civil War era, and as the demand for the metals increased, so did their importation. In 1840 the United States imported $7.1 million worth of iron and steel, including firearms, which was 8 percent of the nation's total imports.

In 1850 the figure was $17.5 million, which was 11 percent, and in 1860, $21.2 million and 6 percent. Without Europe's steel, American industries would have been severely crippled.

The United States needed iron and steel, and had the natural resources for their production. Small furnaces were started in all parts of the nation, and there were literally hundreds of them in operation in the 1850s. Most resembled the back-yard operations the Chinese attempted in the 1950s and early 1960s, and like these, they were economically unfeasible and highly inefficient. Even then it was recognized that iron and steel would become large-scale operations, and that the small furnaces, tended by two or three men, would give way in time to large operations employing dozens, if not hundreds, of workers.

But American businessmen lacked the capital for such complexes. Foundries would be formed, attempt to sell products, fail, and then be purchased by new men, who would go through the experience all over again. Writing of his experiences in the late 1840s, one ironman lamented:

> . . . so they quit, gave up the whole thing as a failure, leaving machinery and everything standing there. I bought the whole thing for a small sum, took it down and moved it to Youngstown, built the Falcan furnace and used the Welshman's machinery and everything else I could use. I had saved up $700 of my salary and I thought I was rich enough to be an ironmaster on my own account. I found out later that $700 was not anything like enough money to build and run a blast furnace; so after running one year I sold out. . . .

Despite many such failures, the iron industry grew rapidly in the 1850s, sparked by an ever increasing demand for its products. Or perhaps the failures actually helped the industry develop, for the smaller, less efficient, and poorly capitalized units gave way to larger and more efficient foundries. Statistics for this period are difficult to come by, and are usually somewhat inaccurate. The best estimates, compiled by the American Iron and Steel Association, indicate that production in 1850 stood at 564,755 tons, which came from 404 foundries. In 1860 the nation had fewer iron works—only 286—but these turned out 919,770 tons.

By 1860 the industry had become more concentrated in a few states, as the smaller units in areas poor in ore, coal or charcoal, and limestone began importing their iron from the better-endowed ones. Almost 60 percent of the nation's iron came from Pennsylvania in 1860, and that state had 125 blast furnaces. Ohio was second, and had 48 furnaces, with New

A general view of the Novelty Iron Works, New York (Harper's Weekly, *1851*).

York's 15 furnaces putting it in third place. The iron pigs would be sent from the furnaces to all parts of the nation, to be turned into finished products. Massachusetts, which produced little in the way of iron, became a leader in the wire industry, for example. But for the most part, iron was fashioned into finished products in the same areas in which the pigs were formed.

The nation's iron foundries were considered architectural wonders, and attracted tourists as well as businessmen and customers to their doors. To Americans of the 1850s, these were the epitome of the coming age of the factory. One writer, describing the Allentown Iron Company's steam furnaces, thought they threw "to the shade many of the castles of Europe."

> No finer object of art invites the artist. The still huger pile of the Crane Works on the opposite side of the river a little higher up is rendered less striking by the vicinity of the hills; the Allentown Works rise unobstructed and unrivalled by surrounding sights, a world of stone and iron in the air, its summit crowned with tall chimneys like the turrets of Caernarvon, flames issuing from its tunnel heads, and cars travelling up and down its planes, long trains of ore mules passing to and fro across its lofty bridges, while other trains of railroad cars wait below to carry off its iron. The repose of bygone centuries seems to sit on its immense walls, while the roaring energy of the present day fills it with a truer and better life than the revelry of Kenilworth or the chivalry of Heidelberg. Its archways conceal a perfected alchemy where the spirit of the wind converts earth to iron and dross to gold, condensing around this pile of matter a little world of intellectual and moral happiness and energy to which poets and statesmen might profitably travel to learn more than is read in books or declaimed in Congress.

Mercantile Agency credit reports can tell us more of the actual operations of such plants, however, and of the nature of the business. In 1858, for example, the leading producer in the Pittsburgh area was Zug & Painter, which according to a credit report of that year "sold more iron in the past 12 mos. than any other company here." The already famous Tredegar Iron Works of Richmond, Virginia, was reported on in 1856. "Foundry here do a heavy bus. Men of high character ... plenty of means." Charles Scranton of Warren County, New Jersey, was the subject of reports throughout the decade. In 1850 he "made a large purchase of land for $60,000. We don't know where he will get the money to pay for it, presume he has friends in N.Y. who furnish the money." A year later we learn that Scranton "is doing a tremendous business, of course his friends furnish the money." Then, in 1852, "he is doing a heavy business." And so it would go for the next few years, until the credit reporter dropped references to Scranton's friends, signifying he had paid off his debts and was now on his own.

TABLE 4

BAR, SHEET, AND RAILROAD IRON PRODUCTION, 1860*

State	Bars	Plate and Sheets	Railroad Iron	Misc.	Total
Pennsylvania	112,276	20,000	133,577	400	266,253
Massachusetts	9,425	6,000	24,000	1,500	40,925
Ohio	20,495	1,200	19,000		40,695
New York	22,825	1,450	14,000		38,275
New Jersey	9,561	7,725	11,000	900	29,186

* Source: *Manufactures of the United States in 1860*, p. clxxxiii.

Steel production presented other problems besides the ones already mentioned. Americans and Europeans recognized that steel was preferable to iron in most industrial applications. But the processes used in transforming bar iron into steel were inadequate, and there were few Americans skilled in the art of steel production. In the early 1830s there were only fourteen steel furnaces in the entire country, three each in New York and Baltimore, at the time the centers of steel production. The furnaces were capable of producing 1,600 tons of steel a year, less than was being imported from England. This steel was produced by placing wrought iron in beds of fine charcoal and heating it to around 1300° F., until the carbon from the charcoal entered the iron. The process, known as cementation, was tedious, inexact, and could take as long as seven days. If too much carbon entered the iron, the product would be brittle; too little meant the producer had relatively soft wrought iron. A successful run produced small amounts of "blister steel," which was then further worked into small, expensive items, such as men's razors.

In the early 1850s some steel men experimented with the crucible process, which required further finishing of poor grade blister steel, usually in clay and plumbago "pots," which were imported from Europe. It was in this period that Pittsburgh took the lead in both blister and crucible steels, and led the nation in the application of steel technology to many finished products, springs in particular. One ironmaster of the time wrote:

> The blister steel made at Pittsburgh was sent all over the west, and was used by the country blacksmiths for the pointing of picks, mattocks, etc., and for plating down into rough hoes, etc. ... German steel [a term that signified a fine Pittsburgh product] was simply blister steel rolled down. The two leading applications of German steel were springs and ploughshares. The business was very large at one time. G. & J. H. Shoenberger

pushed this brand vigorously from about 1840 to 1860. Meanwhile quite a number of other concerns entered into the competition at various times.

Demands for steel increased as its superiority to iron became more evident. This spurred research, and in the 1840s and 1850s several men and teams worked to perfect a new process. One of these was William Kelly, an American, who had the idea that by forcing air through molten pig iron, the oxygen in the air would combine with the carbon in the iron, producing gases and leaving steel in the "blaster." Henry Bessemer and Robert Mushet, both Englishmen, had the same idea, and it was Bessemer who applied for the first American patent, in 1856. Kelly disputed Bessemer's claim to having uncovered the process:

> The reason why I did not apply for a patent for it sooner than I did was that I flattered myself I would soon make it the successful process I at first endeavored to achieve, namely, a process for making malleable iron and steel. In 1857 I applied for a patent, as soon as I heard that other men were following the same line of experiments in England; and although Mr. Bessemer was a few days before me in obtaining a patent, I was granted an interference, and the case was heard by the commissioner of patents, who decided that I was the inventor of this process, now known as the Bessemer process, and a patent was granted me over Mr. Bessemer.

Yet both the Kelly and Bessemer processes would have been useless were it not for Mushet's additions. It was not enough to burn out the impurities; the amount taken out and left in had to be measured precisely, so that an exact amount of carbon would be left in the molten mixture. Mushet's innovations along these lines, patented in 1856 and 1857, made this possible, and at a low cost.

Still, the work of all three men had no significant impact

on the steel industry in the 1850s. Not until 1864 would Bessemer steel be produced in any meaningful amounts in the United States.

Most of the iron and steel produced in America in the 1850s was used for the production of what was classified as "machinery." This is somewhat confusing, since machinery included such products as farm implements and stoves as well as sewing machines and a variety of products used by the railroads. It might also be argued that iron and steel and machinery should be lumped into a single category, since machinery could not be produced without the metal. If this argument were accepted, "metal of all kinds" would emerge as the nation's largest industry in the 1850s.

Accepting the broad definition of machinery, we find that production boomed in the 1850s. Almost each new housing unit required a stove of one kind or another, and versions produced by the Franklin, Rathbone, and Nott companies were popular in many parts of the nation. Over 200 individual companies were in the field by 1860, and these consumed some 200,000 tons of pig iron annually. Manufacturers of farm implements prospered, as the West opened to new settlers and the cotton culture of the South expanded. Farmers, lumbermen, and construction workers required hand tools, especially saws, and though most of these were produced from imported high quality iron and steel, the domestic metal was used for cheaper versions. Henry Disston, an English mechanic who resettled in Philadelphia, produced some of the highest quality saws in the nation. Toward the end of the decade he began experimenting with native steel, and by 1861 was producing high quality saws, entirely American-made, which set the standard for quality in the East and whose fame

114

quickly spread through the nation. Boyden, Dayton, and Risdon water wheels and turbines could be found in most major flour mills and lumberyards, and during the 1850s some were exported to England, where they were well received, much to the chagrin of local craftsmen.

In the 1850s Americans continued to industrialize their economy, most of the time not comprehending where it would lead, what forms it would take in the future, the rewards to be gained, or the price to be paid. A nation that in the time of Washington and Jefferson seemed destined for agriculture was well on the road to industrial greatness during the presidencies of Zachary Taylor and Millard Fillmore. In the early 1830s it appeared manufacturing could become an adjunct of farming; two decades later it was evident that this was not to be, but instead industrial America would challenge the farms for dominance and control of the national destiny. For the most part, Americans accepted this change well, and anticipated the benefits to be derived from it. The English poet Charles Mackay, who visited America in the late 1850s, applauded the railroad, "the fruitful progeny/Ushering the daylight of the world's new morn."

> Blessing on Science, and her handmaiden Steam!
> They make Utopia only half a dream;
> And show the fervent, of capacious souls,
> Who watch the fall of Progress as it rolls,
> That all as yet completed, or begun,
> Is but the dawning that precedes the sun.

Gustaf Unonius, who had arrived in America from Sweden a few years earlier, was amazed at the cities, "which seemed to have come into being by magic." In them he saw the birth of a new civilization, not merely an economy, and one that was spiritual as well as earthly. After a visit to Rochester, New York, he wrote:

> Here, as in all the new cities we passed through, we were surprised to notice the great number of *churches and banks*—evidence . . . of the greater intensity of both spiritual and material activity here than in older communities. While in the smaller European cities only one or possibly two church buildings may be found, and very seldom a bank, it is impossible to walk very far along these newly planned streets, where the mortar and paint have hardly had time to dry on the new houses, without almost in every block coming across some temple erected for the worship of either God or Mammon.

And at the center of all this was the factory, the symbol of the new age. Earlier many Americans had begun to work on the *content* of the emerging industrial economy. The factory, which provided its *form*, began to come into its own in the 1850s. A new America was emerging alongside the old. William Ferguson, a botanist and entomologist, caught a glimmer of this situation on his visit to Terre Haute, Indiana, in 1855.

> We drove south of the town to look out upon the prairie. From a gentle eminence covered with thick natural grass we looked down upon the fields, some green with wheat, most still shewing the intense blackness of the soil, with the maise coming up in intercepted lines of green—the whole plain stretching out till, in the dim distance, a cordon of wood, the old forest, shut in the horizon. To the right, from close by where we stood to the aforementioned forest, a line of buttonwood trees marked the course of the Wabash River. Behind them the sun was setting. A western prairie! A dream realised! And those flashing rays were coming bounding over miles and miles of such, over billow after billow of these wide-spread earth-oceans, and bathing a continent, comprising kingdoms, in the rich evening light.
>
> Away up and down other streets, past flour-mills and porkhouses, and iron foundries—all signs of the giant-life struggling into active being in the "Prairie City."

116

5 / THE FINANCIAL CONTEXT

THE NATION ENTERED THE 1850s ON THE CREST OF AN economic boom, fueled by California gold, bountiful harvests and good farm prices, a developing industrial economy, and the railroad's march westward. All of these spurred the growth of the insurance and credit reporting industries. At the same time, however, they served to mask weaknesses in the banking system.

One of the major difficulties of the banking system was that it wasn't a system at all, but rather a patchwork constructed to take the place of the Second Bank of the United States, destroyed by President Andrew Jackson after the 1832 election. At first several states attempted to replace the BUS with chartered institutions, led by prominent individuals, often with political connections. Some, though not all, were soundly run, and did their tasks well, but the idea of special charters for the rich ran counter to the Jacksonian ideology, and in state after state the cry for "free banking" was heard. If accepted, free banking legislation would permit anyone with "sufficient capital" to set himself up as a banker, accept deposits, make loans, and issue bank notes. The result was the creation of many banks with unsound finances and often unscrupulous leadership.

Despite this, the system of chartered banks and free banks managed to provide the nation with a satisfactory if not trouble-free financial bloodstream. Indeed, banking not only survived in the early and mid-1850s, but flourished. The number of banks of all kinds increased rapidly, as did total assets, loans, investments, and cash. A system of correspondent banks, which began in the mid-1840s, was extended in the 1850s, so that businessmen in one part of the country were

TABLE 5

SELECTED BANKING STATISTICS, 1848-1856*

Year	Number of Banks	Total Assets or Liabilities	Loans	Assets Investments	Cash
		(millions of dollars)			
1848	751	512	345	27	112
1849	782	479	332	24	97
1850	824	532	364	21	115
1851	879	597	414	22	132
1852	913	620	430	23	137
1853	750	577	409	22	127
1854	1,208	795	557	44	163
1855	1,307	817	576	53	155
1856	1,398	880	634	49	167

* Source: *Historical Statistics of the United States: Colonial Times to 1957* (Washington, 1958), p. 624.

An unidentified California goldminer c. 1850.

able to discount notes drawn on banks in other sections without too much trouble.

Poorly financed and led by men often willing to break the law to turn a profit, many of the local banks of the free banking variety lasted only a few years before closing their doors. In Indiana alone fifty-one banks failed between 1852 and 1857, and other states of the Northwest had records almost as bad. In Michigan local banks made a practice of deceiving bank commissioners about the amount of gold they had on hand by transferring boxes and bags of specie from one bank to the next, always a step ahead of the examiners. As one commissioner wrote, "Gold and silver flew about the country with the celerity of magic; its sound was heard in the depths of the forest, yet, like the wind, one knew not whence it came or whither it was going." In the case of one frontier bank it was discovered that a box supposedly filled with gold actually had only a thin layer of gold dust on top of nails and broken glass.

Such a banking situation could hardly have been expected to survive a period of economic distress. Even those who tried to defend it admitted as much. But there was no such problem in the early and mid-1850s, a period of growth, confidence, and heavy investment. The country was not short of funds in this period; if anything, it faced difficulties as to how best use the flow of gold that poured into America from both west and east.

The western flow came from the California gold fields, which peaked in 1853 but continued high through the next few years. During most years of the 1848–1856 period the

TABLE 6

AMERICAN GOLD PRODUCTION, 1847-1856*

Year	Production (1,000 fine troy ounces)
1847	43
1848	484
1849	1,935
1850	2,419
1851	2,661
1852	2,902
1853	3,144
1854	2,902
1855	2,661
1856	2,661

* Source: *Historical Statistics . . .* , p. 371.

120

View of one of California's gold mines in 1858: Cromwell's Claim, Maine Bar, Middle Fork of the American River.

state banks' stocks of gold increased, not so much because of a new conservatism or a desire to become more solvent, but rather because people trusted their notes in a period of prosperity, and found them more convenient to deal in than bars or bags of gold.

Gold also flowed into America from the east—Europe. News of the great American economic expansion resulted in an outpouring of investments, not only in railroads, but factories as well. In 1851 only $6 million came from overseas for the purchase of American land and businesses; in 1853 foreign investment peaked at $56 million. The aggregate foreign indebtedness, which crossed the $200 million level in 1850, was $366.9 million in 1856.

Good times enabled the federal government to reduce the gross national debt from $63.5 million in 1850 to $32 million in 1856, a time when it seemed the debt would be completely wiped out in a matter of a few years. Never before had the country seemed so solvent, and never before had the economic prospect been so pleasing. Of course, no vista is ever one of unalloyed beauty. Prosperity brought inflation in its wake, with the cost of living index (reconstructed) rising from 54 in 1850 to 68 in 1856. But few complained, since wages were rising even more rapidly, as were profits.

In such a climate the wildcat banks not only survived, but expanded. Bank notes in circulation rose from $131 million in 1850 to $215 million in 1857, and in the same period the total currency went from $221 million to $374 million. It was the sharpest rise in outstanding financial paper the nation had known to that time. Yet few eyebrows were raised, and few voices heard in protest. Old diehards, remnants from the old days of the BUS, warned the structure was unsound, and given the slightest push, could collapse like a house of cards. For the time being, they were ignored. So was James Gordon Bennett of the New York *Herald*, who railed against the wild speculation on Wall Street and throughout the nation.

> What can be the end of all this but another general collapse like that of 1837, only upon a much grander scale? The same premonitory symptoms that prevailed in 1835-6 prevail in 1857 in a tenfold degree. Government spoilations, public defaulters, paper bubbles of all descriptions, a general scramble for western lands and town and city sites, millions of dollars, made or borrowed, expended in fine houses and gaudy furniture; hundreds of thousands in the silly rivalries of fashionable parvenues, in silks, laces, diamonds and every variety of costly frippery are only a few among the many crying evils of the day. . . . Thus, as this general scramble among all classes to be rich at once, and by the

122

shortest possible cut, extends and increases, our rogues, defaulters and forgers are multiplied. The epidemic and its attending evils must run their course.

Prosperity and industrialization enabled a weak banking structure to service the nation's needs in a satisfactory manner, while reforms were put off and ignored. These same forces had an opposite effect on the various aspects of the insurance industry, obliging the companies to rationalize their operations and become more responsible. In 1830 the nation had a strong banking system and weak insurance companies; a quarter of a century later the situation was reversed.

As the nation industrialized, fire insurance became an increasingly important field. This is not to say that America lacked fire insurance companies prior to the rise of the factory. Indeed, the first such firm in America, the Philadelphia Contributionship, had been founded in 1752, with Benjamin Franklin one of its sponsors. But this organization, and others like it in the early national period, were operated more on hunches and guesses than accurate knowledge of risks, were badly capitalized with small reserve funds, and could not survive a major flood of claims.

Such fire and casualty insurance operations were adequate to the needs of a village economy, but hardly met those of a rapidly developing industrial and commercial nation. A firm located in New York in 1800 might know all of its policyholders personally, and write policies on a handful of buildings, each for a few thousand dollars. After the War of 1812 and the coming of the factory system these insurance companies were called upon to write larger policies, often for companies far from the home offices. The companies had little experience in setting rates, and none in what today would be called scientific insurance. The insurance firms had no agents or engineers prepared to visit companies desiring insurance, and later on, when they did, the men often did not know what to look for. Fire companies were not required by law to maintain reserve funds, and few did, with most hoping to pay claims out of current income. Finally, as a national economy emerged, the companies were unprepared to write policies for businesses outside their home areas.

Rapid change in the insurance industry began in 1835, the result of a great fire in New York, which destroyed structures valued at $26 million. A good many of the gutted buildings had been insured, and their owners presented claims soon after. Most fire insurance companies lacked funds to meet these claims, and as a result, twenty-three of New York's twenty-six fire insurance concerns went bankrupt, as did several others located in nearby states that had written policies in New York.

The New York disaster forced the old companies that survived to reconsider their methods of operation and new companies that were formed during the next few years to prepare for business more carefully than the earlier ones had.

The Manufacturers Mutual Fire Insurance Company, founded soon after the New York fire, offers an example of this change. From the first the company insisted on careful inspection of sites to be insured, attempted to set realistic premiums with at least 75 percent of all premiums placed in a reserve fund, and set about hiring engineers whose job it would be to visit "various manufacturing establishments and distributing proposals for insurance, and to solicit those who want insurance to make their applications as early as convenient."

Most of the changes, however, were initiated by the older firms. The Aetna of Hartford, Connecticut, was one of these. Founded in 1819, it had been a local firm during its early years. Then the Aetna expanded along with the economy. The Aetna was one of the first to realize that competition between insurance companies for policies could work to the detriment of all concerned. On the eve of the New York fire, for example, several companies would offer coverage to the owner of a warehouse along the East River, who would play one company off against the others, in the end signing on with the firm that offered the lowest premium. The fire insurance firm that wrote the policy would have little to place in its reserve fund, if indeed it had one at all. So when the fire struck, the insurance company would go out of business, leaving the warehouse owner without recourse in law.

Aetna tried to convince other fire insurance firms of the desirability of standardized rates. At a time of unbridled competition, this was difficult. And even had the companies agreed to standardization, which company or agency would set the rates? What criteria would be used? There were no answers forthcoming to these questions.

In 1849 St. Louis was struck by a disastrous fire, after which the insuance firms became more interested in Aetna's proposals. Now they were prepared for standardization, but lacked the expertise to obtain it.

Edwin Ripley, who became president of Aetna in 1857, had long been interested in the creation of accurate risk tables and the more scientific assignment of risks. Soon after coming to office he was surprised to learn that Aetna's officials did not know whether the company had made money on the insurance of paper mills. Ripley ordered a study made, and others followed. By the end of the decade, both the concept of classified risks and the use of statistics in rate setting were being developed. And in the process Aetna's home city of Hartford was becoming recognized as the fire insurance capital of America.

Aetna was also interested in expanding its operations to other parts of the country, and by the mid-1850s had written policies throughout the Midwest. In 1858 the company established a branch in California, while at the same time exploring the possibilities of entering other branches of insurance, including life. But such business presented other pitfalls, which together with its rivals Aetna was not yet fully prepared to meet.

The Insurance Company of North America, founded in 1792, was one such rival. By the early 1840s the Philadelphia company was engaged in a wide variety of business, and pioneered in several. It was particularly concerned with fire and marine coverage, and through trial and error had become expert in both fields. This may be seen in instructions to agents in St. Louis in 1849. Edward Brooks, the company's agent for that part of the country, passed on the word that the firm would insure cargoes only, not boats and ships, since the losses on the latter were too high:

> You may insure goods on board of first class steamboats not over two years old, to the extent of $15,000, when the waters are high and no ice is to be encountered. But when the waters are low, you must not exceed $10,000. When the navigation is obstructed by ice, we should prefer, if you can do it, that you should avoid taking risks altogether. By Steamboats of inferior grade, you will reduce the amount of risk in proportion to their age and character, avoiding, if possible, the lower class entirely. Be careful in all cases to exercize prudence and caution. Espe-

cially would we have you make yourself thoroughly acquainted with the standing of your Masters and Pilots. No premium is adequate to the risk of insuring property under the care of an intemperate or unprincipled man. . . .

You may adopt the same rates of premium which the Companies of your city are charging, not submitting to any reduction for the purpose of securing business. The latter is bad policy. With regard to the settlement of premiums you can follow the course usually pursued in your city. All premiums under fifty dollars ought to be paid in cash. However, do in this matter as your neighbors do.

Brooks had difficulties in dealing with an application from Pierre Chouteau, who as we have seen was a member of one of St. Louis' leading families. At the time Chouteau was one of the city's leading fur dealers, trading for pelts over a vast expanse of territory. But the company had little experience in this kind of insurance, and instructed Brooks to abandon hope of getting the account. "The Board decided to decline whatever applications that might be made for insurances of this character." Brooks protested the decision, but the Board's decision held.

Companies like the Aetna, Insurance Company of North America, and other large fire and casualty underwriters found themselves in desperate need of information regarding individuals with whom they dealt, and companies asking for coverage. As the eastern firms expanded into the West, they discovered themselves writing policies with enterprises well known in their own cities, but without reputations in New York, Hartford, or Philadelphia. This placed a premium upon credit reporting of the highest caliber, and new demands upon agencies dealing in such information.

The same situation prevailed in the rapidly growing area of life insurance, which like fire and casualty underwriting, was still in its infancy in the 1840s, and came to early maturity in the 1850s. The 1840s was the decade of the mutual life companies, as the beginnings of economic recovery after the depression of the late 1830s and early 1840s revived interest in low-cost insurance. To this were added the problems and challenges of the California gold rush at the end of the decade, when many firms were called upon to insure prospectors and others who planned to make the journey west. The boom continued into the 1850s, so that by 1855 there were twenty-one American companies with more than a million dollars worth of life insurance in force. Mutual Life of New York and Connecticut Mutual, the industry's leaders, each had $20 million in policies, and they were followed closely by Mutual Benefit, New York Life, and New England Mutual.

At the time it appeared the mutual companies would force the stock companies out of business. Potential policyholders realized that profits of stock companies were either retained or passed on to stockholders, while those of mutual companies were distributed to owners of policies. Thus, in practice, mutual policies cost less than the same coverage from a stock firm. And the dividends to policyholders were generous, with each company competing with the others for record returns. Dividends of fifty percent a year were not unusual in the early 1850s, and some went as high as sixty percent.

A similar situation existed in fire insurance, where companies would compete for policies by offering lower rates, at the expense of reserves. The high-dividend payers in mutual life often had weak reserve positions, and a plague or a natural disaster such as a hurricane or fire could and did place them

128

in insolvent positions. More than half the mutual life companies founded in the 1847–59 period failed, and this cast a pall over that segment of the industry for a while.

But the situation also led to reforms at the surviving firms and more prudent practices on the part of newcomers. By mid-decade, mutual dividends were declining, reserves were higher than before, and failures less common. Aetna Life, which began operations in 1850, showed the way with its careful reserve policy. Two stock companies, Manhattan Life and Charter Oak, challenged the mutuals, and although not very successful at first, gave new impetus to that part of the industry.

It was during the 1850s that American life insurance produced its first two giants—Henry Baldwin Hyde and Elizur Wright—who within a few years changed the outlook of the industry and its methods of doing business.

Henry B. Hyde was the son of Henry H. Hyde, who was associated with the Mutual Life Insurance Company and was considered by its president "the first general agent of his company to achieve a national reputation in spreading the principles of mutual insurance." In 1850 the son, then sixteen years old, went to work at a dry goods establishment in New York. Two years later he quit the post and went to work at Mutual Life. He rose rapidly in the company, so that in 1858 he was its cashier, receiving a then munificent salary of $1,-800 a year. But young Hyde was unhappy at Mutual Life. For one thing, he thought the company's policy of paying high dividends unwise; he would have preferred to build up reserves and use more money in sales efforts. Hyde also opposed the company's policy of limiting policies to $10,000, at a time when it seemed larger ones could be sold. Finally, the young man had a strong desire to run his own company, to get out from under his father's shadow.

In early 1859 Hyde asked Mutual's President Frederick S. Winston for advice concerning his idea for a new life insurance company. Winston was shocked by the suggestion of new competition for Mutual, and soon after Hyde left the company. Hyde and several associates banded together, raised $100,000 in guarantee capital, and formed the Equitable Life Assurance Society of the United States. Hyde set up offices in the same building as Mutual, and erected a sign advertising Equitable that dwarfed that of the older company. But before that—even prior to acceptance of the charter—Hyde solicited business. The twenty-five-year-old insurance company president sent letters to friends asking them for policy placements that were models of their kind.

> *Equitable Life Assurance Society of the U.S.*
> *98 Broadway, New York, June 1, 1859*
>
> *My dear Sir,*
>
> *Allow me to ask your friendly cooperation in our enterprise in the success of which I am deeply interested. I have the honor to be associated with a number of the most respectable and responsible merchants of this, and other cities, who aim to establish "The Equitable Life Assurance Society of the United States." The preliminaries of organization are nearly perfected, and it is proposed to commence business on or about the first day of July next. The Capital Stock is almost all subscribed, and there will be no difficulty nor delay in completing that part of the organization. It is deemed important however that the Company should enter upon its career with a reasonable amount of business secured to it, and I have assumed heavy responsibilities in this direction to meet which I am compelled to solicit sympathy and assistance from my friends in this, and other cities.*
>
> *Organized upon principles purely mutual and managed by gentlemen whose names must command public confidence, the*

new company will present unrivalled inducements to insurers and its policies will possess all the desirable features of this favorite method of accumulating a certain provision for those who may otherwise be left without help or helpers.

I ask you therefore as a personal friend to authorize the issue of a policy upon your life for such an amount as your judgement may approve, or in case of your being already insured for the desired amount that you will interest yourself in obtaining one, or more applications for insurance upon the annexed paper, and return to me in the enclosed envelope by the 20th of June.

By prompt action in this regard you will place me under obligations which I shall not be slow to acknowledge, and which my official position in the Company will enable me fully to discharge.

Very truly
Your obdt. Servant
Henry B. Hyde

Hyde proved most adept at securing business. Within a year of its founding, the Equitable was able to announce it had $1 million in insurance in force.

Mutual Life was not the breeding ground only for Hyde, but for Charles Gill and Sheppard Homans as well. Gill was an actuary who made the first studies undertaken by a modern life company on the mortality ranges. Upon Gill's death in 1855, his apprentice, Homans, continued the work. It was Homans who stressed the value of developing precise tables based on actual mortality statistics rather than using English or other models then available. Homans compiled preliminary tables that were used by other actuaries throughout the nation.

The work of Gill and Homans proved preliminary to that of Elizur Wright, whom some consider "the father of American life insurance." Wright was a multifaceted individual. He was a mathematician who translated French literary classics into English, an active participant in the antislavery movement, and an editor of several journals in the field. For a while he was sponsored by Arthur Tappan, the wealthy New York merchant who was one of the proprietors of the Mercantile Agency. Wright was poetic and practical at the same time, and above all, intrigued with the emerging science of life insurance.

In 1853 Wright compiled a set of reserve valuation tables for the use of New England Mutual Life. This was the first major American contribution to the field; up to that time American firms had used English tables or relied upon bargaining for charges and guesses for probabilities. These practices had two results, each dangerous for the company and the policyholders. If rates were too low, the firms would lose money and so become dangerously unliquid; if rates were too high, few policies could be sold, and the companies might die from lack of business. Wright's work marked the beginning of the end for such problems.

Wright's second contribution was the innovation of cash surrender values for policies. Up to the early 1850s it was quite common for a policyholder to lose his entire investment if he defaulted on payments. Under Wright's prodding, some American companies initiated the practice of assigning surrender values to their policies. New England Mutual was the first to advertise this, and the company's success led others to imitate it soon after. Most used Wright's reserve valuation tables in figuring cash values, and so Wright's influence was spread throughout the industry.

Wright was a tireless worker for life insurance reform and the introduction of scientific methods in the industry. Toward this end he even invented a calculating machine to speed the work. Together with others at New England Mutual, he lobbied for legislation requiring state supervision of the industry. Massachusetts was the first state to pass such a law, and in 1858, Wright was named to the post of insurance commissioner for the state. He proved a vigorous commissioner, throwing corrupt companies from the state, helping establish scientific rate schedules, and in general helping honest and well-run firms as best he could. The Massachusetts example was followed in other states, so that by the end of the decade, it could truly be said that life insurance was a maturing industry in the nation.

Credit reporting agencies did little in the way of investigating insurance firms in the 1850s, since such companies rarely went in search of credit. But a few companies were reported on, and Mercantile Agency entries for them offer an illuminating picture. In 1852, for example, the Aetna was characterized by a reporter as "one of our best companies if not the best," but the reporter added that "such cos are of course subject to great fluctuations." Later on he added that "This Co has sustained a loss by the late fire in Springfield, Sangamon Co., Ill.," and paid claims promptly. In 1857 the reporter believed "There is not a safer insurance company in the Union. Their capital stock of 500m$ all paid in—their surplus is 500m$. They have in bank 200m$. Subject to call. Their stock is 160$ a share or more on 100$ shares."

The Great Western Insurance Co. of Philadelphia was not so well considered. The company wrote marine and fire insurance, a risky business under the best of circumstances. The Mercantile Agency reporter found that it was led by prominent and respected people, but in 1856 the company was engaged in risky practices. "Have been exchanging paper with the International. Lookout!" Two years later we learn "The standing of this Co. is improving. Bus. is under new management. Own the bldg. they occupy. Cons. safe and reliable." Finally in 1859, the reporter wrote with satisfaction that "as a general thing they are prompt in the payment of losses and enjoy a good name."

Banking, fire, casualty, and life insurance were all deeply affected by the rapidly developing industrial economy of the United States, and may properly be considered the handmaidens of industry in the 1850s. But none was more important than the business of information, which also grew rapidly during the decade. Without credit reporting, business could have stagnated, causing banks to collapse and insurance companies to limit their scope and activities. Industry in general could have been retarded were it not for the information industry, which also grew rapidly in the 1850s.

Like all other great industries, credit reporting rose to serve a strongly felt need on the part of its users. During the early nineteenth century—a time of poor communication when most businesses were small and often shaky—businessmen were faced with harsh choices when dealing with their counterparts in other sections of the country. One could rely upon hearsay and rumors regarding the other's honor and integrity, or refuse to do business unless certain financial guarantees were given. The latter situation rarely obtained, and from the first businessmen recognized that more accurate and less biased reports were needed. So it was that several credit reporting agencies were organized and grew in the antebellum period. One of these, the Mercantile Agency, was founded in 1841 by Lewis Tappan, a prominent New York

Benjamin Douglass, successor to Lewis Tappan, founder of The Mercantile Agency.

merchant. Tappan was well respected and trusted, and in addition was a good businessman. The Agency expanded rapidly, opening a Boston branch in 1843, followed by branches in Philadelphia in 1845, Baltimore in 1846, Cincinnati in 1849, St. Louis in 1850, and New Orleans in 1851.

As the Mercantile Agency grew, Tappan added to his personnel. One of the most promising of his new associates was Benjamin Douglass, a young man who joined the firm in 1846 and became a partner the following year. Douglass was a southerner and sympathetic to the views of the planter aristocrats of that section, while the Tappan family was a major force in the abolitionist movement. Despite their political differences, Douglass and Tappan worked well together. Indeed, the differences actually assisted the Mercantile Agency's operations, since Douglass concentrated his efforts and travels in the South, while Tappan charged himself with the North. This arrangement continued even after Lewis Tappan retired and was replaced by his brother, Arthur. At the time, Arthur Tappan viewed the Agency as a business whose primary concern would be to serve large merchants along the Atlantic coast, while Douglass was convinced the real growth lay in the West. The addition of the Cincinnati, St. Louis, and New Orleans branches were testimonies to Douglass' growing influence in the firm.

By 1851, the end of the first decade of Mercantile Agency work, the company had a network of reporters throughout the nation, and was the largest operation of its kind by far. The reporters, who often were local businessmen, lawyers, and other professionals, would send their reports to the New York office, where they were received by the thirty or so clerks who worked there. The reports would be organized, condensed, and then entered by longhand onto large ledgers. The reporters were expected to submit regular reports, with special ones when significant changes in the status of a reported firm occurred. For example, the New Orleans reporters, in writing of Charles Odier & Co., commission merchants, in July, 1848, noted that the firm's "French house failed some 4 mos. ago, caused by the Revolution." But Odier survived his losses, and in 1852 the firm was characterized as "A vy rich German & French house, long established." An addition in 1852 said of the company: "Have never failed, they only refused to pay or draw on France during the revolution, the house is w. 500 m$." Odier & Co. "Were obliged to suspend some yrs. ago on a/c. of the disturbances in France. This was not really anything vs. them. Now considered a worthy reliable house, worthy any cr. they will be likely to ask." The reporter noted several trips to France on the part of the firm's members, and Odier's connections with a French firm of the same name. In 1858 Odier of Paris collapsed, and news of its fall was received in New York. What would this mean

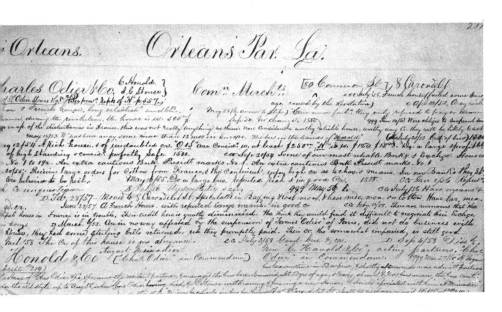

A Mercantile Agency credit report on Charles Odier & Co. covering
the period 1848–1858.

BAKER LIBRARY AT HARVARD UNIVERSITY

to the New Orleans concern? Eastern merchants who extended credit to Odier needed information regarding this,
and it had to be accurate. Subscribers to the Mercantile
Agency could learn, in March, 1858, that the New Orleans
company "Are in no way affected by the suspension of 'James
Odier' of Paris, did not do business with that house, they had
some sterling bills returned, wh they promptly paid. Their
cr. tho somewhat impaired, is still good." But this report was
followed by another, the same month, which noted a swift
change in the situation. "The cr of this house is in abeyance."
Then, in July, "Good bus. and credit." Without such information, by unbiased and reliable sources, businessmen in other
parts of the country would have dealt with Odier and similar

137

firms at the wrong time, in the wrong way, and probably to the detriment of all.

Most businessmen using the service recognized the value of knowing their counterparts better, but some resented having reports written about them for use by others. John and Horace Beardsley of Norwalk, Ohio, involved in a libel action, called upon Douglass to testify at the trial, which was held in New York. Douglass refused to answer some questions, on the grounds that they would require him to violate confidences. For example, he would not offer the name of his correspondent in Norwalk, even when ordered to answer by the judge. Douglass was found guilty of contempt of court, and went to jail for twenty days because of it. But it was a small price to pay to establish the principles upon which credit reporting were founded. As his attorney, Charles O'Conor, put it, trust and confidentiality were the bedrock assumptions of credit reporting, without which the industry could not survive. O'Conor went on to offer a rationale for the industry:

> What is the operation of these agencies? The country dealer who comes to any of the cities needs some evidence that he is worthy of trust and confidence. The ancient practice was for the country dealer to bring with him a certificate of his minister of the Gospel, or a letter from some country lawyer, or, perhaps, from some fellow-merchant; and then he would spend a week perhaps in New York, trying to satisfy the persons with whom he dealt that he was worthy of credit—in establishing for himself, as well as he could, a good character. What has been the result of establishing these agencies? Why, a merchant from this little town of Norwalk, Ohio, walks into the store of a wholesale merchant in New York, or Boston, or Philadelphia, and says: "I should like to purchase from you such and such goods." The city merchant replies: "Well, sir, look at our goods and whatever you desire to purchase shall be laid aside for you." After spending

perhaps half an hour in making his examination and selection of goods, he goes back to the desk or counting room to talk about terms of payment and credit, etc. He asks, "How long a credit do you allow?" The answer is, "Well, we give four or six months." "Do you require an endorser?" "No, sir." This answer, if the country dealer knew nothing about what is going on in the business world, might very much surprise him for perhaps he never was in the store before, and so far as he can tell, he is wholly unknown there. He gets his goods and goes home. He is independent of lawyer and minister and everybody else, so far as this world's mere temporal interests are concerned. Upon the strength of his good character, if he has one, he gets credit. A person of doubtful reputation receives a different answer.

This whole thing is done with a promptitude which is amazing and to all honest people in the country very delightful. They find indeed that "a good name is better than precious ointment," and "rather to be chosen than great riches"; that it accompanies them everywhere. And all this is through the action of these mercantile agencies. While the country merchant is looking at the goods, the mercantile agency reports that he is a man perfectly worthy of confidence, and upon the strength of this report the New York merchant is willing to trust him; and he does so with a pleasantly confiding manner, which is as gratifying to the pride of the country dealer as it is comfortable to propriety.

The Mercantile Agency survived this and similar attacks, as Douglass and Tappan defended it with vigor. The establishment of western branches continued and, in 1857, offices were set up in Montreal and London, to assist in the development of the nation's rapidly growing foreign trade.

In 1851, on a trip to Ohio, Douglass met with Robert Graham Dun, soon to become his brother-in-law. On that occasion Douglass arranged for Dun to enter the Mercantile Agency. Dun rose rapidly in the firm, and on June 1, 1854, became a full partner. This was made possible when Arthur Tappan left the organization, selling out to Douglass, who

promptly renamed it B. Douglass & Co. Five years later Dun took over at the credit reporting firm, which was again renamed, this time R. G. Dun & Co.

Dun was the largest credit reporting concern in the nation, but it had rivals. One of these was Bradstreet's Improved Commercial Agency, founded in 1855 by John M. Bradstreet, a Cincinnati dry goods merchant. Actually, Bradstreet was well versed in credit reporting prior to opening his establishment. Always interested in law, he sold his shop in the mid-1840s and set up practice as an attorney. In 1848 Bradstreet was asked to dispose of an insolvent estate. While doing so he came across much in the way of credit information, relating to the estate's creditors and debtors. Bradstreet found the information interesting, so much so that the following year he established a credit information service. Based in Cincinnati and serving Ohio and neighboring states, the service did well. It was this success that encouraged Brad-

With the opening of his Brad-street's Improved Commercial Agency at 237 Broadway, New York City, in 1855, John M. Bradstreet quickly became a rival of Douglass and Dun.

street to relocate to New York and, in effect, become Dun and Douglass' major competitor.

Bradstreet introduced innovations into the profession. Recognizing the need for better classification techniques, he developed a coding system that enabled far easier reference than had been possible earlier and that was a major step in the development of "scientific" reporting, comparable to what Elizur Wright was doing in insurance. In 1857 Bradstreet published a credit directory—*Bradstreet's Improved Commercial Agency Reports*—which was 110 pages long and contained 17,100 references. The volume was referred to in an advertisement for its 1862 successor:

> In 1857 we printed our first volume of "Commercial Reports." This volume contained reports of the business men of the Cities of New York, Philadelphia, Boston, Baltimore, Cincinnati, Louisville, St. Louis, and Chicago, and we have issued a volume every six months since, adding reports of other cities and towns in each succeeding volume, until Volume XI issued in July, 1862

Headquarters of The Mercantile Agency: (left) 111 Broadway, 1854–1857, and (right) 314 Broadway, 1857–1864 and 1878–1898.

contains reports of nearly 200,000 business men in six thousand and four hundred of the cities and towns of the North. . . . We own and set the type for our books and sheets—the paper used in making the books is manufactured expressly for us. . . .

Bradstreet's volumes were successful, and led the other credit reporting agencies to imitate him. In 1859 Dun published his first volume of reports, and others followed. Now a competition began. Bradstreet had been interested primarily in businesses in larger cities, while Dun, and before him, Douglass, attempted to cover the entire nation. Bradstreet obliged Dun to intensify his work in the large cities, while the desire to compete with Dun meant that Bradstreet had to engage reporters in the small towns as well as the big urban centers.

The two firms would continue to compete for seventy-eight years until, in 1933, Dun & Co. acquired the business of The Bradstreet Company, to form Dun & Bradstreet, Inc.

The business prosperity of the first half of the 1850s served to encourage banking and insurance expansion. The boom enabled the Mercantile Agency to increase its business and helped prompt John Bradstreet and others to enter the field. By 1857 the credit reporting and insurance industries were not only secure, but were innovating in several important areas, while at the same time becoming more responsible members of the business community. No similar or related development was taking place in banking, which remained a barely disguised weakness of the nation's financial structure. Soon after, this weakness not only would become apparent, but would create havoc in all parts of the land.

6 / THE BUSINESS OF NEWS

FOREIGNERS VISITING AMERICAN CITIES OFTEN WERE struck by the large number of newspapers available and their wide circulation. Universal literacy, an announced national goal, appeared capable of achievement at mid-century, and all Americans who could read seemed to be purchasing newspapers, reading them avidly, and then passing them on to others. Philip Hone, the aristocratic New Yorker who considered newsmen scoundrels, nonetheless thought a wide variety of newspapers a natural condition for a republic, in which all citizens were supposed to maintain an interest in public affairs.

If reading newspapers was an expected and even admirable trait, the journals themselves seemed "disreputable." In 1837, Hone attacked the New York *Evening Post*, published by William Leggett. "This unblushing miscreant makes himself popular and sells his paper by administering to the vitiated appetites of his fellow men nauseous doses of personal slander, disturbing the peace of the living and raking amongst the ashes of the dead, and calls it plain-dealing." Three years later Hone went to a ball at the Brevoorts', one of the city's leading families. He was surprised at first to find a reporter from the New York *Herald* in attendance. Then he learned that the Brevoorts had invited him, so as to avoid "unpleasantness" that might result had they been less hospitable. This episode led Hone to issue a diatribe against James Gordon Bennett, editor of the *Herald* and "the evilest man in the land."

> Whether the notice which they took of him, and that which they extend to Bennett when he shows his ugly face in Wall Street, may be considered approbatory of the daily slanders and unblushing impudence of the paper they conduct, or is intended to purchase their forbearance toward themselves, the effect is equally mischievous. It affords them countenances and encouragement, and they find that the more personalities they have in their paper the more papers they sell.

Charles Dickens was horrified by the vulgarity and persistence of American newspapermen. Writing of the press after his American visit of 1842, he said:

> While that Press has its evil eye in every house, and its black hand in every appointment in the state, from a president to a postman; while, with ribald slander for its only stock in trade, it is the standard literature of an enormous class, who must find their reading in a newspaper or they will not read at all; so long must its odium be upon the country's head, and so long must the evil it works be plainly visible in the Republic.

Why was this so? The European press seemed more responsible, less willing to peer into individuals' private lives,

145

New York Herald *editor James Gordon Bennett.*

and on the whole more literate. In political affairs it appeared, on the surface at least, to prize objectivity. Not so in America, where newspaper editors and reportors thought themselves as much a part of the nation's governance as its legislators and executives. Alexis de Tocqueville, that most perceptive observer of American ways, thought this was so due to the peculiar nature of American democracy.

146

The extraordinary subdivision of administrative power has much more to do with the enormous number of American newspapers than has the great political freedom of the country and the absolute independence of the press. If all the inhabitants of the Union were electors, but the suffrage only involved the choice of members of Congress, they would need only a few newspapers, for the occasions on which they had to act together, though important, would be very rare. But within the great association which is the nation, the law has established in every province, each city, and, one may almost say, each village, little associations responsible for local administration. The legislature has thus compelled each American to cooperate every day of his life with some of his fellow citizens for a common purpose, and each one of them needs a newspaper to tell him what the others are doing.

This view of the press, published in 1835, would seem to indicate that the nation's newspapers were political adjuncts of local, state, and national parties. So most of them were; this was the great age of the political press. When de Tocqueville visited America, the nation had some 1,200 newspapers, or three times as many as Britain or France, and no American newspaper had a circulation of more than 5,000. Then followed what might be called the first great revolution in American newspaper history. By 1860 there were 3,000 general newspapers in the United States and hundreds of more specialized journals. Bennett's *Herald*, which so angered Philip Hone, had a circulation of 77,000, and was the world's largest daily by far. The New York *Weekly Tribune*'s circulation was 200,000, and was read by many more people, since it was passed on to others by most subscribers. The New York *Ledger*, which specialized in pirating stories from other newspapers and boasted of being a digest of the best to be found in all journals, was a phenomenon. This first of the weekly news magazines had a circulation in 1860 of 400,000.

The weak, feeble, and almost always financially pressed newspapers of the 1830s and 1840s could not have survived without political sponsorship. The large and well-financed newspapers of the 1850s had little need of such support. Indeed, they thrived because they attacked the powers that were, and not by supporting them. Editors and publishers of large newspapers were often as important as senators and governors. Many had political ambitions, and one, Horace Greeley of the *Tribune*, would become a confidant of presidents, and himself run for the presidency on the Democratic ticket in 1872. The emergence of this new kind of newspaper, and a changed style of journalism, was notable in the 1840s and came to full flower in the next decade. It was a major cultural development, which would have wide implications in other areas as well.

No single factor serves to explain this great transformation in journalism. Rather, there were four interrelated developments, taking place over a period of years and not all at once, that turned the small political press of the 1830s into the giants of the 1850s.

The growth of population, translated into more readers, was a clear reason for enlarged circulation. The 15 million Americans of 1835 were avid readers, as de Tocqueville noted; so were the 27.4 million of 1855. In 1840 the nation's illiteracy rate was 11 percent; two decades later it was 9 percent, one of the lowest in the world, and this too encouraged the growth of newspapers. The very nature of Jacksonian America, glorifying as it were the "average man," led the population to take government more seriously than it had earlier in the century, and the great debates on slavery, immigration, and western expansion increased interest among readers.

But these changes and developments by themselves might have accomplished little were it not for the transformation in the industry, which came about as a result of a new view of the role of newspapers in a free society, technological developments, and lower costs. In the process the feeble political newspapers of the early 1830s, selling for five cents or more a copy and offering little news and much political propaganda, either failed or were transformed into larger journals selling for a penny, which though lower in price contained far more news, features, editorials of an independent cast, and reports on a wide variety of subjects.

Newspaper editors of the early 1830s realized that without a lowering of subscription prices, which hopefully would result in larger circulation, and in turn would attract more advertising, they could not hope to break away from their political sponsors. In 1833 the New York *Sun* appeared, selling for a penny, and hoping to remain independent in this fashion. Like other newspapers of the time, the *Sun* used clumsy, expensive, slow-moving Napier flat presses, capable of turning out a hundred or so impressions an hour. The newspaper installed faster Napiers in 1834, but these could do no more than produce 400 copies an hour. This meant labor costs would be high, and by the time the news reached the readers, it would be rather stale.

As early as 1840 Richard Hoe and Sereno Newton had experimented with a new press, one that combined several functions in a single machine and might easily be harnessed to steam power. The Hoe press, capable of producing from

149

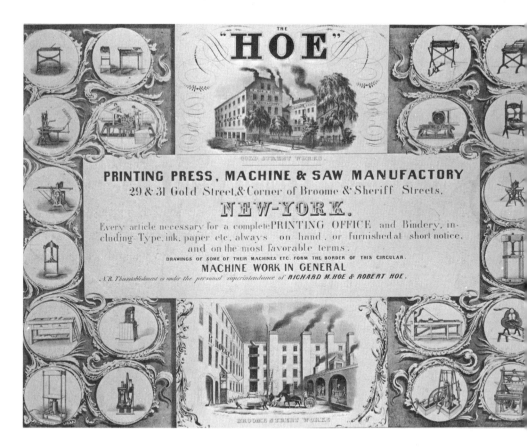

Advertisement for Richard M. Hoe's factory, producer of the famous Hoe printing presses.

2,000 to 3,000 copies an hour, was installed at the *Sun* in 1835. Armed with the new machine, the newspaper lowered its subscription costs, increased its readership to 30,000, and became one of the most famous journals in the nation. Other newspapers followed the *Sun*'s lead, and Richard M. Hoe & Co. became one of the busiest concerns in New York.

The penny newspapers proliferated, and as they grew, the market for Hoe presses expanded. Now Hoe began to develop new machines, faster than the original, and also more costly. The "Lightning," which made its appearance in 1847, produced four pages with each revolution. It was first used by the Philadelphia *Public Ledger*, and was soon in use throughout the Northeast. This was followed by an improved version that utilized ten cylinders, and turned out 22,000 pages an hour. The New York *Tribune* took the first of these in 1852, paying $25,000 for the machine. The "Hoe revolution" was in full swing by then, and the penny newspapers in command of the press.

But population increases and technological changes in newspaper production would not suffice to explain the transformation from the New York *Courier and Enquirer* of the mid-1830's, which sold for six cents, had a circulation of 3,300 and advertising revenues of $65 a day, and was judged the most influential journal of its time, to the *Tribune* of 1855, a million-dollar operation with a circulation close to 200,000 and a price of a penny, which was five times as big in terms of news carried. Of course, given the Hoe presses, newspapers could print several editions a day, each slightly different from its predecessor, carrying the latest news as received at the desks and analyzed by the editors. Had news gathering, reporting, and distribution remained the same as they had been in the days of the *Courier and Enquirer*, the penny newspapers would merely have been larger and less expensive versions of their predecessors. Such was not the case, however, and these changes, like those brought by the new presses, were due in large part to technology and human responses to it.

Newspapers of the mid-1830s were not very different in appearance and the kinds of news carried from those of pre-revolutionary days. Reports from overseas, received from incoming ships, shared the front pages with small advertisements, local news gathered in an occasional fashion by the editor, part-time reporters, and even printers. Much of the news was brought to the journal by interested parties and printed as though to fill space. Commercial reports were believed far more important, for these were of interest to businessmen, a prime market for the journals of that day. One did not read the newspaper to find out what *was* happening outside of the business world, but rather what *had* happened, perhaps weeks earlier.

Recognizing the need for faster reporting of news events, Daniel Craig of Boston, a printer's apprentice, ordered some passenger pigeons that had been trained in Europe and began a news reporting service. Craig would meet incoming ships at sea, gather news from abroad, and send it winging to shore by means of pigeons flying as fast as sixty miles an hour. Subscribers to his "pigeon post" were able to report news faster than their rivals, which led to increased circulation. Bennett enthusiastically adopted the service, and in the mid-1840s had pigeon posts in Washington, Baltimore, Philadelphia, and Albany. The "scoop" had been born, and the search for still better means of news delivery was on.

The telegraph, invented in 1835, was in operation in several cities a decade later, and clearly was an improvement over pigeon post. Several New York newspapers, the *Herald* among them, recognized that through its use, news could be sent and received almost instantaneously from every part of the country. But telegraph costs were high, and even the rapidly growing penny newspapers could not afford the devices. It was also clear that at a time when the United States was engaged in a war with Mexico and European capitals were besieged by revolutionaries, the public demand for fresh news would have to be met. So the newspapers took the plunge, and some of the leaders began to use the telegraph.

It soon became evident that the telegraph was being used only for the most important transmissions, such as presidential proclamations. Then twenty and more reporters would send essentially the same report and transcript to their editors, to be published simultaneously in the journals. This was clearly a waste; a single transmission would do just as well, if only the newspapers could agree to it. At least, this was the thought of David Hale, of the solid and respectable New York *Journal of Commerce*, who is usually credited with suggesting a cooperative news gathering and reporting agency. Hale, who had contempt for Bennett and other penny newspaper editors, swallowed his pride and went to the *Herald*'s office to put forth the proposition. Bennett agreed, and later on the two men met with representatives from the *Sun*, the *Tribune*, the *Express*, and the *Courier and Enquirer* to present their proposition for unified newsgathering, reporting, and transmission of foreign and distant news.

As might have been expected from men used to competing with one another, agreement on cooperation was hard to come by. Still, in 1848, the editors did come together to arrange for cooperation in procuring telegraph reports on foreign news received in Boston. Later on the *Herald* purchased a ship, the "Naushon"—renamed "Newsboy" by Bennett— which was placed in the service of the group and used to obtain news from incoming European passenger ships. Cooperation was not achieved in a season, or even a year, but rather over a period of probing and experimentation. Finally, in

1851, the Harbor News Association, one of several cooperative ventures, released the following statement:

> It is mutually agreed between G. Hallock of the *Journal of
> Commerce*, J. and E. Brooks of the *Express*, J. G. Bennett of the
> *Herald*, Beach Brothers of the *Sun*, Greeley and McElrath of the
> *Tribune*, and J. W. Webb of the *Courier*, to associate for the
> purpose of collecting and receiving telegraphic and other intelli-
> gence.

Naturally enough, the new combination was called the
Associated Press, although for a while it was also known as
the General News Association. The association grew rapidly,
albeit painfully, in the 1850s, so that by the end of the decade
Americans in large cities received news more rapidly than citizens of any country in the world.

Finally, the federal government assisted the newspapers as
a group, and the New York press in particular. In 1852 Congress passed and the President signed a new Post Office Act,
one provision of which was to lower newspaper postage
charges by half when prepaid. The new act enabled the big
city papers to compete more easily with their small-town rivals. Postage service had been poor in the 1830s and 1840s,
but was improving in the 1850s. An Albany subscriber to the
New York *Herald* might now receive Monday's paper on
Wednesday and read news not yet picked up by his local
dailies and weeklies. With the lower postage rates, the cost of
the *Herald* would be the same, or even lower, than that of
many local newspapers. Cheap distribution enabled New
York's publishers to dream of covering the entire nation in
time, as some London and Paris newspapers already were
doing in their countries. It also meant higher advertising rates
and increased subscriptions.

The penny newspapers now embarked on a competition for readers and advertisers. The two were tied together. Advertisers preferred newspapers with a wide readership, while readers often were attracted by advertisements. In the 1850s, the level of advertising in penny newspapers sank to a new low, both in truthfulness and form. Patent medicines, real estate offerings, and merchandise for sale advertisements were replete with lies, exaggerations, and deception. And some were amusing in their obvious appeals. In 1851, for example, Radway's, a medium-size soap manufacturer, concocted the following ad:

> Thus Alexander knelt at beauty's shrine
> And Anthony thought Cleopatra's charms divine:
> Celestial beauty—daughter of the skies—
> Fair-skinned, rose-cheeked and lily-necked arise!
>   Try RADWAY'S CHINESE MEDICATED SOAP!
> This, this alone each form will purify
> And make the ugliest handsome to the eye!
> This for pimples, blotches, tetters, rheum,
> Will banish all before its rich perfume . . .

Finally, the new postal act encouraged editors to enlarge their coverage, both in terms of geography and features, and their ambitions in the area of politics. The New York *Sun* of the 1830s and 1840s concentrated on foreign and local news; the New York newspapers of the 1850s were concerned with events in all parts of the nation, and offered wide coverage of business, politics, fashion, sports, literary news, and the like. The editors of the Jacksonian era wrote for their political patrons, and served them; their counterparts in the 1850s were freed from such patronage, and hoped for national careers of their own.

But all this cost large sums of money. The Hoe machines

made it virtually impossible to start a newspaper on a shoe-string. Without mass circulation the large city journals could not have survived. Now advertisers and subscribers replaced political parties as patrons of the press, while editors were obliged to retain the penny price in order to reach such a market. In some ways it was a healthier situation than that which had prevailed in the early 1830s, but it still did not guarantee a free and unbiased press. If anything, the general level of newspapers fell as a result, though there were notable exceptions to the rule.

Mass marketing and high capital requirements helped make journalism big business in America for the first time in

The composing room of Leslie's, *one of the leading illustrated news-papers* (Frank Leslie's Illustrated Newspaper, *August 2, 1856*).

Leslie's *pressroom.*

the nation's history. In order to produce the kinds of newspapers the public demanded and for the price people were willing to pay, big city newspapers had to expand their staffs, regularize their operations, and become more efficient in every way. James Parton, the historian, noted this in observing the press room of the New York *Tribune* in the mid-1850s:

> The editorial rooms ... have become intense. Seven desks are occupied with silent writers, most of them in the *Tribune* uniform—short sleeves and moustache. The night-reader is looking over the papers last arrived, with scissors ready for any paragraph of news that catches his eye. An editor occasionally goes to the copy-box, places in it a page or two of the article he is writing, and rings the bell; the box slides up to the composing room, and the pages are in type and corrected before the article is finished. Such articles are those which are prompted by the event of the hour; others are more deliberately written; some are weeks in preparation; and of some the keel is laid months before they are launched upon the public mind.

The editor was the key person at such newspapers. More often than not he was its owner or part owner, publisher, chief reporter, *de facto* head of the advertising and employment bureaus, publicizer, and expert on printing, paper procurement, and the evaluation of equipment. Above all he was the lord of the castle, the defender of its interests (which he would delineate regularly on the editorial page).

During the 1850s editors of leading newspapers were as powerful as senators, governors, and even presidents, and at times even more influential than such elected officials in molding public opinion on such issues as the tariff, land policy, internal improvements, public morals, and the key issue of slavery. Thurlow Weed of the Albany *Evening Journal* divided his time between the tasks of editorship and those of directing the Whig Party, determining who should be its nominees and what they should think. Greeley of the New York *Tribune* would mold public opinion for four decades, with more influence than any president of his time except Lincoln. Henry Raymond of the New York *Times*, Bennett of the *Herald*, Webb of the *Courier and Enquirer*, and William Cullen Bryant of the *Evening Post* had influence far beyond Manhattan. Out-of-town editors of large newspapers were also respected, especially if they were the leaders in their cities, as were J. W. Fornay of the Philadelphia *Press* and Joseph Medill of the Chicago *Tribune*, while Samuel Bowles of the Springfield *Republican*, though based in a small town, was known throughout the land. Most of these men were individuals of strong beliefs and personalities; they stamped these indelibly on their journals, which in many ways they considered reflections and extensions of themselves, embodiments of their ambitions and dreams. In writing of Greeley, Parton said:

> The Editor-in-Chief is at his desk writing in a singular attitude, the desk on a level with his nose, and the writer sitting bolt upright. He writes rapidly, with scarcely a pause for thought, and not once in a page makes an erasure. The foolscap leaves fly from under his pen at the rate of one in fifteen minutes. He does most of the *thinking* before he begins to write, and produces matter about as fast as a swift copyist can copy. Yet he leaves nothing for the compositor to guess at, and if he makes an alteration in the proof, he is careful to do it in such a way that the printer loses no time in "overrunning"; that is, he inserts as many words as he erases. Not infrequently he bounds up into the composing room, and makes a correction or adds a sentence with his own hand. He is not patient under the infliction of an error; and he expects men to understand his wishes by intuition; and when they do *not*, but interpret his half-expressed orders in a way exactly contrary to his intention, a scene is likely to ensue.

Greeley served a long apprenticeship before founding the *Tribune* in 1841, at which time he was thirty years old. Starting out as a printer, he went to New York, learned the ropes, and in 1833 founded his first newspaper, the *Morning Post*, which failed in three weeks. For the next eight years Greeley edited an influential but insolvent newspaper, worked for Thurlow Weed by editing two Whig journals, and became known as a key member of the Weed-Seward-Greeley alliance, which dominated the state's politics.

Greeley founded the *Tribune* in order to have his own power base, and also because he did not perform well in harness with others. As he put it later on:

> My leading idea was the establishment of a journal removed alike from servile partisanship on the one hand and from gagged, mincing neutrality on the other. Party spirit is so fierce and

intolerant in this country that the editor of a non-partisan sheet is restrained from saying what he thinks and feels on the most vital, imminent topics; while, on the other hand, a Democrat, Whig, or Republican journal is generally expected to praise or blame, like or dislike, eulogize or condemn, in precise accordance with the views and interest of the party. I believe there is a happy medium between these extremes. . . .

In his time Greeley supported a host of reform movements, from utopian socialism to labor unionism, women's rights, food faddism, prohibition, and abolition, and his views found expression on the *Tribune*'s editorial page. Perhaps more than any other important public figure of the 1850s, Greeley was identified with reform, with the lot of the poor, with the sentiment that the nation needed some kind of spiritual regeneration. His was a powerful voice, one imitated by other editors and picked up by ambitious Republican politicians. And in the process, the *Tribune* became the most important and influential newspaper in the land.

In writing of his desire to steer a middle course between "servile partisanship" and "mincing neutrality," Greeley might have been thinking of two of his major rivals, James Gordon Bennett of the *Herald* and Henry J. Raymond of the *Times.*

Bennett was born in Scotland, arriving in America in 1819 at the age of twenty-four. After a brief attempt at teaching, he turned to newspaper work. He was a reporter for several journals, among them the Charleston *Courier* and the New York *Enquirer*, both of which were prosouthern and pro-Andrew Jackson. Bennett became an enthusiastic Jacksonian in 1828, and for the rest of his life championed the cause of the "common man." At the same time he was

160

Horace Greeley, New York Tribune *founder.*

proslavery, at a time when the great debates on that subject were just beginning.

In 1832 Bennett started his own newspaper, the New York *Globe*, which supported Jackson in his reelection campaign. Bennett was a strong and often vicious writer, traits that led others to distrust him. When the *Globe* failed, he found it difficult to obtain employment at another journal. After several false starts, Bennett founded another newspaper, this one the *Herald*, in 1835.

Two years later, Bennett wrote, "Shakespeare is the great genius of the drama, Scott of the novel, Milton and Byron of the poem—and I mean to be the genius of the newspaper press." Certainly the *Herald* gave evidence of this ambition.

Bennett produced what some consider the forerunner of the modern newspaper. His was the first daily to have a detailed financial section, including prices at the New York Stock and Exchange Board, "muckraking" stories on a regular basis by reporters whose task it was to seek out corruption and expose it, and special features for children, women, and others who did not ordinarily read newspapers in those days. Before Bennett, editors had vilified one another. Bennett raised such battles to an art, charging his rivals with all sorts of foul deeds. At first his major target was James Webb of the *Sun*, with whom he had broken in 1832. A few years later, in what his readers had come to expect as a typical editorial, Bennett wrote:

> As I was leisurely pursuing my business yesterday in Wall Street, collecting the information which is daily disseminated in the *Herald*, James Watson Webb came up to me on the northern side of the street, said something which I could not hear distinctly, then pushed me down the stone steps leading to one of the brokers' offices, and commenced fighting with a species of brutal and demoniacal desperation characteristic of a fury. . . . My damage is a scratch about three quarters of an inch in length, on the third finger of the left hand, which I received from the iron railing I was forced against, and three buttons torn from my vest, which any tailor will reinstate for a sixpence. His loss is a rent from top to bottom of a very beautiful black coat, which cost the ruffian $40, and a blow in the face, which may have knocked down his throat some of his infernal teeth, for anything I know. Balance in my favor, $39.94. . . . As to intimidating me or changing my course, the thing cannot be done. Neither Webb nor any other man shall or can intimidate me. I tell the honest truth in my paper, and I leave the consequences to God. Could I leave them in better hands? I may be attacked—I may be assailed—I may be killed—I may be murdered—but I will never succumb—I will never abandon the cause of truth, morals and virtue.

162

Bennett was convinced "books have had their day—the theatres have had their day—the temple of religion has had its day." The future belonged to newspapers. "A newspaper can be made to take the lead of all these in the great movements of human thought and of human civilization." And as though to prove his point, Bennett set about establishing the finest news-collecting operation in the business. In this, as in other areas, he ran afoul of Greeley, whom he considered little better than an anarchist or a traitor.

Luncheon meeting of Horace Greeley (left) and James Gordon Bennett (right) at the Everett House, Union Square, New York. (Frank Leslie's Illustrated Newspaper, *October 18, 1856*).

Greeley tended to stand for intellectuals who desired reform, often was pro-big business, antislavery, and a Whig-Republican, while Bennett favored reforms that originated from the masses themselves, and was vehement in his hatred of big business, especially Wall Street. As might be expected, Bennett was a favorite of Tammany Hall in New York and a Democrat. Greeley thought Bennett the paid tool of the Democratic Party, while the older man thought the *Tribune* was the vehicle for every crackpot scheme that came along. Their struggles against one another were a preview of what would befall the nation in the 1860s, but at the time, the rivalry obliged both papers to improve their reporting and features, making them the best and most quoted in the nation.

Henry J. Raymond tried to take another path. In 1838, at the age of eighteen, Raymond traveled to New York from his study at the University of Vermont, seeking employment at the *Evening Journal*. Raymond worked on several newspapers, the most important of which was the *Tribune*, where he rose quickly to become one of Greeley's most important associates. Then he broke with Greeley to join the *Courier and Enquirer*, and began criticizing other editors for their lack of objectivity and seeming unwillingness to report events as they occurred. Raymond also engaged Greeley in a series of debates, conducted on the editorial pages of their respective papers, on such questions as utopian socialism and other reforms, in which he showed himself the master of the newspaper titan. Then Raymond left newspapers entirely, hoping for a political career. He won election to the state legislature as a Whig, but soon found the work in Albany boring. In 1851 he and a friend, George Jones, considered starting a new journal. One day, when the two were walking across the

The New York Times *editor Henry J. Raymond.*

frozen Hudson River, Jones mentioned that he had learned the *Tribune* had earned over $60,000 in 1850. Convinced that he could make a go of it at a new paper, and that the enterprise would be profitable, Raymond surveyed the scene in New York. The *Journal of Commerce* was dull and behind the times, while the *Sun* was read primarily by "domestics in quest of employment and by cartmen dozing at street corners waiting for a job." The *Evening Post* seemed interested only in the tariff, while the *Express* was "stodgy," and the *Commercial Advertiser* barely read at all. Bennett's *Herald* contained much "printed filth," while Raymond thought the

165

Tribune "had got into bad ways" through Greeley's advocacy of a variety of reforms.

Raymond and Jones raised $70,000, and on September 18, 1851, put out the first issue of the New York *Times*. In those days, an editor was expected to issue a statement of principles at such a moment. Raymond refused. Instead, he hoped to present the news in an unbiased, impartial fashion, and refrain from being drawn into lengthy and often unproductive disputes with other newspapers. Although the term "newspaper of record" was not to be coined for many decades, it seems Raymond was aiming for that distinction even then. "There are few things in the world which it is worth while to get angry about," he wrote in 1851, "and they are just the things that anger will not improve." This, at a time when the great national debate on slavery and western expansion was heating up. Of course, Raymond had his beliefs, which were stated—and understated—in his editorials. For example, Raymond was not opposed to slavery, and felt the North should mind its own business in this regard. But where Bennett would castigate the abolitionists, Raymond merely editorialized that the *Times* could not "countenance any improper interference on the part of the people of one locality with the institutions, or even the prejudices, of any other."

But Raymond could change his mind more easily than could Greeley or Bennett, perhaps because he did not bring their emotional fire to his newspaper. Later in the decade Raymond would convert to Republicanism—indeed, he helped write the party's first platform in 1856—and support the Free Soil movement, considered the scourge of the plantation South. Then too, Raymond returned to politics in 1854, serving a term as lieutenant governor and being offered the

Engraving of The New York Times *Building at Park Row, Nassau, and Spruce Streets, erected in 1857–1858.*

Republican nomination for the governorship two years later. He refused, turning his attention instead to the *Times*, already an influential newspaper of national reputation. Perhaps he realized, as did Greeley and Bennett, that the editor of a major newspaper had more power than most governors in the 1850s.

Raymond's quest for objectivity in reporting, Greeley's ability to catch the national mood, and Bennett's innovations in reporting and features influenced newspapers throughout the nation, and even each other. Bennett's business and financial reports, for example, were most popular with businessmen, even though their tone was decidedly antibusiness. Greeley and Raymond noted this and began running reports of their own, but their coverage could not match that of the *Herald*.

The apparent desire for business and financial news was not lost on other editors and publishers, especially in the mid-1840s, when recovery from the panic and depression seemed complete. Isaac Smith Homans and Edwin Williams, two reporters and editors, believed the time was ripe for a weekly newspaper devoted to business interests, one that concentrated on business news and offered more complete financial coverage than even the *Herald*. In 1845 they introduced the *Banker's Weekly Circular and Statistical Record*, the first business paper devoted to banking interests. "We have long felt that there has been wanting in this commercial metropolis a weekly paper, established upon a liberal footing, and devoted to the great money interests of our country," they wrote.

> It is true, that the New York daily journals furnish, in the aggregate, nearly all the information which it is proposed to give in the *Banker's Weekly Circular*, but it is in such a scatter shape, that valuable as the information is, it cannot be used for reference without a large accumulation of unwieldy papers. Now we propose to give a bird's eye view of these important topics, and in convenient shape to file away for reference.

The *Banker's Weekly Circular* did far better than even its founders had anticipated, and soon achieved a wide though limited circulation. Its success encouraged other business journalists to enter the field, while at the same time older, small business weeklies and monthlies saw their circulations and profits increase in the 1850s.

Although the business and financial press produced no figure comparable in power to Greeley, Bennett, or Raymond, Rufus Porter did come to dominate the field. Porter was born in Massachusetts in 1792, worked at a variety of occupations—most of them involved with technology—and in 1841 became the editor of the near defunct *New York Mechanic*. Porter put the journal on its feet and, finding himself intrigued with the possibilities of business and technical reporting and editing, went on to found several other journals in these fields, among them the *Scientific American*, the first copy of which appeared in 1845. Perhaps the most interesting of Porter's journals was the *Aerial Reporter*, which he produced in 1852. This was the first business newspaper devoted entirely to aviation, and was read by thousands even before the Wright brothers were born. The *Aerial Reporter* was devoted to news of a technological nature, but also included items of interest to businessmen who might wish to invest in new firms devoted to the production of balloons. In August, 1852, Porter reported somewhat hopefully on the performance of a company in which he had an interest. Writing to his shareholders on the front page of the *Aerial Reporter*, Porter said:

> The main difficulty in forwarding the progress of this work, and which has occasioned our disappointment in regard to the time required, has consisted in the necessity of deferring some branches or parts of the work until other branches were finished, thus employing but a limited number of hands at the same time. Having procured the construction of the engines, boilers, saloon, cabin, elevating car, smoke-pipe, propelling wheels, and rudder,

and having varnished and prepared the fibrous material, and made the longitudinal rods for the float, nothing more could be done until the strips were sewn together, in which branch, from the nature and position of the work, only five or six persons could be employed at the same time, and, consequently, much time was required to sew 8,000 feet of seams. . . . Having been considerably deceived with regard to the time required, I will not venture another guess, but continue to expedite the work as much as possible to completion, well knowing that all my kind patrons have a good share of patience (as well as myself,) and are more desirous to have the work well and properly done, than to have it over pressed.

With regard to the cash account, I need only say that the various items of expenses have from the commencement been "too numerous to mention," and that the original $1,500 have been "pretty well used up"; but that there are yet apparently sufficient funds on hand, and that, moreover, there is still a demand for shares, (extra,) and that I may consent to sell a few more at the original price ($5,) though I see no reason to doubt that they will soon command at least $100 each. Confidence in the success of the enterprise is advancing, and many of those who were formerly disposed to deride it, now freely express their confidence in its feasibility and ultimate success.

Needless to say, Porter's company did not become a giant of the aviation industry, for one would not exist for another half century. Nor did the *Aerial Reporter* survive for more than another few issues.

As might have been expected, the journals devoted to railroading did much better. Henry Varnum Poor of the *American Railroad Journal*, who increased circulation from 1,200 to more than 5,000 in the period from 1849 to 1854, did more to spread interest in and information about railroading than any other American of the 1850s. Poor was indefatigable in his encouragement of financiers and others to spread a network of rails across the countryside. At the same time,

Poor insisted on accuracy in reporting and stressed the need for up-to-date information, without which business decisions would be impossible and railroading discredited.

During the 1850s Americans witnessed the first of several "information explosions," this one concentrated in the press. Bennett's vision of a newspaper replacing all other forms of the arts and literature was exaggerated, to be sure, but Americans were reading more newspapers and journals than ever before, and rarely since. It was a time when the great issues of the day were reported upon and analyzed in thousands of newspapers across the land. Opinion, often disguised as fact, could and did sway thousands of readers to one or another side of a public issue. But at the same time an even more important development was taking place—the business of news was becoming more a part of the business of information than ever before. Without information, the nation's political life would have been crippled; without information, business decisions would have been made blindly, especially as the national economy developed. This information was provided by many sources, among them credit reporting firms such as the Mercantile Agency and Bradstreet's. The role of newspapers was an uncertain one in the 1850s, as the differences between men like Greeley, Raymond, Bennett, and Porter indicate, but a start had been made.

7 / EMPEROR WHEAT AND KING COTTON

MUCH OF THE NATION APPARENTLY WAS DESTINED FOR agriculture, as was most of its population in 1850. A family could obtain a large farm, with excellent soil, sufficient rainfall, and a climate that permitted the raising of more than a single crop a year—all of this at a price that was a small fraction of the cost of an inferior and smaller farm in Europe. If the farm were on the frontier, it might cost nothing at all. Little wonder, then, that America seemed a utopia for farmers, or that so many Americans were attracted to the soil rather than to the cities. So it would remain for another seven decades. Not until 1920 would a majority of Americans live in urban places.

But these were not sedentary farmers. There were, to be sure, farmers who loved their small plots of land, worked them carefully, rhapsodized about hard work under God's sky on the good earth. In the East in particular such individuals spoke of their semimystical love of the land. Such men were cited as typical by intellectuals in the cities, who themselves usually knew little of the rigors of farming. Far more significant was the businessman-farmer, who would purchase a farm near the frontier at a small price and work the land until settlement arrived to force its price up and poor farming methods had leeched the soil of much of its vitality. Then the farmer would sell out, move farther west to cheaper land, cultivate it, and repeat the process. In this way a family might relocate two or three times in a generation. The mobile American was not a development of the highly industrialized late twentieth century; he was here at the founding. "The Americans carry over into agriculture the spirit of a trading venture," wrote de Tocqueville, "and their passion for industry is manifest there as elsewhere."

> It is unusual for an American farmer to settle forever on the land he occupies; especially in the provinces of the West, fields are cleared to be sold again, not to be cultivated. A farm is built in the anticipation that, since the state of the country will soon be changing with the increase of population, one will be able to sell it for a good price.

Far more than their European counterparts, Americans tended to be in the business of farming, rather than viewing agriculture as innately superior to any other occupation. While it was true that American farmers viewed urban dwellers as unnatural men, and preferred the hardships and rigors of the countryside to the squalor and crush of the cities, they nonetheless expected that their work would bring material rewards, in the form of high incomes, economic abundance, and the ever increasing value of their land, equipment, and cattle.

This attitude can largely be explained by the way the factors of production came together in the United States in the mid-nineteenth century. The most important element was the seemingly unlimited amount of good, cheap land. Virgin soil, usually untouched by the Indians who only hunted the land, was there for the asking. And should it be wasted, raped by overplanting and underfertilization, the farm could be abandoned, for beyond the next ridge or over the next river lay more virgin land, also free or available for a very low price. The cheapness of the land could be seen by one of the eastern farmer's last acts before moving on. He would burn down his log cabin, not as a brutal act or in rage, but rather to remove from the ashes the most valuable part of his old dwelling—a handful of nails, which cost far more than the lumber. America was built on the misuse of natural resources, not because Americans were stupid or malevolent, but rather because land, like air and water, seemed limitless, while capital and labor were dear.

In 1850, the average American farm was 203 acres, larger than its counterpart in Europe. Many western farms, owned by families who did not consider themselves wealthy, ran into the thousands of acres, or at least so it seemed, for the owner was not certain where his holdings ended and the next farm —or the wilderness—began. Europeans who knew something of farming were shocked by the waste they saw on such farms. One wrote that the land in America was not farmed as much as it was mined. Crops were extracted from the soil, which was then left to fall under. Another writer estimated that from the first white settlements to 1851, Americans had wasted a half billion dollars worth of soil (how he arrived at this figure is unknown). "There are whole counties, and almost whole States, which would once have yielded an average of twenty bushels of wheat or forty of Indian corn to the acre, yet would not (unmanured) average not more than twenty of corn and five of wheat," wrote the New York *Tribune* in 1851. " 'The virtue has gone out of them.' They have been gradually robbed of their fertility by false, miserable, wasteful culture." And a third writer, a reporter for the *National Intelligencer*, estimated that of the 125 million tilled acres in the United States, four-fifths were being depleted at a rapid rate and only one-fifth sustained or improved.

If land was cheap, labor was dear. The population was rapidly rising, but not fast enough to keep pace with the nation's economic development. "Hands are always scarce in harvest, and demand good wages," grumbled an Indiana wheat famer in 1852, sounding much like a Massachusetts factory owner complaining of labor shortages in busy seasons. In feudal Europe his counterpart would have had little land and cheap labor; the availability of resources was switched in capitalist America. So the businessman-farmer set about seeking solutions to his problems, just as did the businessman-manufacturer. He would mechanize. Continuing on, the Indiana wheatman wrote:

> Machines are being introduced, now for harvesting wheat, and some of them are designed to thresh, and partially clean it, also. They are truly labor-saving. The sickle has been laid aside, and the scythe and cradle will most probably soon give place to this machinery, worked by horse or steam power.

Such a man may have loved his land, but it shared his affection with the machine. In time he might move on, leaving the land with scarcely a backward glance and taking his carefully tended machines to the next farm.

Without such machines, the large-scale farms of Pennsylvania and upper New York would have been difficult to maintain, if not impossible to work economically. And as farmers moved westward in the 1840s, to Indiana and Ohio, and in the 1850s to Illinois and Wisconsin, they settled on still larger farms, needed even more machinery. The wheat growers recognized this more than any other group. The *Prairie Farmer*, a midwestern journal of the period, wrote in 1850:

> The wheat crop is the great crop of the North-west, for exchange purposes. It pays debts, buys groceries, clothing and lands, and answers more emphatically the purposes of trade among the farmers, than any other crop. The corn is the main crop in home feeding, the pork and beef, butter and cheese, all go to enrich particular districts, but the wheat is the reliance of the democracy of agriculture.

The newspaper wrote of the fine wheatlands of the western states, especially those of Illinois and Wisconsin, and encouraged eastern farmers to sell their holdings and relocate on lands a quarter as expensive and four times as productive as the tired soils of the East. Most New York wheat growers considered a yield of 50 bushels an acre extraordinary, while 70 bushels was above the norm for Pennsylvania and 85 for Ohio. In contrast, returns averaged over 130 bushels in Iowa, 160 in Illinois, and 220 in Wisconsin. Or at least, so it was claimed.

As Americans recovered from the depression, they began to move west. The excitement of the Mexican War added fuel to the movement, as did the allure of California gold after 1849. By 1853 the nation was in the grips of another of its periodic attacks of land fever. In the process, the wheatlands benefited. In 1849, the nation raised slightly more than

100 million bushels of wheat; in 1859, it produced 173 million bushels. The leading wheat states in 1849 were Pennsylvania, Ohio, New York, and Virginia, in that order. Ten years later they were Illinois, Indiana, Ohio, and Wisconsin. In this decade Illinois's production rose from 9.4 million bushels to 23.8 million, and Indiana's from 6.2 million to 16.8 million. The Mississippi valley had become the nation's granary.

The farms of that region—vast, flat spreads, often thousands of acres in a single holding, worked by gangs of agricultural laborers at hire and equipped with the newest in machinery—were as much factories as the shoe and textile establishments of New England. These were expensive machines, and the men who worked them were well paid for the time. An agricultural worker of 1820 could be had for $13 a month. Midwestern machine operators could expect as much as $2 a day. But the higher price of labor was more than compensated for by its productivity, given the new machines. In 1820 it would take fourteen men armed with hand reapers to clear fifteen acres of wheat in a day. Given the equipment available in 1856, nine men could do the job, and in the process harvest more wheat, since machine harvesting was less wasteful than doing the task by hand. Writing in the *Country Gentleman*, a midwestern farm journal, one farmer catalogued his experiences with both hand and machine mowing:

In the first place, in this section of the country, for several years past, no good mowers could be hired for less than $1.50 a day and board, and I never saw five mowers together that would average over one acre each, daily, and seldom that where the acre would yield two tons of dry hay, and if cut as close and even as the machines, not near that. For years before we had mowing machines, I often let my mowing by the acre, and paid from $1.25 to $1.50, beside board. Now I could get any quantity I ever had, or ever will have to cut, done for 62½ cents per acre by horses, and they will cut ten acres per day. The difference of board of ten men in place of one man and one pair of horses, is no small item. . . .

Such a farmer might own his own equipment or, as was becoming more the rule in the Midwest, would use the services of a jobber, one who owned a variety of machines and hired gangs of men to go from farm to farm, servicing the farmers at planting and harvest times. An Illinois farmer of 1853, who owned a large spread, wrote of the experiences of that time and place:

At first farmers owned their own threshers, but now they mostly belong to jobbers, who go about threshing and cleaning grain at a certain price per bushel, thus saving the farmer the cost of a fanning mill and the labor of recleaning and rescreening as was the case until a few years ago. As the great mass of farmers on the prairie have no barns this system of threshing has great advantages and the farmer is at no outlay of capital for machines. Farmers who have large barns generally own a different style of machine, these are called horse-power and are adapted to one, two, or three horses. Some of these have only separators attached so as to separate the straw from the chaff and grain. In this case the threshing progresses according to the demands of the stock for straw and chaff. . . . Steam threshers were introduced here and there before the close of the period, but they can hardly be said to have come into common use.

Without this wedding of men and machines, the large-scale business-farms of the wheat belt would have been difficult to maintain, if not impossible to work economically. The more than 70 percent increase in production that occurred in the 1850s could not have been recorded unless hand labor was replaced by that of machines. And such a change in a basic American industry could not avoid affecting other parts of society and the economy. Farmers and jobbers borrowed heavily from banks to purchase machines, so that a good deal of the public's debt by 1860 was for farm equipment. The increasing demand for machines invigorated the factories that produced them, and in the process created great fortunes, business dynasties, and a managerial class, almost as a byproduct of the wheat fields. This marriage of wheat, capital, and iron gave impetus to mining, smelting, and metal working in all their various aspects, as well as to foreign trade. Finally, the manpower released from the farms would, in the next decade, provide the armies of the Union. It would not be much of an exaggeration to say that the road to Appomattox passed through the wheatfields of the Midwest.

The American grain farmer recognized that expensive labor and cheap land dictated mechanization a full generation before the 1850s, and he acted upon this knowledge, eagerly purchasing the newest in implements. As early as 1839 Judge Jesse Buel, a leading expert in wheat farming, wrote:

> The disparity between old and new implements of culture is great, not only in the time employed, but in the manner in which they do their work, and in the power required to perform it. The old plough required a four-cattle team, and two hands, to manage it, and the work ordinarily was but half executed. The improved plough is generally propelled by two cattle, requires but one man to manage it, and when properly governed, performs thorough work. Harrows and other implements have undergone a like movement. Besides, new implements, which greatly economize the labor of tillage, are coming into use, as the roller, cultivator, drill-barrow, etc., so that a farm may now be worked with half the expense of labor that it was wont to be worked forty years ago, and may be better worked withal.

Other improvements followed, and in rapid succession. Seed drills produced by William T. Pennock of Pennsylvania and Henry W. Smith of Ohio were sold in the Midwest, and their possession by large farmers was considered a sign of "progressiveness." Disk harrows, seeders, field cultivators, and other machines made their appearance in this period. In the 1850s John Deere's steel plows were the standard for excellence in the upper Midwest. In 1856 he and his 65 employees were producing them at a rate of 13,400 a year at the Deere plant in Moline, and having no trouble in selling the product, despite strong competition.

There was even more competition in the field of threshers. In the 1840s John and Hiram Pitts, Maine-born farmer-inventors, produced a new model that became popular throughout the Midwest. The brothers organized J. B. Pitts & Co., erected a factory in Dayton, Ohio, and produced several models in the 1850s. One of these, a giant powered by from six to eight horses, was advertised as being capable of threshing 300 bushels of wheat a day. The *Ohio Cultivator* reported, in 1856, that "almost all the grain is threshed and cleaned, if not by one operation, at least by one machine, so that a fanning mill, as a separate machine, amounts to little else than a superannuated implement."

The Pitts brothers had competition from several firms, one of which, headed by Jerome I. Case, produced mechanical threshers in Racine, Wisconsin. Not only were the Case machines superior to the Pitts in some respects, but they were better advertised and merchandised. Case advertised in farm journals, saying, "If you know of anyone in your vicinity who wishes to purchase a threshing machine, you will confer a favor on him, his neighbor and myself, by inducing him to examine my machines before purchasing elsewhere." A Case thresher could cost from $290 to $325 at the factory, a high price for all but the most successful wheat farmers. Case recognized this, and worked out an "easy payment plan." Farmers would pay $50 down, $75 after the fall harvest was sold, an additional $100 on the next January 1, and the balance after the next harvest. But if the farmer had a bad year, Case would defer payments, often visiting the farm in person and cheering his customer as best he could. In this way, Case not only enhanced his reputation but aided his business.

The reaper was the most important of the farm machines of this period, the one that did the most to transform the family farm into the farm-factory. The importance of a machine to cut and gather wheat was recognized in the late colonial period, when several farmers experimented with simple contraptions, none of which seemed to work. Robert McCormick of Virginia, a weaver and farmer, constructed a reaper that was used in the harvest of 1816, but it was not

Sketch of McCormick's reaper in an 1851 edition of The Illustrated London News.

commercially or mechanically viable. The work continued, and by 1831, 58 inventions—33 English, 22 American, two French, and one German—were on record as being in various stages of development.

Cyrus McCormick, Robert's son, developed his reaper in 1831, at which time he used it in field trials. While McCormick and his father worked to perfect the machine, Obed Hussey of Cincinnati patented his, filing the necessary papers in 1833. Hussey demonstrated his machine in July, and it was received warmly. Encouraged, he established a factory and went into production. By 1840 the Hussey machines were in use in New York, Pennsylvania, Illinois, and Missouri.

It was not until 1840 that McCormick produced his first reaper, and he sold but two that year. Turning out the machines at his Virginia farm, McCormick sold them to well-known farmers in the vicinity. And all the while he made improvements, knowing he had to compete eventually with the Hussey machines. By 1844 the McCormick reaper was perfected, and 50 were sold. Now McCormick set about organizing a distribution network. He demonstrated the machine in western New York, Ohio, Illinois, Wisconsin, and Missouri, and at the same time established machine shops for their production in Brockport, New York, and in Hussey's own preserve of Cincinnati. McCormick produced over two hundred reapers in 1846, and five hundred in 1847. By then, his domination over Hussey had been established. On the other hand, new manufacturers entered the field, and the competition became fierce. Nine reapers, each from a different maker, vied with one another at the Geneva, New York trials of 1852, and the Burrall machine bested McCormick's. Soon after, at a trial in Springfield, Ohio, the Densmore reaper received the prize. Machines constructed by at least a dozen makers competed in the Midwest, with all the agents taking aim at the McCormick men, attempting to wrest the lead from them.

McCormick prepared for the contest. In 1847 he had established his new factory in Chicago, so as to be closer to the wheat fields. Now he concentrated his attention on perfection of his machines and the sales effort, leaving other problems to his associates and the rest of the country to licensees. J. B. McCormick, a cousin, who had become a traveling representative in 1845, stepped up the effort in the Midwest, and McCormick hired territorial supervisors to coordinate the work of the field men. These went through a training period, followed by a tour of the district at the side of a seasoned man. Then he was sent out on his own, to compete against four or five other reaper manufacturers' representatives. The McCormick salesmen did well, not only because they had a good machine, but because they were better trained in presentation. For example, D. R. Burt, an agent in the 1850s, developed a technique to use against representatives of a machine produced by John Manny:

> I found in the neighborhood supplied from Cassville quite early in the season one of Manny's agents with a fancyfully painted machine, cutting the old prairie grass to the no small delight of witnesses, making sweeping and bold declarations about what his machine could do and how it could beat yours, etc., etc. Well, he had the start of me, I must head him somehow. I began by breaking down on his fancy machine, pointed out every objection that I could see and all that I had learned last year ... gave the statements of those that had seen the one work in my grass ... all of which I could prove. And then stated to all my opinion of what would be the result should they purchase from Manny. You pay one half money and give your note for the bal-

ance, are prosecuted for the last note and the cheapest way to get out of the scrape is to pay the note, keep the poor machine and in a short time purchase one from McCormick. . . .

Having said this in regard to the Manny machine and that company's business methods, Burt concluded by observing the virtues of the McCormick reaper and outlining the way the company did business:

> Now gentlemen, I am an old settler, have shared all the hardships of this new country with you, have taken it Rough and Smooth ... have often been imposed on in the way I almost know you would be by purchasing the machine offered you today. I would say to all, try your machine before you [pay] one half or any except the freight. I can offer you one on such terms, warrant it against this machine or any other you can produce, and if after a fair trial ... any other proves superior and you prefer it to mine, keep [it]. I will take mine back, say not a word, refund the freight, all is right again. No Gentlemen, this man dare not do this.

As a result of this kind of offer, Burt sold twenty machines in Lafayette County, and the Manny man, none.

Increased wheat exports as a result of the Crimean War in Europe, a shortage of labor created by farmers leaving for the California gold rush, and an increase in the price of wheat all helped McCormick in the early 1850s. The McCormick works turned out 4,600 machines in the 1851–54 period, making McCormick Chicago's leading citizen, not only a living symbol of that city's growing power, but a major purchaser of wood and iron from local establishments and a hirer of workers. The Mercantile Agency credit reporter agreed with those who thought McCormick a sound businessman, and in 1853 he wrote:

> Been here 6 or 8 yrs has a v fine prop. large brick building with steam engine, cant have less than 100 hands to work—is consid[d].

A Mercantile Agency credit report on Cyrus H. McCormick covering the period 1852–1865.

w. 200m we thk him w. $150m clear. His patent is w a fortune
  tho' it costs him a gd deal of money to defend it   manfrs from
  12c 1500 reapers a yr. which he sells at $120 each.

By 1858 the reporter had raised his estimate of Mc-
Cormick's net worth to $200,000, and believed him to be the
wealthiest man in the Midwest. Yet McCormick did not
dominate the large farm equipment market, since there was
no discernible industry in 1860; most farm implements of all
kinds were made and used locally. In that year some $21 mil-
lion worth of farm machinery and tools were produced in the

United States; the manufacturers ranged from McCormick who by then was the symbol of the rapid rise of wheat in the Midwest, to the blacksmith in a New England village.

Some claimed the reaper had done for wheat what the Whitney cotton gin had accomplished for cotton. This was an exaggeration, for the reaper did not create a new kind of farming or revive an old, but rather added to the benefits of what had already existed. One of McCormick's biographers, noting his birth in 1809, wrote, "That was a great year for the world. Poe and Tennyson, Chopin and Mendelssohn, Darwin, Gladstone, and great Lincoln were born then—and McCormick, if he may be judged by his services to humanity,

An ambrotype by Alexander Hesler of grain elevators at the mouth of the Chicago River, 1858.

is none too small a man to share their birth year." Few would accept such a statement as this today. But large wheat farmers in the American Midwest in the late 1850s might have felt otherwise, as might the millers and shippers of Chicago, which became a great flour center in the 1850s, in part as a result of the reaper.

TABLE 7

SHIPMENTS OF FLOUR AND GRAIN FROM CHICAGO, 1850-1860*

Year	Total, Flour and Grain (in bushels)
1850	1,858,928
1851	4,646,521
1852	5,873,141
1853	6,422,181
1854	12,902,320
1855	16,633,645
1856	21,583,221
1857	18,032,678
1858	20,040,178
1859	16,768,857
1860	31,109,059

* Source: *Eighth Census of the United States, 1860: Agriculture*, p. cxlix, Table H.

As powerful as the upward surge of wheat appeared to be in the 1850s, there seemed no way by which grains could challenge cotton as the leading American crop. This, at least, was the tale told by the statistics. Cotton production increased substantially in the 1850s, with the first 3-million-bale year recorded in 1852. Seven years later, in 1859, 4.5 million bales were produced, a record that would stand until 1877.

TABLE 8

COTTON PRODUCTION, 1850-1859*

Year	Production (1,000 bales)
1850	2,136
1851	2,799
1852	3,130
1853	2,766
1854	2,709
1855	3,221
1856	2,874
1857	3,013
1858	3,758
1859	4,508

* Source: *Historical Statistics of the United States: Colonial Times to 1957* (Washington, 1958), p. 624.

TABLE 9

VALUE OF TOTAL EXPORTS AND COTTON EXPORTS, 1850-1859*

Year	Total Exports	Cotton Exports
1850	$144,376,000	$ 71,984,616
1851	188,915,000	112,315,317
1852	166,984,000	87,965,732
1853	203,489,000	109,456,404
1854	237,044,000	93,596,220
1855	218,910,000	88,143,844
1856	281,219,000	128,382,351
1857	293,824,000	131,575,859
1858	272,011,000	131,386,661
1859	292,902,000	161,434,923

* Source: Douglas C. North, *The Economic Growth of the United States, 1790-1860* (New York: Norton, 1966), p. 233.

In this same period, cotton retained its position as the nation's leading export and earner of foreign currencies. Grains and manufactured goods were becoming increasingly important in the area of foreign trade, but at the end of the decade, cotton still reigned supreme.

These statistics told only part of the story, however. In fact, they masked deep problems in cotton production, difficulties the planters struggled to overcome and which were worse at the end of the decade than they had been at its beginning.

One of the most important problems involved the nature of the crop. Cotton cultivation tended to leech the land of its vitality. This difficulty might have been overcome through crop rotation and intense use of fertilizers, and indeed some farmers, especially those in the eastern states, employed both. But most plantations were heavily mortgaged, and these practices lowered the farmers' incomes, often to the point where they could no longer meet the interest on their debts. A far simpler solution was to abandon the eastern farm, or sell it for a low price, and move westward, to virgin and often better soils. And many made the move. One of these, Curtis B. Sutton of Virginia, made his move to Texas in the late 1840s. By the 1850s Texas was in the midst of a new cotton empire, cultivated largely by men like Sutton—emigrants from Virginia and other southern seaboard states. There one field hand could produce ten bales, which could be sold at New Orleans for $400, a profit of $300 per hand. In 1853 Sutton wrote to a friend, William Lyons, of his feelings:

> I could not myself live in Virginia after seeing what I have and
> as to the advantages of a young man in a new country, I like a

Southern life, there is an excitement in the Southern people that I admire. Old Virginia I shall never forget and what son of hers was ever known to forget her, God bless her. I can look back and appreciate her openness of character, liberality, and hospitality—Old Virginia, if I had money, forever is my motto, but she presents no encouragement to young adventurers.

"Who can clear $300 on that poor land of the Slashes of Hanover?" asked Sutton. For this reason, above all, men of the old South relocated to the new. Texas, Alabama, Mississippi, Arkansas—these states were becoming the heart of the cotton kingdom in the 1850s.

TABLE 10

NUMBER, ACREAGE, AND AVERAGE SIZE OF FARMS, 1850-1860*

State	Number		Acreage		Average Size	
	1850	1860	1850	1860	1850	1860
Alabama	41,964	55,128	12,137,681	19,104,545	289	346
Arkansas	17,758	39,004	2,598,216	9,574,006	146	245
Florida	4,304	6,568	1,595,289	2,920,228	371	444
Louisiana	13,422	17,328	4,989,043	9,298,576	372	536
Mississippi	33,960	42,840	10,490,449	15,839,684	309	370
Texas	12,198	42,891	11,496,339	25,344,028	942	591
United States					203	194

* Source: *Eighth Census of the United States, 1860: Agriculture*, p. 222.

But even the good, productive, virgin soil of the Southwest could not bring prosperity to the plantation owners, for costs were rising in this period, while the price of cotton appeared to be in a long-term decline. After the War of 1812, cotton fetched over thirty cents a pound; in the mid-1840s it fell as low as five cents. Then the price leveled off, and actually rose somewhat. Cotton was eleven cents in New Orle-

Engraving of a slave hut on a cotton plantation during the 1850s.

ans in 1849, fell as low as seven cents in the early 1850s, rose
to fifteen in 1857, and then declined to ten cents in 1859.
And all the while other prices—factoring costs, transportation, labor, and goods needed on the plantation among others
—either remained stationary or rose. Labor cost, meaning
slaves in this case, was an especially vexing problem. In the
1850s over 200,000 slaves were taken from their old homes in

the upper South and sent to new ones in the Southwest, usually by means of slave auctions in New Orleans. Plantation owners had to increase production to show profits, and to do this had to purchase more slaves, which in turn forced their price upward, and then the process repeated itself. In 1855 a Georgia planter noted that "Negroes are 25 percent higher now with cotton at ten and a half cents than they were two or three years ago when it was worth fifteen and sixteen cents," and he predicted "a reversal will come soon." Such was not to be. Instead, the continuing demand for slaves forced their prices upward, so that at the end of the 1850s, prime field hands cost over $2,000 at the New Orleans auctions. The net worth of southern slaves in 1850 was in the neighborhood of $1.6 billion; by 1860 the sum was closer to $4 billion, and headed higher.

Faced with such a situation, compounded by rising costs elsewhere, southern planters either expanded, sold out, or resigned themselves to becoming members of the class of poor farmers. Some, a relative few, succeeded in transforming their plantations into agricultural factories along the lines of the large wheat fields of the upper Mississippi valley. Such people were in a dilemma. In order to lower costs, they might try to produce all they needed on their plantations. But to do this they would have to divert land and other resources from cotton, and so lower income as well. At first many plantation owners attempted to become self-sufficient, but by the mid-1850s they seemed to give up in order to concentrate on cotton. Stephen Duncan, owner of one of the largest plantations near Natchez, Mississippi, recorded the purchase of 135 barrels of pork, seven of flour, as well as other agricultural products, in 1857, even though his farm was well suited for the raising of wheat and hogs. In 1859 Duncan purchased 939 bushels of corn, 12 of oats, 135 barrels of pork, among others. And his example was typical of the nature of large plantation farming.

The division of southern planters into the large cotton farm-factory owners and the small, struggling self-sufficient farmers created social and economic tensions. A small farmer near Natchez told Frederick Law Olmstead, then traveling through the area, that he disliked the plantation class. "Big plantations, sir, nothing else—aristocrats; swell-heads I call them, sir—nothing but swell-heads. . . . Must have ice for their wine, you see, or they'd die; and so they have to live in Natchez or New Orleans; a good many of them live in New Orleans." And their offspring were just as bad. "You can know their children as far back as you can see them—young swell-heads! . . . They do want so bad to look as if they weren't made of the same clay as the rest of God's creation."

Southern businessmen, especially those attempting to create an industrial climate in the South, sharply criticized the plantation class for its apparent lack of interest in the section and unwillingness to purchase its goods. The *Mississippi Free Trader* believed:

> The large planters—the one-thousand-bale planters—do not contribute most to the prosperity of Natchez. They, for the most part, sell their cotton in Liverpool; buy their wines in London or Havre; their negro clothing in Boston; their plantation implements and supplies in Cincinnati; and their groceries and fancy articles in New Orleans. The small planter has not the credit nor the business connections to do this; he requires the proceeds of his crop as soon as it can be sold; and he purchases and pays for, cash in hand, almost every necessary wanted during the year, in the same market where he sells his cotton. The small planter hoards no money in these times; he lends none

at usurious rates of interest; he buys up the property of no unfortunate debtor for a few dollars; but he lays it all out for the purchase of supplies, and thus directly contributes his mite to the prosperity of our city.

A social revolution—one that would pit the plantation class against the small farmers and businessmen—was not in the making in the 1850s, but social tensions between these classes were on the rise.

For their part, the large plantation owners blamed their difficulties and those of the South in general on cotton factors and merchants, many of whom represented northern interests. Cotton was the key to America's prosperity and growth, they claimed, but it was in bondage to northern interests, who contributed little to the national well-being but took the cream from the South. To the large planters, they seemed like leeches on the economic body. W. C. Daniell of Savannah, Georgia, spoke for his class when he castigated such individuals:

> Our adversaries herd in the public marts; they fill up the highways; they combine; they control public opinion; they command the press, and exercise, not always, a just and wholesome influence over the opinion of the factors who sell our crops. They estimate our productions, and too often regulate the prices, upon data made for the occasion. We do not, perhaps we cannot, combine.

But the attempt at combination was made. Beginning in 1851, the planters held conventions, aimed at formulating a common policy against their perceived enemies. There was talk of a common purchase policy, withholding crops from markets until the cotton price rose, and political action through the Congress. And all the while, the planters came to look upon the North as their natural enemy. This was not so much the result of abolitionist protest, though that played a part. Rather, it was economic subordination—a belief that the South was becoming a colony of New York, Boston, and Philadelphia—that concerned the delegates. At the New Orleans convention of 1855, Albert Pike, a leading planter, exclaimed:

> From the rattle with which the nurse tickles the ear of the child born in the south to the shroud that covers the cold form of the dead, everything comes to us from the north. We rise from between sheets made in northern looms, and pillows of northern feathers, to wash in basins made in the north, dry our bodies on northern towels, and dress ourselves in garments woven in northern looms; we eat from northern plates and dishes; our rooms are swept with northern brooms, our gardens dug with northern spades, and our bread kneaded in trays or dishes of northern wood or tin; and the very wood which feeds our fires is cut with northern axes, helved with hickory brought from Connecticut and New York.

There was a cry for a beginning of a concerted effort at creating a large manufacturing complex in the South, but little came of it. In Mississippi six textile factories were charted in 1850, and in Alabama twenty between 1849 and 1854. The total capital invested in southern cotton factories in 1840 was less than $6 million, and this figure doubled in the next two decades. Still, it was far behind that of the North and Midwest. Capital invested in manufacturing in the South was nearly 20 percent of the national total in 1840, 17.6 percent in 1850, and less than 16 percent in 1860. In addition, little of the southern growth in manufacturing was in textile and related factories, but rather in lumber, tobacco processing, and flour milling.

In the 1850s the cotton South suffered from scarce capital and labor, complicated by the many problems revolving around the slave labor situation. Its only salvation seemed to be in increased production of cotton, which would be sold by the factors to bring in money, which the cotton South would use to purchase goods from other sections of the country and overseas. Cotton was king, but it was in chains too. Even if the cotton kingdom were to tread water and not advance, it would need more land to replace worn-out acres and add to the cash crop. That land, so it was believed, was in the West.

But the farmers of Minnesota, Iowa, Illinois, and other wheat states had the same desire. To whom would the West belong? The Kansas-Nebraska Act of 1854 seemed to answer that question. Stephen Douglas had all but obtained the transcontinental railroad for Illinois and the Midwest. Iowa and Minnesota wheat farmers would filter into Nebraska, and in time that territory would enter the Union as a free state. But Kansas would belong to the South and to cotton. It would be settled by plantation owners, some from the lower South, many from Missouri. In time Kansas—cotton Kansas—would join the nation as a slave state. The equation seemed to favor the North somewhat, but on the surface at least appeared to benefit all sections. Yet below the surface were the many emotional aspects revolving around southern slavery and northern abolitionism. Free and slave—wheat and cotton—would contest for Kansas, with both sides recognizing the need for the land, not only for economic reasons, but ideological ones as well.

8 / THE POLITICS OF MORALITY

IN ANOTHER, QUIETER PERIOD OF AMERICAN HISTORY, THE contest between wheat and cotton might have been settled without fanfare. During the great debates of 1850, for example, Henry Clay had told southern delegates that even had slavery been permitted in California, that state was destined to have a free status due to its soils and climate, which he believed would not support a cotton culture. A majority of southerners either accepted this argument or, understanding it, would consider the question calmly and prepare for future compromise. There were, of course, politicians on both sides prepared to argue the moral issue of slavery as well, but in 1850, this question was unspoken.

Such was not the case in 1854. By then cotton and wheat no longer were mere crops, but symbols of civilizations, complete with moral codes. And political discussions that year were not of compromise and conciliation, but of morality, and the possibility of an armed clash between forces of good and evil. One might reconcile economic differences, but how could good come to terms with evil without becoming evil itself? So ran the conversations among Wilmot Proviso Whigs, who met to discuss politics and morality in their rooming houses near the Capitol, while in other houses and rooms, southern fire-eaters did the same. Men like Douglas and, for a while at least, Jefferson Davis still hoped the differences could be resolved. But neither man had the prestige or talent of a Henry Clay. And even a Clay might have been thwarted by the growing atmosphere of hate in Washington, as grim-faced legislators went from caucus to caucus, all but convinced that an armed conflict between cotton and wheat, South and North, slavery and freedom, was about to commence, with Kansas the battlefield.

Residents of the Northeast and old Northwest also discussed the issues of Kansas and the spread of slavery, and often with great fervor. But for the majority the questions were academic and philosophical rather than matters that touched upon their everyday lives. Most Americans of these sections had never seen a slave and would never consider relocating beyond the Mississippi. This is not to say the slavery debate was unimportant, but rather that, to many, it was abstract.

Such individuals also discussed another matter, one that did touch upon their lives directly, one they could see if they lived in the Atlantic port cities, and which evoked more interest in the early 1850s than the Washington debates. To these people the threat to the nation's integrity came not from the clash between northern and southern values and cultures, but from the confrontation between native-born

198

Americans and immigrants. In Washington, legislators discussed the possibility of a war over the extension of slavery; their constituents in the eastern cities seemed more concerned with the possibility of an armed conflict between native Protestants and immigrant Catholics.

The statistics of slavery interested native Americans of the early 1850s, but those relating to immigration were more foreboding. One in particular caught the public's attention. In 1851 the nation's population stood at 24 million, and in that year, 221,000 Irish immigrants arrived in America, of a total of 380,000. Approximately three out of every two hundred Americans had arrived in the country within the past year. One of every hundred Americans was a newly arrived Irish Catholic. In 1850 one out of every twenty-two Americans had been born in Ireland, and since most Irish-Americans were concentrated in the Northeast, their presence there seemed far more obvious than in other parts of the country. And their numbers were growing all the time, leading many native-born Americans to feel engulfed by the "Irish tide." "Since the period when the Gothic tribes, under their hereditary kings, strode down the banks of the Borysthenes, and overwhelmed Greece and Germany and the whole empire of Rome, no migration of men has occurred in the world at all similar to that which is now pouring itself upon the shores of the United States," wrote the *Democratic Review* in 1852, in an article entitled, "Revolution or Migration —The Irish Question." "In a single week we have again and again received into the bosom of our society, numbers as great as a Gothic army."

There were those who noted a similarity in the situation of the black slaves of the South and the "white slaves" of the

North. Almost all Irish immigrants were poor. Most found employment in menial occupations at below the wages paid native Americans. They lived in hovels in the worst parts of town. Native-born Protestants often viewed them with mistrust and fear. Just as the plantation whites came to believe the blacks were in some ways subhuman, so the industrial-commercial North wrote of the "simian-like" qualities of the Irish Catholics. Leaders of both sections feared armed uprisings on the part of the workers against their masters. Yet northern industry could not do without Irish workers, just as the plantation South insisted slaves were needed for the cotton crops.

As early as 1836 John C. Calhoun recognized this situation, and he called upon "the sober and considerate" northerners to support the plantation class against abolitionists. The plantation South was the natural ally of the industrial and commercial North, he claimed. In effect, he invited the upper-class northerners to support plantation slavery, in return for which the plantation owners would be their allies against the working-class northerners. In 1847 he repeated the invitation, reminding conservatives of the North that the abolitionist who today called for an end to slavery might tomorrow lead a worker rebellion against northern factories. Wealthy northern Protestants had an interest "in upholding and preserving the equilibrium of the slaveholding states." "Let gentlemen then be warned that while warring on us, they are warring on themselves." In 1849 Calhoun exclaimed that an end to slavery would be a prelude to class war in the North, when that section would "be subject to all the agitations and conflicts growing out of the divisions of wealth and poverty," and he told Josiah Quincy that "the interests of the *gentlemen* of the North and of the South are identical."

There were some signs that such an alliance might indeed develop. In 1842 a Native American Party was formed in Louisiana. It was directed against French Catholics, but had aspirations for national power as well. During the next two years the movement spread northward, where it found even greater favor. The Native Americans of New York, which was the largest Irish Catholic city in the nation, elected James Harper as mayor in 1844. The same year six Native Americans were elected to the House of Representatives, all from the Northeast, with the contingent led by Lewis C. Levin, a Philadelphia lawyer who was also editor of the rabidly anti-immigrant Philadelphia *Daily Sun*. Levin's announced intention to press for immigration restriction won support from some southern spokesmen. The governor of Virginia noted that "foreignism brings 500,000 who settle annually in the free states with instincts against slavery, making fifty representatives in ten years to swell the opposition to the South . . . our highest duty to the South is to discourage immigration." A southern slaveholder echoed the sentiment, adding: "The mistake with us has been that it was not made a felony to bring in an Irishman when it was made piracy to bring in an African."

In time the Native American movement would engulf and help destroy the southern Whig Party. Yet an alliance of plantation owners and factory owners never developed. Paradoxically, a good many Americans who viewed slavery as a moral crime were among the leaders of the virulent anti-Catholic crusades in the North, while leading spokesmen for immigrant causes would defend the southern plantation owners. Then, as before and since, politicians asking for moral crusades and deep societal changes found audiences only when the changes sought were to take place far from their constituencies. The abolitionists calling for freedom for the slaves came from northern states where there were no slaves; those who criticized the Native Americans often could be found in areas untouched by immigrants. Such were the vagaries of moral politics in the 1850s.

The Native Americans flourished in the eastern cities and midwestern towns. They formed semisecret and secret clubs and organizations, known by such names as Sons of '76, Druids, Foresters, Sons of Sires, and so on. The leading such organization, concentrated in New York, was the secret Supreme Order of the Star Spangled Banner. Horace Greeley dubbed this group the "Know-Nothings," since its members were under strict orders to say they knew nothing when asked of the organization's activities. The name stuck, even though the Native Americans abandoned their secrecy in 1853 and came out into the open.

The Know-Nothing view of Catholic immigrants was both simple and direct. Thomas R. Whitney, a leading party spokesman, divided all immigrants into four categories, and found none of them acceptable. The first consisted of those who came to America to make money, intending to return home after a while. Such individuals were not really Americans and had no desire to become Americans, while taking jobs from native laborers. Then there were workers who intended to stay and accepted work for lower than prevailing pay, and so demoralized native workers. The third class consisted of "Papists—men who will obey their priests *first*, and the laws of the country afterwards." Clearly all such people should be barred, said Whitney. Finally, there were the paupers and criminals, the first living off the labor of taxpayers, the second making the cities unlivable.

In the early 1850s Irish-American youth gangs prowled the street at night, when even policemen feared to walk their beats. Mike Walsh's Spartan Band and the Empire Club vied for the West Side, while the Dead Rabbits and the Bowery Boys aimed at controlling the entire city. To fight them the

A "Bowery Boy" (left) and a "Dead Rabbit" (right) depicted in Frank Leslie's Illustrated Newspaper, *July 11, 1857.*

Know-Nothings formed their own gangs, which included the Black Snakes, Blood Tubs, Plug Uglies, and Hard Times. Some citizens protested that they too were guilty of lawlessness, but Know-Nothing advocates and members claimed they were only fighting fire with fire, and sought to protect the rights of decent, law-abiding citizens. The view of the immigrant as a lawbreaker became prevalent and was reflected in the words of a New York judge who, on passing sentences of murder in 1851, said:

> Eight persons have been arraigned at this term for murder. Five of you have been convicted, and upon three of you the last punishment known to our law is denounced. All of you owe your crimes to your indulgence in the ruinous habit of intoxication. All of you are foreigners, who have sought our soil that you might enjoy the benefits of our free institutions, and, in return for the protection which our laws so freely offer you, violate them without scruple, and apparently without remorse, even unto the shedding of blood. The preservation of peace and good order among us, and the security of human life, admonishes us, in a peculiar manner, under such circumstances, to enforce the law upon you.

By 1854 the Know-Nothings had erected a national coalition, and were attempting to rationalize and clearly define their objectives. The Catholic immigrant would be opposed because he was not, and could not become, a true American, due to his allegiance to the Roman Church. Increased crime and taxes appeared wherever he settled, and he acted to the detriment of native-born workers. It was to these native-born Protestant workers that the Know-Nothings aimed their primary appeals. The Whigs, they claimed, represented a business aristocracy, while the Democrats spoke for the cotton aristocrats. The Know-Nothings would defend the rights of free, native labor.

In order to broaden their appeal, some Know-Nothing leaders tried to formulate a policy toward the western lands and slavery. This caused difficulties, since southern party members were for slavery and northern ones against it. In 1854, however, it appeared the party was headed in the direction of opposing the spread of slavery into the territories while accepting it in the South.

Thus, what began as an anti-Catholic and anti-immigrant movement in the early 1840s had within a decade broadened its appeal to include a class bias in favor of workers and a group appeal directed at midwestern farmers. The movement even had its "bible," *Foreign Conspiracy Against the Liberties of the United States*, by Samuel F. B. Morse, the noted artist and inventor. Little wonder that the Know-Nothings looked forward to the presidential and congressional elections of 1856, at which time the party would field a full slate of candidates. The strategy was clear: in 1856 the party would establish itself as one of the two major political coalitions, the other being the Democrats. Then, through alliances with others, it would capture the presidency and the Congress in 1860, and then carry through on its programs of immigrant exclusion.

The nativists represented one of the major emerging moral-political forces of the mid-1850s. As such, it vied with the antislavery movement for public support. Older, better established, and wider in appeal than the nativists, the antislavery forces also suffered from divided leadership, disputes over tactics, and an inability to agree on methods of procedure. But it did have an arena, a place where it could contest its politics and morality, and it also had a book and a fanatic. Both excited and inflamed the nation.

At the beginning of the 1850s the antislavery movement appeared to have reached its zenith. In 1848 Martin Van Buren had been placed in nomination for the presidency by the Free Soil Party, and had received 292,000 votes, or 10 percent of the total cast. Drawing from both the Whigs and northern Democrats, adding the ballots of the short-lived Liberty Party of 1844, it seemed the Free Soilers might replace the Whigs as the nation's second most powerful political party by 1852. But the party faced problems of direction. Some of its leaders insisted slavery could be ended peacefully, while others, convinced the white South would never yield on the issue, called for armed struggle. Not all antislavery people felt the institution could be banished from the South and were content to attempt to fight its spread into the western territories, and these were opposed by firebrands calling for guerrilla war against the slaveholders in the heart of the South. Politics was the road to success, said one branch of the movement; direct armed action was the only answer, said others. Many antislavery people seemed content to talk and do little else.

The Compromise of 1850 both discouraged and excited the antislavery forces, and provided its members with a new battlefield. Accepted by moderates in some sections, it appeared to end the antislavery debate for the time being. The nation's attention was turning to other matters, and the Know-Nothings, not the antislavery forces, seemed a greater threat to the two-party system. But the passage of the Fugitive Slave Law gave the antislavery forces a new cause. Many of them protested the legislation and prepared to fight it in a direct fashion. The underground railroad enlisted hundreds of volunteers, both black and white, and through its operations slaves were encouraged to flee the plantations and helped to find refuge, usually in Canada. White southern leaders were enraged by the activity and demanded stricter enforcement of the law. And with each protest, the antislavery forces were further encouraged in their work. The Compromise of 1850 thus crippled those abolitionists who believed in political action and aided those who favored a more direct approach. The legalists in the movement were depressed, while the extremists were encouraged. And in the process, abolitionism gained in moral fervor even though it lost in its number of adherents. The victory of the extreme wing was sealed in 1852, when Free Soil presidential candidate John P. Hale received only 156,000 votes, or less than 5 percent of the total cast, half that of Van Buren four years before.

If the moderates lost their election, the radicals received their bible—*Uncle Tom's Cabin*, by Harriet Beecher Stowe, which was serialized in the *National Era* in 1851, published in book form the following year, and which within a year had sold 1.2 million copies. The novel was a phenomenon, and the widest-read American book since Tom Paine's *Common Sense*.

Harriet Beecher Stowe was an abolitionist, but not one of the radicals. Daughter of the famed preacher Lyman Beecher and wife of abolitionist scholar Calvin Ellis Stowe, she grew up and lived in an atmosphere dominated by discussions of the injustices of slavery. For a while she was content to write short stories, most of them dealing with subjects other than slavery, such as "Sunny Memories of Foreign Lands." Then, in 1851, she read of the death of a slave named Uncle Tom. It was then she decided to write her novel. After conducting careful research into plantation life and consulting with for-

Abolitionist Harriet Beecher Stowe.
Her Uncle Tom's Cabin *was published in 1852.*

mer slaves, including Frederick Douglass, but without visiting the South itself, she began work. Apparently Harriet Stowe herself had little idea of how popular the book would become, or that it would be discussed, analyzed, and debated by scholars and literary figures to the present day.

The novel was not a great work of art, and was written with much Victorian sentimentality. Its characters—the kind slaveholder St. Clair, the cruel Simon Legree, the saintly Little Eva, the slave child Topsy, and Uncle Tom, the kindly and badly treated slave—were painted in the blacks and whites so popular in that period's novels, without the subtlety demanded by a future generation or the insights and awareness of complexity one finds in her contemporaries, such as Nathaniel Hawthorne and Herman Melville. Southern readers, even those sympathetic to abolition, observed that the author's portrayal of plantation life and slaves was unreal and overidealized, while the whites in the book were barely recognizable and two-dimensional. But having said this, it must be recognized that to many northerners, who had never seen a plantation and were used to this genre, *Uncle Tom's Cabin* was reality, and Uncle Tom and Eliza real people. More than all the broadsides of William Lloyd Garrison and the preachments of hundreds of northern ministers, Harriet Beecher Stowe touched the conscience of the North. There is no way of knowing how many converts to antislavery she was responsible for, or the number of formerly uncommitted people she helped into the antislavery camp, but there were doubtless many. To what was probably a majority of northerners, *Uncle Tom's Cabin* was a true picture of southern plantation life, which was immoral. And to as many white southerners, it seemed the North was filled with people who believed them moral cripples, and the institution they defended one that had to be obliterated.

It has been said that Abraham Lincoln read *Uncle Tom's Cabin* and understood it, Charles Sumner and other abolitionist political leaders knew its message before it was written, and Stephen Douglas never heard of the book. Like all such statements, this one is grossly exaggerated. Certainly Douglas knew of the book and its impact. But he clung to the belief that a majority of Americans of both sections would accept compromise as an alternative to a bloody civil war. It was in this hope that he steered the Kansas-Nebraska Act through

Congress and spoke in its favor after the measure had been signed into law.

Such was not to be. Although Nebraska was rapidly settled by free farmers, a contest developed for Kansas. Slaveholders entered the territory from the lower Midwest, while free farmers, urged on by the abolitionists of the New England Emigrant Aid Society, also came to Kansas. Despite Pierce's efforts to maintain peace and favor the slaveholders, conflict developed between the free farmers in the northern part of Kansas and the slaveholders in the south. By early 1855 armed clashes between the two groups were common; a year later actual civil war erupted in "Bleeding Kansas." Tempers rose in the South and North, and reached a boiling point in Washington, where legislators took to carrying weapons wherever they went. Would Kansas be slave or free? Would it eventually enter the Union allied to the North or South? The future direction of the national destiny seemed to hinge on answers to these questions.

The Kansas issue shattered the uneasy political peace, and with it, the remaining shreds of the northern Whig Party. The Democrats had taken their stand in favor of the Kansas-Nebraska Act and southern power in Washington. The old party of Henry Clay, ever hopeful of compromise, could not survive in the growing moral atmosphere of the times. Abolitionists and Free Soilers in the Midwest found many Whigs joining their banners. Together these forces helped form a new political party, the Republicans. Several local clubs contended for the honor of being the first Republican organization, but most historians agree that the leading claimant was the one in Ripon, Wisconsin, headed by Alvin E. Bovay. The midwestern Republicans were a union of several antislavery

210

groups, farm organizations, and intellectuals, though most of the latter preferred to remain Whigs for the time being. Moderate Republicans called for passage of the Wilmot Proviso, while radicals—usually former Free Soilers—demanded an end to slavery throughout the United States.

In most respects the Republican programs were diametrically opposed to much of what the Know-Nothings professed. Yet appeals were made to Know-Nothings too, for at least a temporary alliance in order to restructure the nation's priorities. The time seemed ripe for radical politics. By 1855 it was no longer a struggle between North and South, but was evolving into one between radical and conservative. For example, Southern fire-eater Robert Barnwell Rhett and abolitionist spokesman William Seward had opposite views on slavery, but both agreed the question was a moral rather than political problem, one that could be decided by war. They considered their rivals to be Alexander Stephens and Stephen Douglas, two moderates seeking political solutions. In a similar way, the Know-Nothings and Republicans were allied in believing an alien group was destroying the nation. The Know-Nothings hated the foreigners, while the Republicans concentrated their ire on the slavocracy. *Uncle Tom's Cabin* and Morse's *Foreign Conspiracy* were moral tracts. Readers of both books were willing to see the nation dismembered before surrendering their moral beliefs.

The first session of the Thirty-fourth Congress met on December 3, 1855. Immediately sides were drawn on the Kansas issue. The factions argued over the selection of a doorkeeper for the House and a sergeant at arms for the Senate. There was a prolonged battle over the speakership; not until March did Nathaniel Banks of Massachusetts take the post.

Interestingly enough, Banks had begun his political career as a Democrat, then in 1854 had switched to the Know-Nothings, and shortly thereafter had become a Republican. Later on, he would rejoin the Democrats, and finally end his life as a Republican. His career was not unusual for politicians of that turbulent period.

Congress named a committee to investigate conditions in Kansas, a measure supported by moderates in the hope that a knowledge of the facts and the passage of time would help cool conditions in Washington. But the Kansas debates opened before the committee could report, and they became more fiery as each day brought new reports of atrocities from Kansas. Southern and northern legislators hurled harsh epithets at each other; senatorial courtesy, an old tradition, was another casualty of the fighting. In a speech on Kansas, Charles Sumner called Douglas "a noisome squat and nameless animal," and Senator David Atchison of Missouri was characterized as a "Cataline." Senator Andrew Pierce Butler of South Carolina spoke of the northern abolitionist legislators as "mental pigmies." His opponents replied by accusing him of drunkenness, and Sumner spoke derisively of "the loose expectoration of his speech." Some senators were shocked, and roundly criticized Sumner. But Congressman Preston Brooks of South Carolina, seeing the insult as a matter to be avenged, reacted as an antebellum southern gentleman might be expected to. He walked into the Senate and beat Sumner over the head with a cane until he was unconscious. The entire nation was aroused. Northerners considered Brooks a coward, but in the South he was a hero.

While they talked, news reached the congressmen of further bloodshed in Kansas, this the work of the leading fanatic

Senator Charles Sumner of Massachusetts.

of the abolitionist cause, a man who already had become a symbol of the extremists of that movement. John Brown, a man of strong religious fervor and dubious sanity, had worked for the abolitionist cause for several years, speaking of his dreams of leading the slaves in a bloody revolt against their masters. As the Kansas fighting intensified, Brown saw his chance in that territory. Shortly after learning of a southern attack on the Free Soil town of Lawrence, Brown, his sons, and several followers went to Pottawatomie County, a southern preserve. There they killed five settlers, mutilated

213

their bodies, burned their houses and barns, and then rode off on stolen horses. The Pottawatomie raid was so brutal that several Free Soil and Republican leaders disavowed Brown. But that year violence was coming to replace debate, and more would follow.

It was also a political year, one in which the nation would select its next president. By then it was clear the Whig Party was finished, with the Know-Nothings and the Republicans fighting for the corpse, and the right to contest the Democrats for national power.

The Know-Nothings met first, in Philadelphia, in February, 1856. The party's leaders realized their opportunity for power had come, but they didn't know how to handle it. So long as the party had been a small organization, concentrating on one issue with little chance of national power, it held together. Now, with a large and growing group of discontented former Whigs, potential Republicans, and disaffected Democrats in the van, the leaders searched for some means of broadening their appeal to take in other elements, while at the same time retaining the support of the original anti-Catholics.

The convention itself was mobbed, with fist fights breaking out regularly and speakers unable to capture the attention of the delegates. Southern delegates demanded a plank opposing the antislavery movement; without it, they could do nothing against their area's Democrats. Northern members, many sympathetic to the abolitionists, asked for support of the free forces in Kansas. The southerners wanted to water down the previous anti-Catholic resolutions, while northern Know-Nothings wanted to strengthen them. In the end, the convention attempted to find a compromise. Many southerners appeared willing to accept this, but the northern Know-Nothings rebelled, and threatened to walk out unless stronger anti-Catholic and antislavery planks were written. In part to appease this wing of the party, the southerners accepted former President Millard Fillmore of New York as the presidential nominee. But Fillmore, who had taken strong stands on no single issue, and was considered above all a man of compromise, was not acceptable to the northerners. Seventy-one northern and midwestern delegates left the convention, vowing to meet again in June, at which time they would decide whether to continue on their own, or join the Republicans. In this way, the Know-Nothing bid for national power died aborning.

Between February and the Democratic convention in Cincinnati in June, the Brooks attack and the Pottawatomie raid had taken place. Once again the Democrats sought unity and attempted to find a political solution to the slavery issue. Pierce was passed over; he was scarred by the Kansas issue, and distrusted by leaders in both sections of the country. In particular the northern Democrats opposed his plans to annex Cuba and Lower California, which they assumed were destined to become slave states, while southern Democrats felt he had blundered in his attempts to assure Kansas as a slave state. Douglas was ruled out for similar reasons, as were other congressional Democrats associated with the Kansas-Nebraska Act.

After seventeen ballots, the party finally selected James Buchanan, the sixty-five-year-old minister to Great Britain, whose major recommendation was that he had been out of the country for the past four years and had fewer enemies than most. Buchanan had served in both houses of Congress, had been minister to Russia for Andrew Jackson and secretary of state for Polk. Although a leader of the powerful Pennsylvania Democratic Party, he was more identified with foreign affairs than with domestic politics. Together with two other American ministers he was the coauthor of the Ostend Manifesto, which called for the annexation of Cuba. The document had been denounced by the Administration, but it served to win southern friends for Buchanan and was not forgotten at the convention. Once again, the Democrats selected a northerner with southern principles. And as if to seal the bargain, John Breckinridge of Kentucky, another moderate, was chosen as his running mate. The platform called the Kansas-Nebraska Act "the only sound and safe solution of the slavery question" and supported southern economic programs.

The new Republican Party had done well in local and congressional elections in the North and Midwest in 1854, and so entered the presidential year with high hopes. The leadership's ability to obtain the House speakership for Banks spoke well for its organizational talents, while reports of new Republican clubs forming in the Midwest and the defection of old Whigs to the party cheered the members.

The Republicans of 1856 had aspirations that were at the same time more modest and far more ambitious than those of the Know-Nothings. Unlike the other new party, it would not attempt to form a nationwide organization; there would be no Republican clubs below the Mason-Dixon line. This would limit the party's scope, but would at the same time make ideological harmony easier to achieve. The Republicans would fashion an alliance of North and Midwest—of New York and Chicago—to defeat that of the South—St. Louis and New Orleans. In this party would be farmers, antislavery intellectuals, and former Whig businessmen. Appeals would be directed to northern workers, but the Republicans were realists, and knew the Know-Nothings were strong with the Protestant laborers of the Northeast, while the Catholics were true to the urban Democratic machines.

The Philadelphia convention, which began on June 17, was a carefully planned affair, both in terms of the program and the maneuverings of candidates and platform writers. Less than two weeks prior to the opening, the "North American" Party—the new name for the antislavery Know-Nothings—had met and selected Nathaniel Banks for the presidency and William Johnston of Pennsylvania for the vice-presidency. But theirs was not to be a permanent selection, and the Republicans knew it. Banks understood he had no chance for the Republican nomination, and had allied himself with a man who did—John C. Frémont of California, the dashing soldier-explorer, who had made a heroic if overstated reputation during the Mexican War. Frémont was known to oppose the spread of slavery into the territories, but at the same time was not considered a radical, and so might attract moderates to the new party. If the Republicans selected Frémont, Banks would step aside. Then new Republicans, old Whigs, and discontented Democrats and Know-Nothings might form an alliance that would sweep the northern and midwestern states in November. In their first presidential bid, organized as a sectional party, the Republicans believed they could capture the White House.

Frémont was not the only possible candidate. Seward and Chase worked for the nomination, but party leaders considered them too radical to be accepted by the middle-of-the-road voters. Supreme Court Justice John McLean had ambitions, as did a long line of old Whigs, who had recently joined the party. By convention time, however, Frémont's nomination seemed assured. Even the New York *Herald* favored him, a rather strange situation since its publisher, Bennett, was known to be sympathetic to the southern cause.

The first order of business was to write a platform. This was accomplished without much difficulty. The Republicans condemned the Kansas-Nebraska Act and the Ostend Manifesto. They called for the immediate admission of Kansas into the Union as a free state. In an attempt to win the business vote, the party came out in favor of a transcontinental railroad. Then, in a reiteration of its antislavery stance and an appeal to anti-Mormon voters, it declared that Congress had a duty to prohibit "those twin relics of barbarism—Polygamy and Slavery" from the territories.

With this completed, the convention proceeded to nominate Frémont for the presidency and William Dayton of New Jersey for the vice-presidency. Then Banks and Johnston dropped out of the race in favor of the Republican nominees, and the North Americans dissolved. This seemed to signal a pact between moderate antislavery forces, old Whigs, and northern Know-Nothings. And with this, the campaign began.

For the first time in a generation the issues were clear cut. If Frémont won, Kansas would be a free state and the Wilmot Proviso would become the central issue at the new Congress. The victory of James Buchanan would mean administration support for the slave forces in Kansas; a drive for annexation of Cuba, probably as a candidate for eventual ad-

John C. Frémont,
Republican presidential candidate in 1856.

mission to the Union as a slave state; and southern domination of national politics. It was widely assumed as the campaign developed that Fillmore could not hope for victory in November; the only question seemed to be whether he would draw more votes from Buchanan or Frémont. As a result, both men attempted to avoid the Know-Nothing issue, fearful of saying something that might alienate potential voters.

The Republicans attacked Buchanan as an old party wheelhorse, ignorant of the issues and morally blind. The Democrats responded by charging that Frémont was a Catholic. They also warned northerners that his election would mean war and an end to the prosperity the nation was then enjoying. At a time like this, they said, America needed an experienced statesman, not a wild young man capable of all kinds of radical actions, the nominee of an uncertain and unstable new sectional party.

The Democratic campaign was effective. Buchanan carried every southern state as well as most of the border states. Illinois, Indiana, Pennsylvania (his own), and New Jersey went Democratic. Even California chose him over Frémont, who had been that state's first senator.

On the other hand, Frémont did better than many Democrats had expected. He swept New England and carried New York and most of the Midwest. Buchanan had captured the Irish-American vote in the East, but Frémont did almost as well with first-generation Americans in the Midwest. Frémont received 114 electoral votes to Buchanan's 174, and 1.3 million popular votes to Buchanan's 1.8 million. Significantly, the Democrats received only 45.3 percent of the popular vote, the lowest percentage for a victor since 1824.

Fillmore also did well, surprising many Democrats who were certain that the Know-Nothing rank-and-file would choose Buchanan in fear of a Frémont presidency. He won a majority in only one state, Maryland, which not only had a large anti-Catholic population but was a border state, fearful of both northern and southern domination. In New York and Massachusetts, where anti-Catholic feelings were high, he ran strongly, as he did in Tennessee, Kentucky, and other border states, which feared destruction should civil war erupt. There Fillmore was the candidate of moderation, the choice of people who hoped a war would be avoided, and who viewed Buchanan, as much as Frémont, as a sectional candidate.

Fillmore received eight electoral votes and 874,000 popular votes. In the process, he helped establish the Know-Nothings as an important political force, but his inability to do as well as Frémont indicated that the Republicans, not the Know-Nothings, would succeed the Whigs as one of the nation's two major parties. Still, the Know-Nothing votes were the margin of victory in eight states with 92 electoral votes. Had the Know-Nothings voted for Buchanan, the Republicans would have been reduced to a small sectional force, with power only in New England and parts of the Midwest. United with the Republicans, the coalition would have placed Frémont in the White House.

This situation was not lost on leaders in either the South or the North. Southern politicians, such as Governor James H. Adams of South Carolina, recognized that if nothing else, the election demonstrated that the nation was polarizing. "Slavery and Free Soilism can never be reconciled," said Adams soon after the election. He continued:

> Our enemies have been defeated—not vanquished. A majority of the free States have declared war against the South, upon a purely sectional issue, and in the remainder of them, formidable minorities fiercely contended for victory under the same banner. The triumph of this geographic party must dissolve the confederacy, unless we are prepared to sink down into a state of acknowledged inferiority. We will act wisely to employ the interval of repose afforded by the late election, in earnest preparation for the inevitable conflict.

Abraham Lincoln, the Springfield, Illinois lawyer, came to a similar conclusion. Lincoln had served a single term in Congress, had barely missed receiving a senatorial nomination in 1854, and then, soon after turning Republican, had received a scattering of votes for the vice-presidency at the 1856 convention. After the election he said:

221

> All of us who did not vote for Mr. Buchanan, taken together, are a majority of four hundred thousand. But in the late contest we were divided between Frémont and Fillmore. Can we not come together in the future? Let everyone who really believes, and is resolved, that free society is not and shall not be a failure, and who can conscientiously declare that in the past contest he has only done what he thought best, let every such one have charity to believe that every other one can say as much. Thus let bygones be bygones; let past differences as nothing be; and with steady eye on the real issue, let us reinaugurate the good old "central idea" of the republic.

Lincoln, of course, was speaking of the Frémont-Fillmore coalition, which he hoped would develop and lead to a victory in 1860. He saw no hope of bringing the North and South together, but rather would concentrate on obtaining an electoral mandate to limit slavery, hoping that men like Adams were in a minority in the South.

It remained for James Buchanan, the last American president to be born in the eighteenth century, to attempt to find arrangements acceptable to the two sections. The task seemed impossible, even for a miracle worker, and Buchanan was no such individual, but rather an old, weary, sick, and often insecure politician who seemed to be from a bygone age. He had been elected, but realized he had no mandate to rule, and that made his task all the more difficult. Still, Buchanan was a master at survival, and that by itself required no small degree of skill. And he indicated determination to bring the nation together. Speaking to an audience of Franklin and Marshall college students and faculty shortly after his election, he said his administration's object "would be to destroy any sectional party—North or South—to harmonize all sections of the Union under a national and conservative government, as it was fifty years ago." The best he could offer, then, was an attempt to return to the past. Buchanan had few plans for a future that included issues like Kansas, and individuals like John Brown, Preston Brooks, and Harriet Beecher Stowe. Buchanan's enemies conceded he knew every trick in the book. Neither they nor he could realize, however, that the old book had been discarded, and a new one opened. It was a volume Buchanan could not decipher. Governor Adams' pronouncement seemed more in keeping with the age of moral politics then in full swing. And so were those of Senator Seward, who in addressing a New York audience shouted, "I know, and you know, that a revolution has begun."

9 / THE PANIC OF '57

SINCE THE SNOWS CAME EARLY TO MAINE, THE STATE'S citizens voted in September, and their choice was made known to the rest of the country weeks prior to the general election day. "As Maine goes, so goes the nation." It's an old saying, the origins of which have been forgotten by most. Actually, Maine was and is a pretty poor barometer for political sentiment. Still, a Maine victory was rightly considered good publicity by politicians.

For this reason, and because their party could not afford to lose a single northern state, the Republicans organized a large-scale campaign in Maine, which in any case was Free Soil by inclination. From the first the Democrats conceded the state, while the Know-Nothings had only a small base there. But the country was not prepared for a landslide, which was what took place. The Republicans cheered, and claimed the rest of the country would follow Maine's example. Northern Democrats observed that only in Maine had the Republicans a strong state organization. The situation would be different elsewhere in the North, which they confidently expected to sweep.

But Governor Henry Wise of Virginia, a loyal Democrat, feared his northern colleagues were mistaken; a Frémont victory in November was a distinct possibility. What then? Already the lower South buzzed with rumors of slave uprisings, timed to coincide with the election, followed perhaps by a Republican invasion of the South, led by a uniformed Frémont. Talk such as this was clearly exaggerated, but seemed more plausible in 1856 than it would have appeared a few years earlier.

On September 15, Wise wrote his fellow Democratic southern governors, calling them to a conference at Raleigh, North Carolina, "to admonish ourselves by joint counsel, of the extraordinary duties which may devolve upon us from the dangers which so palpably threaten our common peace and safety." Then Wise ordered the Virginia militia into a state of readiness. "If Frémont is elected there will be revolution," he wrote. Senator James Mason of Virginia shared his concern, writing to a South Carolina group that "in the event of Frémont's election, the South should not pause but proceed at once to 'immediate, absolute and eternal separation.'" "I am a candidate for the first halter," said the fifty-eight-year-old Senator.

Few agreed with Wise and Mason. Only Governor Adams of South Carolina came to Raleigh, while Governor Thomas Bragg of the host state was annoyed by the call, and not surprised by its failure. The vast majority of white southerners disliked the Republicans and would have regretted a Frémont victory. However, only a handful in 1856 would have looked upon it as a clear signal for secession.

There were three major reasons for this lack of revolutionary fervor. Clearly in 1856 most southerners did not believe Kansas was worth destroying the Union for. The conflict there raised sparks and debate, but not fire. Why should small farmers, especially those with only one slave or none at all, living far from Kansas and not likely ever to go there, risk death and destruction for the sake of a cause that didn't seem to affect them? Southern farmers enjoyed peace and prosperity in 1856, as did their counterparts elsewhere in the nation. While it was true that peace might be threatened, prosperity was real enough. If the first went, so would the second. Southerners weren't interested in making so great a sacrifice that election year. Finally, there was the obvious material superiority of the North-Midwest combination *vis-à-vis* the South. These sections were more heavily populated than the South. According to the 1850 census, there were 14.2 million people living in the North and Midwest and only 9 million in the South, of which 3.4 million were slaves, who might revolt in time of war. The North was mechanizing rapidly, and appeared powerful financially. All power seemed to emanate from New York, not New Orleans or St. Louis. "Every beat of this great financial organ is felt from Maine to Florida, and from the Atlantic to the Pacific," wrote the Louisville *Courier,* while the South was still agrarian and relatively undeveloped industrially, and unsure of its power. True, the South had cotton, the nation's leading export crop and earner of foreign currencies. And Southern statesmen were convinced that in case of war, their armies would be better led than the northern brigades, while southern soldiers had long been

226

considered the finest on the continent. Would this be enough? In 1856, the answer seemed "no."

A year later the same southern statesmen who felt their section would not consider secession—that southerners would not sacrifice material prosperity to protect the well-being of a relatively few large slaveholders and to defend a principle and that in such a war the South could not win—had changed their minds. Part of the reason for this change came from Kansas, where the fighting intensified, and from developments in Washington. But more came from New York's Wall Street, which had been considered the powerhouse of the North in 1856.

If the country was in the midst of prosperity during the election season, Wall Street enjoyed a bonanza. With the important exception of the slavery issue, the sky appeared cloudless. Not only did the nation's economy seem solid, but it was improving all the time.

The reasons for the Wall Street boom were known to all in the financial district, and brokers and bankers would tick them off given the slightest excuse to do so. First, there had been Britain's repeal of her Corn Laws in 1846, a major free-trade measure calculated to benefit that country's manufacturers. This led to a sharp increase in American grain exports, while total exports more than doubled from 1850 to 1857, rising from $152 million to $327 million. Then came the American victory in the Mexican War and the acquisition of new territory, capped by the discovery of gold in California. Combined with the free and easy banking situation of that time, California gold boosted the amount of currency in circulation from $221 million in 1850 to $342 million in 1855, with the total standing at $374 million in 1857, for one of the sharpest rises of its kind the nation would ever know. In 1845 the amount of money in circulation per capita was $6.79; in 1857, it was $12.93.

Easy money helped stoke the railroad boom, which in turn made it easier for farmers to get their goods to market. In the process all segments of the economy benefited, as did all sections of the country. There seemed no reason to expect this process to end, and speculators made the rails the glamour stocks of the bull market.

Finally, there was the Crimean War, which began in 1854, and which resulted in an increase of American grain sales to Europe. Foreign investors, seeking safety and growth, sent their gold to Wall Street for investment purposes. The war ended in 1856, but the gold flow continued.

Little wonder, then, that Wall Street's bulls were delighted with the prospects, while the bears went into hiding.

The institutional structure of the financial district was not much different in the mid-1850s than it had been a decade earlier. The nation's most important banks were there, along with insurance firms and large importers. The district was most famous for its speculators, of course, and these might be found in the brokerages that were scattered throughout the district, at the lively outdoor "curb" market at William and Beaver, or at the New York Stock and Exchange Board at 25 William Street. In addition, there were many smaller "exchanges" in the district.

Volume was high in 1856, especially when compared with what it had been in the 1840s. Most of the trading was done at the curb, where volume might soar as high as 70,000 shares a day. Some curbstone reporters claimed volume reached a million shares a month on occasion, but such a figure clearly was exaggerated. Better records were kept at the Stock and Exchange Board, and these indicate that a 9,000-share day was quite "heavy."

As it had since its origins, the Stock and Exchange Board employed an auction system. Twice a day, at 10:30 A.M. and 2:45 P.M., the auctioneer would call off a list of stocks and bonds, and then the exchange members would begin to bid on them. The method was inefficient, but the tradition-minded Exchange would consider no other, even when its brokers and dealers rushed to the streets between calls, hoping to deal in stocks there as well as at the exchange. The auctions themselves were wild affairs, especially during the bull market of 1857. The presiding officer would call out the stock or bond, and the brokers would begin their frantic bidding:

> First broker, "At 41⅝, seller 3." Second broker, "I'll give 45⅝, buyer 60, for 100." Third broker, "I'll sell 100 at 41⅝; I'll sell 100 at 41½." Broker, "Done!" Second broker, "Another hundred," Fourth broker, "I'll take 'em." Second broker, "Fifty more." Fifth broker, "Here, done, done!" By this time twenty voices are going at once. "I'll give 41½ regular"; "41¼, seller 10"; "43⅜, seller 3"; "done"; "take 'em"; "Sell 'em"; "seller 10, 5 up"; "fifty more"; "one hundred more"; "I'll take your lot, buyer four months." A dozen men are on their feet, their arms swinging above their heads . . . and the scene is a perfect Babel to the uninitiated.

The exchange's vice-president would take note of each sale, and prepare a report soon after the session was completed. The list would be given to the newspapers, and be reported the following day. On July 13, 1857—a busy session —the report looked like this:

FIRST BOARD

$11,000	Tenn. 6's	82
38,000	Mo. 6's	78
3,000	"	77¼
1,000	Cal. 7's	53
1,000	Erie R.R.	100
1,000	Lake Erie & Western	47
3,000	Buffalo & St. Louis 7's	90
8,000	Terre Haute 2nd mortgage	63
5 sh.	Hanover Bank	93
60	Del. & Hudson Canal Co.	117
100	Cumberland Coal	16½
100	" "	17
20	La Crosse & Milwaukee R.R.	38
160	" "	36
30	" "	36
20	Pacific Mail Steamship Co.	74¼
30	" "	74
5	New York Central R.R.	81
550	" "	80⅜
50	" "	80⅜
200	" "	80½
10	" "	80⅝
1100	" "	80¾
60	Erie R.R.	27⅞
50	" "	27¾
200	" "	27¾
260	" "	28
100	" "	28
125	" "	28
150	" "	28¼
210	Harlem R.R.	16½
40	Harlem R.R. pfd.	23
10	" "	23⅛
50	Galena & Chicago R.R.	91⅛
100	" "	92⅛
57	Mo. Southern & Nashville R.R.	47⅛
100	" "	47⅛
400	" "	47¾
5	" "	48

100	Mo. Southern & Nashville R.R.	45
100	" "	44
100	Illinois Central R.R.	120
100	" "	118
100	Cleveland & Toledo R.R.	58
300	" "	57¾
50	" "	57⅛
100	" "	57⅜
200	Chicago & Rock Island R.R.	91½
210	" "	91
200	" "	90¾
200	" "	90
10	Milwaukee & Mississippi R.R.	52
50	" "	51½
150	" "	51¼
150	" "	50⅛
6	Panama R.R.	87¾

The afternoon session resembled the morning, but usually was less active, since the brokers had spent the time in between trading and dealing at other markets or at the curb, and so had less interest in Stock and Exchange Board dealings. During the two sessions on July 13, $72,000 worth of bonds were traded and 9,490 shares of stock, of which all but 345 shares were of railroads. The volume leader that day was New York Central, with 2,028 shares changing hands.

But this, of course, was only a small fraction of what was actually being bought and sold. John Bigelow of the New York *Evening Post* reported that he had learned that more than $22 million worth of stock had been traded in one two-week period in 1857, although he did not indicate his source. In an editorial entitled "A Growing Evil—Overspeculation," Bigelow condemned "honest men"—lawyers, merchants, doctors, and even clergymen—who seemed willing to abandon

231

their normal pursuits to engage in wheeling and dealing on Wall Street.

Nor was that all. Speculative fever seemed to be present in all parts of the land. Land prices in the Midwest were rising at a more rapid rate than at any time since the early 1830s—the eve of the panic of 1837. In the North the newspapers told of large-scale imports of jewelry, laces, silks, and other finery from Europe, to feed the appetites of the *nouveaux riches*. Southern observers, such as industrialist William Gregg, noted that "Ladies are seen dashing about the streets and watering places again with their $500 dresses and $1,500 shawls; merchants are seen pulling down princely buildings to vie with each other in the erection of stores, at an expense of three to five hundred thousand dollars; men are seen running to and fro, to find employment for money that has been borrowed at ten to fifteen percent premium; every railroad project, however visionary, may make bonds and find purchasers." That sometimes puritan James Gordon Bennett thundered against such goings-on in the *Herald* of June 27, 1857:

> What can be the end of all this but another general collapse like that of 1837, only upon a much grander scale? The same premonitory symptoms that prevailed in 1835-6 prevail in 1857 in a tenfold degree. Government spoilations, public defaulters, paper bubbles of all descriptions, a general scramble for western lands and town and city sites, millions of dollars, made or borrowed, expended in fine houses and gaudy furniture; hundreds of thousands in the silly rivalries of fashionable parvenues, in silks, laces, diamonds and every variety of costly frippery are only a few among the many crying evils of the day. The worst of all these evils is the moral pestilence of luxurious exemption from honest labor, which is infecting all classes of society. The country merchant is becoming a city stockjobber, and the honest country farmer has gone off among the gamblers in western

land. Thus, as this general scramble among all classes to be rich at once, and by the shortest possible cut, extends and increases, our rogues, defaulters and forgers are multiplied. The epidemic and its attending evils must run their course.

Bennett was not alone in calling for an end to this worldliness. A national religious revival began early in 1857, fueled by uncertainties as to future peace, the moral fervor of the Know-Nothing and Republican crusades, and the extravagances of speculators in New York and throughout the nation. Church attendance was higher than at any time since the great revival swept the nation in the 1840s. Throughout the Northeast ministers demanded the closing of theaters and gaming rooms, while decrying the moral laxity of the times. There were regular prayer meetings on Wall Street itself, and in front of the Stock and Exchange Board, the symbol of the materialistic world the congregations denounced. But as the *Times* observed, while some ministers were out in the streets preaching against speculation, others were in brokerages, buying and selling securities.

Greeley and Raymond were bullish on the economy and the securities markets, and both editors charged Bennett with distortions and exaggerations. Bennett responded that the nation was indeed in serious troubles, pointing to the front pages of the *Times* and *Tribune*, which featured stories on Kansas, conflicts with the Mormons in Deseret, and continued tensions in Washington.

And in the city itself violence was in the air. On Independence Day riots erupted in lower Manhattan, most of them involving the gangs of young Irish-Americans. The police stepped in, but were hurled back by the Dead Rabbit Club, the most notorious of the gangs. The fighting contin-

Brickbats being thrown at police during two weeks of gang rioting in lower Manhattan in the summer of 1857 (Frank Leslie's Illustrated Newspaper, *July 11*).

ued for two weeks, broken by short periods of peace, while the gangs regrouped. On July 13 some five hundred Dead Rabbits attacked the police with pistols and knives, killing several and causing the others to flee in disarray. Not until August would the rioting cease, and then it would stop more through boredom with violence than as a result of strong police action. All of this was reported fully in the *Herald*, which had become the prime organ for Wall Street's bears.

One bear in particular was interested in seeing to it that these stories continued, and that speculators acted upon them. Leonard Jerome, the grandfather of Winston Churchill, was one of the district's leading figures, and at the time believed stock prices were due for a collapse. Jerome sold stock short, in large blocks, and then set about spreading gloom, in the hope that uncertainty would cause the market to collapse and earn him another fortune. Jerome owned stock in the *Times*, and for a while tried to influence Raymond in helping in the drive. But Raymond refused to be budged, and so Jerome entered into conversations with Bennett, starting by giving the editor what amounted to a crash course in the nature of railroad overexpansion and bank weaknesses.

Aided by "inside information" provided by Jerome, Bennett wrote and the *Herald* published a series of articles on the subject in July. Bennett seemed particularly interested in cataloguing those railroads in financial straits—usually those whose stock Jerome had recently sold short. The campaign was not very successful. For example, Bennett was harsh on Michigan Central, and the stock did fall from 81 to 79 from July 3 to July 24, while most other rails were rising. But even the articles could not hold the stock down, and it closed the month at 85. Still, the campaign did affect other editors, who now investigated the economy more closely. Greeley, who in the spring had scoffed at rumors of an economic decline, now began to warn of its increasing possibility, running editorials on the subject that were rather mild in late June, and intensified in feeling by late July.

The signs could be read in the countryside and mill towns by that time. The Crimean War had ended, and with it the great demands for American wheat. The price of grain declined, in anticipation of a slackening of exports, and farmers, who had counted on higher prices, were suffering financially. The market for textiles was weak, while speculators had pushed the price of raw cotton to new highs. Faced with a situation where they could not pass the higher costs of raw material on to the consumer in the form of higher prices, textile factories in New England began cutting back and closing in July. At the same time farmers in all parts of the country began drawing heavily against their bank deposits, in anticipation of the need for funds for the harvest and marketing of their autumn crops. As a result, many New York banks found themselves short of funds by early August.

In itself this would not have been too serious; the banks were used to such a situation, which occurred every year, and they knew the deposits would be returned once the crops were marketed. But it was different in 1857. Lower demands for wheat and the high price of cotton in the face of declining demand created uneasiness in the New York financial community and the nation at large. With all the talk of the importance of manufacturing in the United States, it was still an agrarian country. The farm bonanza seemed to be ending, and doing so at a time when the already poorly structured banking system was at its weakest.

Shortly before noon on August 11, N. H. Wolfe & Co. announced its failure. The news reverberated through the financial district. Wolfe was the oldest flour and grain company in New York, was considered quite conservative in its finances, and ably led. Was the Wolfe failure the prelude to the feared depression? Some bulls seemed to believe so. In any case, activity increased at the Stock and Exchange Board that afternoon, and prices were down.

Bennett viewed the decline as a vindication of his warnings. "The stock market is decidedly sick," he wrote. "There is no health in it. The supply of weak, sickly stock securities pressing for sale is very great, and there are no buyers, no demand from any source. . . ." And he repeated his warnings regarding Michigan Central.

On August 19, Edwin C. Litchfield, president of the railroad, resigned "in order to spend more time on personal matters." Few believed him, and the stock declined. Four days later Bennett stated flatly that "in all human probability, every railroad in the United States will become bankrupt in the course of the next six or eight years." Stocks declined again, as Wall Streeters stopped talking of the opportunities of railroads to concentrate on their risks, especially overexpansion and weak cash positions. The atmosphere was right for panic.

On the morning of the following day—August 24— Charles Stetson, president of the prestigious Ohio Life Insurance & Trust Company, announced that the New York branch of the firm had suspended payments. Ohio Life specialized in investments in western lands, and had been particularly active in channeling eastern and foreign funds into Ohio and Illinois. In addition, the company was heavily invested in railroad securities and was known to speculate considerably in commodity futures. Ohio Life had lost money on poor investments in all these areas, and its collapse provided the signal for the beginning of the panic.

Prices fell sharply at the exchanges and the curb market, although there were some minor recoveries in the afternoon at the Stock and Exchange Board. The decline began again the following morning, slowly at first, but then in a rout. The news was bad—especially the confirmation of Bennett's claims regarding Michigan Central, which announced its insolvency. Now the bear market took on added power, leaving the wreckage of investments in its path.

In effect, the securities markets had finally reflected the economic decline signaled earlier in the year, one that had been compounded by a shaky financial structure and wild speculation in commodities, land, and even slaves. But New York had become the financial capital of the nation, with Wall Street its symbol. Throughout the land many people assumed the speculators—men like Leonard Jerome—actually *controlled* the economy, and could cause the destruction of a major line like the Michigan Central. As the panic intensified, and the nation awoke to the economic problems that had been hidden or overlooked in the past, the search for a scapegoat began. And many Americans—especially southerners, given the climate of politics in 1857—found that scapegoat in the North, in New York, on Wall Street. The St. Louis *Intelligencer* lashed out at Jerome and other bears, as well as at Bennett—they had not only benefited from the depression and financial ruin in the land, but had caused it:

> And all this ruin of families and fortunes has been brought about by the unprincipled course of a set of stock gamblers in Wall Street, New York, who probably never owned, legitimately, one-thousandth part of stock in the road they ruined. They have sold the stock, *to be delivered at a future date*, and then set about inventing the most atrocious and rascally lies in regard to the road and its management; and in the *New York Herald* they found a willing instrument to circulate their falsehoods and thus, finally, after six months of desperate detraction, they have accomplished their work, and brought ruin and distress on thousands of orphans, widows, and aged persons, who have no hope of recovery.

Even Raymond of the *Times* joined in this kind of criticism, though from his background one would have assumed he might have known better. "Why push it to extremes because the Ohio Trust Bank has suspended payments?" he asked. "Does everything in the way of securities go to pieces because one concern has been mistaken or unfortunate in selecting its borrowers?" As far as he was concerned, the blame for the financial distress could be found among the speculators on Wall Street. "The Stock Exchange, as at present managed, is very little more than an enormous gambling establishment—and the whole scale of its operations is quite as ruinous, quite as infamous, as any of the Broadway hells which have recently enjoyed the attention of the Metropolitan Police."

Raymond seemed to derive some satisfaction from the failures of speculators—almost all of them bulls—during the next few days. Da Launay, Iselin & Clark, private bankers, suspended operations on August 25, along with E. S. Monroe and John Thompson, who were described as "speculators." E. A. Benedict and E. F. Post, also "speculators," were unable to meet their obligations the following day, the former losing all when he went long on Illinois Central, the latter a major bull on Ohio Life. Jacob Little, the most famous Wall Street plunger of his day, went bankrupt for the fourth time in his career on August 27, not because he had been wrong on the market—like Jerome, Little was a bear—but rather due to the inability of those who owed him stocks and money to deliver. And through it all, the bears made money, if they could locate those who were obliged to them and force them in one way or another to make good their debts. One of the most successful American businessmen, Cornelius Vanderbilt, who only dabbled in the markets, was on the bear side, and had no trouble getting his money; no one crossed Vanderbilt knowingly. As the Mercantile Agency credit reporter wrote of Vanderbilt: "It would be difficult to find the real wealth of V. It must however be great. He is illiterate and boorish, vy austere & offensive & has made himself vy unpopular with

Cornelius Vanderbilt.

the inhabitants of Staten Island, so much so that his leaving there is subject of great rejoicing by the inhabitants & was manifested by a public jubilee."

In late August, Wall Street learned that Vanderbilt was "going to gold." The great man was taking notes issued by New York banks to their cashiers, and demanding payment in the metal. Others followed his example, as gold went into hiding throughout the nation. The New York banks, which showed deposits of $67.4 million on August 8, had only $57.3 million on September 12. Many were on the verge of bankruptcy, but they held on. Bankers were shaken by the news of the failures of the Delaware, Lackawanna & Western, and Fond du Lac railroads, but still they clung to the hope they would ride out the storm. The next gold shipment from California was due in late September. This, they told reporters, would end the panic in New York.

But even nature conspired against the banks. On September 12 the steamer "Central America" sank in a hurricane off Cape Hatteras. Over four hundred passengers and crew went down with the ship—which had $1.6 million in California gold in its hold.

This news hit the financial community as a blow to the heart. Now the bank failures began, not only in New York, but throughout the nation. Leading institutions in Philadel-

A Mercantile Agency credit report on Cornelius Vanderbilt covering the years between 1853 and 1867.

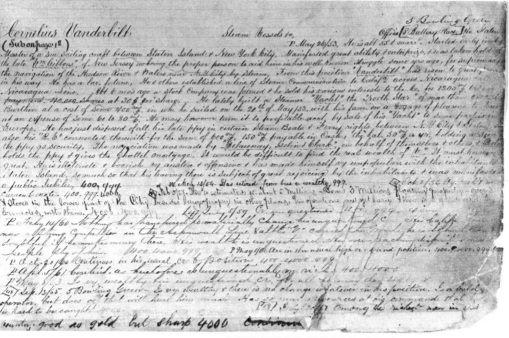

Scene of the catastrophe after the sinking of the "Central America" from a sketch provided by one of the rescued passengers (Frank Leslie's Illustrated Newspaper, *October 3, 1857*).

phia and Baltimore suspended further gold payments on September 25, a certain sign of insolvency, and the *Herald* predicted the New York banks would follow in a matter of days.

Faced with certain ruin, the Treasury acted. The federal government began purchasing state bonds, paying for them with gold, hoping this would restore both bank balances and confidence, at least until the next California gold shipment arrived in New York. But the move didn't work, and on October 13, the Treasury, itself in a poor state of liquidity, stopped its purchases. Now new rumors were spread, these concerning the government, which itself might be forced to suspend gold payments. If this happened, it would mean the

242

United States itself was bankrupt. Americans who only months before were hotly contesting the question of Kansas, now wondered whether there would *be* a United States in 1858. The nation could be destroyed not by slavery, but by bankruptcy.

There were related disruptions in Paris and London, for investors in these European capitals had also invested in American securities, which in a matter of months, perhaps days, could be worthless. The Bank of England's money rate rose 3 percent in less than a month—an unprecedented rise. "All the bubbles, blunders, and dishonesties of five years' European exuberance and experimentations in credit were tested and revealed," wrote Benjamin Disraeli afterward, and this seemed a fair assessment of the situation.

The chain of collapse continued in America. The Erie & Pittsburgh, the Fort Wayne & Chicago, went bankrupt in October, as did the Reading and the Illinois Central. Bennett's prediction that all the railroads would go under now seemed possible—and the banks with them, and the nation too. George Templeton Strong, the diarist, wrote in deep gloom:

> We seem foundering. Affairs are worse than ever today, and a period of general insolvency seems close upon us. People say, "We must reach the bottom soon," but the bottom has certainly come out. Depression and depletion are going on without any sign of limit and promise to continue till we reach zero point or universal suspension. This attack is far more sudden, acute, and prostrating than that of 1837. Will the banks stand it? I think *not*, and predict their downfall within ten days.

New York, which earlier in the year had seemed a bastion of great strength, was in disarray. Mayor Fernando Wood

*New York to Philadelphia Bank: "Going to suspend yourself, eh?
Is that your Brotherly Love?"* (Harper's Weekly, *October 17, 1857*).

promised aid for the starving as winter approached, but
added that none would be given "slackers." He also attacked
the city's wealthy citizens. Most New Yorkers, he said, "labor
without income while surrounded by thousands in selfishness
and splendor who have incomes without labor." By refusing
to aid the poor, and then turning on the rich as responsible
for their distress, Wood encouraged the already lawless gangs
to do their worst. So they did. Mobs broke into stores and
stripped them bare in the pre-Christmas season. Crowds
gathered nightly in Tompkins Square to hear radical speakers
calling for a class war. The crime rate rose spectacu-

"Wall Street, half past 2 o'clock, October 13, 1857," by James H. Cafferty, N.A., and Charles G. Rosenberg. According to an early auction catalogue, Commodore Vanderbilt is the short man at the extreme right. The dominant central figure in a light "drover's" coat is a well-known financier and speculator of the period, Jacob Little.

MUSEUM OF THE CITY OF NEW YORK

larly, as the police appeared powerless to stop the looting and murders. The Dead Rabbits went so far as to seize City Hall itself, eject the mayor and his officials, and hold it for more than an hour before leaving to start another round of mayhem. The next day another group of protesters appeared at City Hall, this one to oppose a measure to provide funds for the construction of Central Park. Wood defended the park program, noting it would provide work for thousands of unemployed men. Still, the tensions continued, and the matter was not resolved, even when Wood was defeated in his reelection bid. Seeking a scapegoat for his defeat, the Mayor blamed it on the "Wall Street interests."

Nothing seemed to help, and as conditions worsened in the nation as a whole, and in the North and New York in particular, those preachers who earlier had called for a turning away from Mammon now claimed the panic and depression were God's retribution on an ungrateful and undeserving people who had turned away from Him. A Reverend Lampshire, a Dutch Reformed minister, called upon businessmen to stop work for an hour a day for prayer. This, he said, might help. Many businessmen did pray. Churches throughout the city were packed, not only on Sundays, but every day, and not only with the poor and homeless, but with the wealthy and influential. Even the *Journal of Commerce*, perhaps with tongue in cheek, printed a poem on the subject:

> Steal awhile away from Wall Street
> and every worldly care,
> And spend an hour about mid-day
> in humble, hopeful prayer.

Theodore Parker, a philosopher-historian of the time, thought the revivalism a "reaction from an overstimulated state . . . whose waters covered the flats left bare by retreating prosperity." "Every race has oscillated between its shop and its temple," he wrote, and now it was time for the temple.

The winter of 1857–58 was harsh, and the suffering great in New York and other northern cities. Recovery began late in 1858, and a year later was on in most industries in most parts of the country. Those banks that survived helped put business back on its feet, and new banks appeared to take the place of the old. The railroads that went bankrupt in 1857 were also refinanced, while most continued to operate even while in receivership.

At the time, however, it seemed that cotton had led the nation out of the depression. American cotton worth $128 million had been exported in 1856; in 1857 the value was $132 million, despite a decline in shipments from 1.4 million pounds to 1 million pounds. The value of cotton exports in 1858 stood at $131 million, and the following year it rose to $161 million. Without this money, earned from foreigners, could the nation have survived the panic and depression? Many southern leaders thought not. On October 16, 1857, at the onset of the depression, the Bedford, Virginia *Sentinel* wrote that since the New York financial community was in difficulty, the entire nation would suffer, so much was the nation controlled by New York. "The great heart of American commerce becomes diseased from a plethora of trade or a stagnation in the arteries of traffic and speculation, beats in unhealthy throbs, and every State in the Union . . . instantly feels the effects of its morbid action." Some southern banks had indeed failed as a result of the New York collapse, but fewer than had in the North or West. These banks had speculated less in railroads and were more closely tied to cotton. The rails were weak; cotton was strong. This was a lesson of the panic. The New Orleans *Picayune* declared with pride:

> In the process of healthy reaction, the banks are stronger than they were when the northern suspensions alarmed the sensitive billholder, and caused that senseless run which produced so much mischief. The steadiness with which these banks sustained themselves against the shock, and the strength with which they have righted themselves so speedily, are proofs of the intrinsic excellence of the principles upon which they are organized; and the endurance and success with which the commercial community stood up under the confidence of inestimable value to their future prosperity and that of the city.

If this was so, why did the South permit itself to fear the North? Or, as the Charleston *Mercury* put it on October 14, 1857:

> Why does the South allow itself to be tattered and torn by the dissentions and death struggles of New York's money changers? Why not trade directly with our customers? What need is there for this go-between to convey to the markets of the world our rich products, for which the consumers stand ready, gold in hand, to pay the full value?

"The wealth of the South is permanent and real, that of the North fugitive and fictitious," wrote *DeBow's Review* in December. "The North is paralyzed," wrote Governor Herschel Johnson of Georgia, while the South "stands calm and unmoved, poised upon the consciousness of her capacity to outride the tempest." Senator James Hammond of South Carolina, who in 1856 had argued for caution in the face of a possible sectional war, now trumpeted a new doctrine to northern colleagues:

> Cotton is king! Who can doubt it that has looked upon recent events? When the abuse of credit annihilated confidence . . . when you came to a deadlock and revolutions were threatened, what brought you up? Fortunately for you it was the commencement of the cotton season and we have poured upon you one million six hundred thousand bales of cotton just at the crisis to save you.

Later Hammond would note that the panic and depression had cost the North and Midwest $142 million; southern losses were less than $17 million. In 1859 banks in New Orleans and Charleston seemed in better shape than those of New York and Philadelphia. "There is no disrupting the fact that the southern portion of the Confederacy is in a highly prosperous condition," wrote the New York *Times'* New Orleans correspondent on March 25, 1859. "The South is getting out of debt and beginning to accumulate surplus capital." To this, the prosouthern *Herald* added:

> We have not thought it necessary to go over Southern states seriatim as we have done with the West. The comparative prosperity prevailing there, the general healthy tone of business, and the absence of excessive and wild speculation, have rendered it in our judgement unnecessary. . . . The accounts from all parts of the South, except portions of Virginia, are uniform in their testimony that trade is in healthy condition.

Considering this situation, it is little wonder that moderate and intelligent southern leaders concluded that the northern economy still was shaky in 1859, and would collapse in time of war were it not for southern assistance. The New York riots of 1857–58 led them to believe that if the North engaged the South in a civil war, northern workers would revolt and become their allies. In 1856 it had appeared possible that a union of antislavery Republicans and anti-Catholic Know-Nothings might control the nation. Three years later the southern Democrats were coming to believe that northern urban Catholics—already Democrats—would more than counter any northern effort to bully the South into submission. Bennett thought as much in late 1857. In view of the fact that the black slaves of the South were being fed while 200,000 northern workers had lost their jobs, "How can any candid common-sense man profess the belief that slavery is a horrible, atrocious, accursed, God-defying sin?" The abolitionists claimed the slaves hated their masters, and yet the slaves were not revolting against them. In the North, however, and in New York in particular, the workers were showing their feelings toward those in power by rioting. Bennett then urged both sections to turn from the issues of slavery to more important problems, like the tariff, currency, "and solid and permanent basis of security upon which all the varied commercial and business interests of the country may repose." Francis Blair, Jr., a member of the House from Missouri, agreed. "I look now to see matters of finance, the tariff, and so on become the leading topics in Congress."

But this was not to be. The many aspects of slavery, and the problems involved in the institution, would come to the forefront once again, soon after the panic had ended but while the depression was still on. The panic of '57 would not lead to the replacement of moral politics by economic and financial debates. Rather, it served to convince the South it had nothing to fear from a weak, divided, and befuddled North–West coalition.

10 / THE EDGE OF THE ABYSS

PRESIDENT-ELECT JAMES BUCHANAN LEFT WHEATLANDS, his Lancaster, Pennsylvania home, on the morning of March 2, a cold and gray day following the snowstorm of the previous night. On to Baltimore and Guy's National Hotel he went, by coach, train, and coach, where he would wait for two days and nights before proceeding to his inauguration in Washington on March 4. All was in readiness for the gala; Buchanan seemed pleased. But the sixty-six-year-old man, who always prided himself on a rugged constitution but nonetheless had suffered his share of disease, was struck down by diarrhea the first night, and although he recovered in time for his great day in Washington, was weak, pale, and visibly tired as he stood to deliver his speech. "We have recently passed through a presidential contest in which the passions of our fellow citizens were excited to the highest degree by questions of deep and vital importance," he said, "but when the people proclaimed their will the tempest at once subsided and all was calm."

But all was not calm, and Buchanan knew it. Still, he spoke of the need for moderation, in the accents if not the words of Henry Clay. "Under our system there is a remedy for all mere political evils in the sound sense and the sober judgment of the people." Was the slavery issue a "mere political evil"? If so, then Buchanan might have been correct when he added, "Time is a great corrective. Political subjects which but a few years ago excited and exasperated the public mind have passed away, and are now nearly forgotten." The new President, six years old when Washington was first inaugurated, a veteran of the War of 1812 who first went to Congress in 1821, had seen much in the way of conflict, and heard even more talk of disunion and the destruction of the nation. One of the last of the great second generation of American statesmen, which had produced Clay, Webster, and Calhoun, Buchanan had seen men who had taken opposite sides in controversies come to terms with one another after a fashion. It could be done again. Slavery could be compromised. He would lead the way. "Let every Union-loving man, therefore, exert his best influence to suppress this agitation, which since the recent legislation of Congress is without any legitimate object." This, when abolitionists were talking of a "higher law" than the Constitution, which they were bound to follow, and southern fire-eaters demanded Kansas as their "moral right."

Buchanan's words that day were familiar. Such had been uttered throughout the early nineteenth century by the nation's great leaders, with few exceptions. By 1857, however, the phrases seemed anachronistic and naïve. The days of

252

compromise were over; those of conscience had begun. Buchanan, the aged, sick man, would be the last of his breed to achieve power, and even as he spoke, he was not quite certain what to do about the moralists, how to convince them of the need for give-and-take, how to block their actions. He would never learn the answers, because for a man of his generation, there could be little communication with those of the next.

Although he used the rhetoric of unity, Buchanan's cabinet reflected the nature of the coalition that elected him. Secretary of the Treasury Howell Cobb was from Georgia, and Secretary of War John Floyd from Virginia. Secretary of the Interior Jacob Thompson had been a Mississippi congressman prior to accepting the appointment. Aaron Brown, the new postmaster general, had been born in Virginia, and had served as governor of Tennessee. And Lewis Cass of Michigan, seventy-five years old when he took the office of secretary of state, was willing to go along with the administration's southerners. This left Secretary of the Navy Isaac Toucey of Connecticut, and Attorney General Jeremiah Black of Pennsylvania (a Buchanan protégé) the only two northerners in the cabinet who at times spoke out for their section, and they did so only rarely and then in muted tones.

The southern orientation of the cabinet reflected that of the Supreme Court. Justices Samuel Nelson, Robert Grier, Peter Daniel, James Wayne, John Catron, and John Campbell, along with Chief Justice Roger Taney, were all either from slave states or considered prosouthern Democrats. Only two—Republican John McLean and Whig Benjamin Curtis—were from the North and declared opponents of the spread of slavery. This was the Court that met in early 1857 to discuss the decision in the case of *Dred Scott* v. *Sandford*.

President Buchanan's cabinet reflected the nature of the coalition that elected him. Only two members, Toucey (center right) and Black (bottom), spoke out for the North (Harper's Weekly, April 11, 1857).

Scott was the slave of an army doctor, John Emerson, who had taken the slave from Missouri to Illinois, and then returned to Missouri. Soon after, Emerson died, and his widow, an abolitionist, transferred Scott's ownership to her brother, John Sandford of New York. Sandford then arranged with some friends to have Scott sue for his freedom, on the grounds that his residency in the free state of Illinois had made him free.

The case was first heard in the Missouri state courts in the late 1840s, and from there worked its way up to the federal courts. In 1854 it was in the United States Circuit Court for Missouri, and by then it had become very political in nature. It was recognized that Sandford had no desire to contest Scott's right to freedom; an abolitionist himself, he could do no less than grant him that right. Rather, Sandford wanted to make a test case of the Scott situation. If Scott indeed became free when he first set foot in Illinois, then the slaveholders had no right to demand of the courts that slaves be returned to their original homes. In effect, the Fugitive Slave Law, which required it, would be struck down. Sandford considered the very fact that the district court heard the case to be a victory of sorts, for the Constitution stated that the federal courts would hear cases involving citizens of one state litigating against those of others. By agreeing to hear the case, the courts were indicating a willingness to consider Scott a citizen, and not mere chattel.

The Supreme Court first heard the case in February, 1856, at a time when Kansas and the forthcoming election were prime topics of conversation. Because of this, some justices wanted to dismiss the case for lack of jurisdiction, in this way preserving the Court from political charges. There

Dred Scott
(Frank Leslie's Illustrated Weekly, *June 27, 1857*).

seemed no way to decide the case without raising the question of slavery, Scott's citizenship, Kansas, and the Fugitive Slave Law. And once this was done, the Supreme Court would become politicized, and perhaps lose its influence thereby.

The seven southern justices agreed to avoid the discussion, but McLean and Curtis, the northerners, indicated they would write dissents, and in them raise the issues. Faced with this situation, the southerners agreed to hear the case, and with this decision they too entered the political arena.

The Court reached its decision in late February, although it would not release it until after the Buchanan inauguration. As expected, a majority, in separate opinions, decided against Scott and for the South, with McLean and Curtis writing vigorous dissents. In what would later on appear a violation of the constitutional mandate for a separation of powers, Justice Catron went to see President-elect Buchanan to tell him of what would transpire. And it was with a knowledge of the decision that the prosouthern Buchanan delivered his inaugural address. In it he called upon all citizens—himself included —to accept the verdict of the courts on the slavery issue. He said ". . . it is a judicial question, which legitimately belongs to the Supreme Court of the United States, before whom it is now pending, and will, it is understood, be speedily and finally settled." Of course, Buchanan knew as he spoke what that decision would be. "To their decision, in common with all good citizens, I shall cheerfully submit, whatever this may be. . . ." Then, as though to throw a sop to the North which would be remembered after the decision was handed down, the new President came out in favor of popular sovereignty, under which the people of a territory would decide for themselves whether or not to have slavery within their borders. Afterwards, the South would have a major victory, while the North would reflect that Buchanan had been on the "right" side, with his hands tied by the courts. "May we not, then, hope that the long agitation on this subject is approaching its end, and that the geographic parties to which it has given birth, so much dreaded by the Father of his Country, will speedily become extinct?" Buchanan expected that the answer would be in the positive.

Two days later the Supreme Court handed down its verdict, and with it, destroyed Buchanan's hopes for a calm and prosperous administration. Recognizing the importance of the issues, each member delivered his own opinion. Taney spoke for the southern majority, however, in declaring Scott not to be a citizen of Missouri, and therefore not entitled to bring suit in federal courts.

Had he stopped with this, as he might easily have done, Taney would have given the South a great victory and the North a blow. The Supreme Court would have dipped its toes in the turbulent political waters of 1857, but would not have gone further than that. But Taney went on, and in the process, plunged the Court deep into political waters, and the country into a new fever.

Would Scott have won the case on its merits had he been permitted to sue? Taney answered the question by saying the verdict would have been the same, since Scott's status depended on the laws of the state in which he resided (Missouri), and not those of Illinois, and these permitted slavery. Finally, the Court's majority declared that the Missouri Compromise, which excluded slavery from areas north of the parallel of 36°30′, was unconstitutional. "Congress could not exclude slavery," wrote Taney, for this would violate due process of law as guaranteed by the fifth amendment. Congress had "only the power coupled with the duty of . . . protecting the owner in his rights." In this way, the Court's majority decided that Scott was property, not a human being under the law. Furthermore, it declared that no state had the right to legislate slavery from its jurisdiction.

The Court's majority had effectively stated that all territorial and state restrictions on slavery were dead letters. So was popular sovereignty, under which a state or people might decide to forbid slavery from its midst. The doctrine upon which many moderates, including Douglas and Buchanan, had erected their arguments and pleas for quiet debate and the democratic process was now shattered by the very Court that only two days earlier Buchanan had agreed to follow.

The new President had hoped the Dred Scott decision, coupled with his speech, would offer something to both sections, and lead to a return to the concept of popular sovereignty and balance. Instead, Taney had given the slave South a far greater victory than it had imagined possible. Men like Sumner and Chase, who had fought to keep slavery from Kansas, were now told that not only would the institution be legal there, but in New York and Ohio as well.

After the Taney decree, the slave states could portray themselves as defenders of the Constitution, while their northern opponents were driven to a choice between acceptance of slavery and the law on the one hand, and opposition to slavery and defiance of the law on the other. There appeared to be no legal means by which one could oppose the expansion of slavery into the territories, including Kansas. The nation seemed poised for a great debate, perhaps to be followed by a civil war, in which segments of the North would call for secession from the Union, dominated as it appeared to be by southern slave interests.

Before such a debate could begin, however, the panic of 1857 and the depression that followed intervened. This proved the second great blow to the North that year, one that turned attention from slavery to more pressing immediate economic needs.

Even in Kansas the situation seemed to be swinging in favor of the South. Buchanan wanted to avoid conflict at all costs. He still believed the Kansas situation could be resolved through discussions and compromise. He had promised the nation to support a free choice in Kansas despite the dictates of the Court. If Kansans selected a free-state status, he would defend their right to do so. On the other hand, should they opt for slavery, he would be equally strong in defense of that choice. It seemed fair enough at the time.

After consulting with Douglas, the President sent Robert Walker to the territory as its new governor. Walker was a former secretary of the treasury, who, though a Pennsylvanian by birth, was a Mississippian by choice and an expansionist by inclination. Walker was considered a fair man, but one who was prosouthern. As a result, the South applauded his selection, while northern Republicans viewed it as yet another sign of Buchanan's antagonism to their cause.

Walker promised the residents of the territory that they would be given a fair chance to select between entering the Union as a slave or free state, and he scheduled a territorial election for October 5. The election was held, but it was fraudulent. Thousands of proslavery voters came into Kansas from Missouri and cast illegal ballots. Walker was shocked by the outright attempt at a steal, said so openly, and threw out thousands of fraudulent ballots, in this way winning support of northerners and earning the distrust of administration insiders. The final results gave free-state advocates majorities in both houses of the territorial legislature. For the moment, at least, it seemed the tide was turning in favor of the North.

Meanwhile, members of the constitutional convention, a majority of whose delegates favored slavery, met in Lecompton to write a constitution for the state. The delegates realized that an outright proslavery document would be rejected out of hand, and so resorted to a clever stratagem. Voters would be given the opportunity to accept a constitution with or without slavery, but in either event, those slaves already in Kansas would be allowed to stay. There was no way by which a voter might cast his ballot for complete free-state status, even though such might have been the choice of a majority.

Immediately voices were raised against the Lecompton constitution in the North, and not only by Republicans. Douglas denounced it as unjust, as did Bennett and others normally considered prosouthern by the Republicans. The white South, as might have been expected, considered the choice fair, especially in the light of the Dred Scott decision. Walker sped to Washington to confer with Buchanan, who earlier had pledged him full support for a vote between slave and free status.

It was a critical moment. Already conventions had been called in Alabama, Mississippi, and South Carolina. Southern firebrands warned that they would fight, perhaps secede, if Buchanan did not support the Lecompton constitution. It had happened before, when Buchanan was a young congressman. In 1832 Calhoun had threatened President Andrew Jackson with what amounted to an end to the Union if Jackson did not comply with southern demands. The President had responded by mobilizing the armed forces. But the crisis passed without war. Buchanan had been horrified by the confrontation, and memories of it lingered. Should he now risk war to preserve the Union, as had Jackson? Or should he back down, and so make certain the nation would not be visited by a civil war?

The President wavered. But in the end Buchanan, who feared war and was practiced in the arts of compromise, opted for the more secure choice. He upheld the Lecompton constitution.

Buchanan's decision was greeted with jubilation in the plantation South, while northerners of both parties united in anti-Buchanan rallies. The President had lost not only his northern support, but his credibility. By compromising his word in the face of southern threats, he had become not only a sectional president, but one who could no longer be believed. B. B. French, former President Franklin Pierce's secretary, a man who was sympathetic to the South but at the same time understood the uses of power, was irate. "I had considerable hopes of Mr. Buchanan," he wrote. "I really thought he was a statesmen—but I have now come to the settled conclusion that he is just the d——dest old fool that has ever occupied the Presidential chair. He has deliberately walked overboard with his eyes open—let him drown, for he must."

As expected, Walker submitted his resignation, which was accepted. Douglas broke with Buchanan, taking moderate northern Democrats into active opposition to the administration. Even John Forney, one of Buchanan's leading editorial supporters, protested. "Mr. Buchanan," he said, "for the first time in our lives we are at variance. I find myself standing by one principle, having followed your lead—and you have deserted it." The President urged Forney to reconsider. "If I can afford to change, why can't you? If you, Douglas, and Walker will unite in support of my policy, there will not be a whisper of this thing. It will pass by like a summer breeze." But it would not pass by. The President had promised justice in Kansas, and most northerners now felt he had not been just. They trusted him once; they would not do so again. "Sir, I intend to make my Kansas policy a test," he told

Forney. "Well, sir," was the response, "I regret it; but if you make it a test with your officers, we will make it a test at the ballot box."

In this way, Forney announced the northern Democrats would oppose Buchanan at the polls if he decided to run again in 1860. More than that, they would deny him the nomination if he attempted to obtain it. Buchanan was now a southern Democrat. The northern elements of the party would have nothing to do with him.

On December 21, Kansas voted on the Lecompton constitution. The free-state forces boycotted the election. The results showed 6,226 for the constitution with slavery, and 2,720 in favor of the constitution with limits as to the further introduction of slaves. And even then, when the South had an almost complete victory in its grasp, fraud was introduced. Some 2,700 of the proslavery ballots were later shown to be illegal.

News of the Kansas vote spread through the nation that Christmas season. In the North there was unrelieved gloom; in the South, white plantation owners and middle-class farmers rejoiced. Within a period of less than a year they had won on the Dred Scott issue and the Kansas constitution. The depression had shown the weaknesses of the North and the strengths of the cotton South. In November, 1856, it appeared the South was on the defensive. Then came the election of Buchanan and the defeat of the Republicans, and since then all had gone better than even the most optimistic might have anticipated. The South controlled the presidency and the Supreme Court. It had great power in Congress; the North-Midwest alliance could not pass legislation in the face of a united southern Democratic contingent. The South also appeared more powerful economically than the North, and better organized.

In retrospect, it might seem that white southerners had confused the appearance of power with its reality. Even then there were faint signs of economic recovery in the North and Midwest. Democratic power in Congress could easily be crippled, especially if many of the anti-Lecompton northern Democrats joined the Republicans, as was widely predicted. Such an alliance, which might also include former Know-Nothings and the remaining Whig remnant, could then go on to capture the presidency in 1860. This would leave the South with only the Supreme Court, and that branch of government would be powerless without the support of a like-minded president and Congress. Finally, it was questionable that the white South was indeed unified. Hinton Rowen Helper, a North Carolina-born journalist, had written a book in 1857 disputing this claim. *The Impending Crisis of the South and How to Meet It* was a fiery attack on slavery, not in the name of the slaves, but rather for the sake of poor whites. The institution of slavery benefited only a small portion of the South's white population, while the rest was degraded by it. In other words, the 350,000 slave owners and hirers of the South were holding the 5.8 million slaveless whites in bondage.

> Non-slaveholders of the South! farmers, mechanics, and work-ingmen, we take this occasion to assure you that the slaveholders, the arrant demagogues whom you have elected to offices of honor and profit, have hoodwinked you, trifled with you, and used you as mere tools for the consummation of their wicked designs. They have purposely kept you in ignorance, and have,

by moulding your passions and prejudices to suit themselves, induced you to act in direct opposition to your dearest rights and interests.

Helper's work was not yet widely known in 1857, but it represented a warning to southerners who supported slavery, one that would become louder and more insistent the following year, when northern Republicans seized upon it, seeing in the book evidence that a truly national antislavery party was indeed possible. And with its creation the slave South could not only be contained, but even destroyed.

In Congress the battle lines were drawn. The issue still was Kansas. Southern Democrats demanded its immediate admission as a slave state under the Lecompton constitution, while northern Republicans, together with a growing group of northern Democrats, opposed them. In the middle were the moderates, most of them northern Democrats and border-state residents, the latter realizing they would suffer most should a civil war between the sections erupt. Many of these rallied behind Douglas. They had opposed the Lecompton constitution, believing some kind of compromise possible. One of their number, Representative William English of Indiana, offered a suggestion: resubmit the Lecompton constitution to the voters of Kansas. If accepted, Kansas would enter the Union as a slave state, and with an eye to encouraging such a vote, English proposed that in such an eventuality, the government would grant Kansas a bonus of four million acres of federal land. Should the constitution be rejected, admission would be delayed until the territory's population reached 90,000.

The English compromise, like so many before it, was

265

designed to defer a decision on the slavery issue until a future date, when hopefully tempers would be cooler than they were in 1858. But the moral temperature was rising in the wake of events of the previous year. Increasingly moderates of both sides were preparing for a showdown, unwilling to give even an inch to the other side. So the English measure appeared a feeble gesture, one that even the Douglas forces were unsure of, and which not all felt they could support, especially in an election year. Nevertheless, the measure passed the House by a narrow margin and was sent on to the Senate.

Now all eyes were on Douglas, the leader of and spokesman for the moderates, the voice of the opposition Democrats. Earlier he had broken completely with the administration. "No Democrat ever yet differed from an administration of his own choice without being crushed," Buchanan had warned Douglas, reminding him of the fate of those who had opposed Andrew Jackson in the 1830s. Douglas had responded that Jackson was dead, and that a new era was opening. His entire career had been marked by a willingness to compromise, to conciliate, to defer judgment on difficult issues if necessary. But Douglas was also the champion of a single principle: popular sovereignty, and this had been flouted by Buchanan's support of the Lecompton constitution. By early 1858 he had reconciled his own advocacy of popular sovereignty with the Dred Scott decision, always with an eye to the South. Douglas would accept the decision —a state could not legislate slavery from its borders. But if the people of a state wanted to ban slavery, they could refuse to pass legislation protecting the institution. What slave owner, asked Douglas, this time with an eye to the North, would bring his slaves into such a state? Thus, during the debate on the English compromise, Douglas had successfully walked the narrow plank between the Scott decision and popular sovereignty.

By early 1858 Douglas' break with Buchanan had led some southerners to burn effigies of the "Little Giant" in towns in the lower South. But most southern Democrats, though supporting Buchanan, recognized that Douglas, the master manipulator, would not lead a drive to end slavery in the territories. On the other hand, moderate Republicans of the North, including the influential Horace Greeley, were talking of supporting Douglas for the 1860 Republican nomination, in this way not only helping to preserve the Union, but saving the party from radicals like Sumner.

But 1860 was a long way off, and Douglas would have to maintain his precarious position until then if he was not only to survive, but to triumph. Now he had to face the English compromise. Could it prove a trap? Douglas was not certain. And after some hesitation and much discussion with allies in all parts of the country, he voted against it. The measure then passed without his support, and was signed into law by Buchanan.

In the South many interpreted Douglas' vote as a sign that he had gone over to the enemy, a belief compounded by the fact that many Republicans had also opposed the compromise, on the grounds that a showdown was needed. A quick canvas of his senatorial colleagues convinced Douglas that his lines of communication with slave-state leaders were intact. Southern Democrats might not prefer Douglas for the presidential nomination in 1860, but if the convention named him, he would have their support against a Republican—assuming, of course, he went no further in the direction of the anti-Lecompton forces than he already had.

Now the Lecompton constitution was placed before the Kansas voters. This time the election was carefully policed, with few outsiders able to cast ballots. The Free Soilers rejected the document, while the proslavery forces favored it. The vote was 11,812 to 1,926 against the constitution. As English and the moderates had expected, the Kansas issue was deferred. It would prove the last compromise of its kind to be successfully carried through, however.

The civil war in Kansas continued, but at a slower pace than before. Both sides seemed to recognize that all alternatives had been explored and found wanting. A new factor had to be thrown into the equation, one that would tip the

Violence in Kansas: pro-slavery settlers gun down eleven anti-slavery citizens in Blooming Grove on May 19, 1858.

scales one way or another. And one was at hand: the congressional elections.

The coming elections were significant for several reasons. In the first place, they would test the power of the rising Republican Party in the North and Midwest. Too, they would enable southern political leaders to canvass their states, to determine the temper of the population. Radicals like Robert Toombs and moderates like Jefferson Davis would journey through several southern states, hoping to uncover the key that would dictate sectional and personal success in the next two years and might help one or the other to rise to the seat of Calhoun as a sectional voice—and perhaps to succeed Buchanan as president. Then there was the contest between the Douglas and Buchanan wings of the Democratic Party, particularly important since Douglas was running for reelection to the Senate from Illinois. Even before leaving Washington for home, Douglas knew he was one of the most popular men in the North. The effigy burnings in the South led many northerners of both parties to believe Douglas was a man who not only could bring the country together, but could do it in such a way as to favor their section. Every time his homeward-bound train stopped at a station, crowds would gather to cheer the Little Giant, shouting encouragement not only for 1858, but 1860 as well, when it was assumed Douglas would lead the Democrats into battle.

The candidate himself was concentrating on matters at hand. Able politician that he was, he understood that only slightly less important than winning the senatorial race was the *way* he won. If, in triumphing, Douglas alienated the South, his presidential hopes would be dashed. Should he lean over too far in placating the plantation South, might not his northern supporters in Illinois turn against him in 1858, and deny Douglas his Senate seat? Should this happen, the presidency would be beyond his grasp. So Douglas had not only to win in 1858, but to do so in a proper fashion.

Greeley understood this, and so had urged Illinois Republicans to allow Douglas to run unopposed. But the Illinois party was independent of the party in New York, and went its own way. By 1858 it was one of the most powerful in the nation, with each clash in Washington or Kansas bringing in new members. The Republicans had a sizable delegation in the state house, and now had reason to believe they could defeat Douglas in his reelection bid, in the process not only destroying him for 1860, but placing the victor in a position to challenge men like Seward, Sumner, Chase, and McLean for the presidential nomination.

The Republicans held their convention in Springfield in June, with two candidates leading all the rest. "Long John" Wentworth, the newly elected mayor of Chicago, the first of his party to assume leadership of a major American city, was one of the two. Wentworth was a former Democrat who had joined the Republicans after passage of the Kansas-Nebraska Act. Although personally friendly with Douglas, he had quickly seized control of the Cook County machine and could count on a great deal of upstate support. But Wentworth was an abrasive man, one who had angered other Illinois Republican leaders. Furthermore, he was considered too moderate for the increasingly radicalized Illinois Republicans.

Abraham Lincoln was the second hopeful. Lincoln had begun his political career as a Whig, a follower of Henry Clay and a man who early in his career was known as a moderate and a compromiser. He was capable of taking strong stands on basic issues, however, even when he understood they might harm him politically. As a congressman he had opposed the Mexican War and, in part because of this, was obliged to step down after serving a single term. From that time on, Lincoln was considered antislavery, though by no means an abolitionist or radical.

Lincoln practiced law in Springfield in the early 1850s, and came to represent several railroads, a sign he was acceptable to the "responsible" elements. He also remained active in politics. After declining an offer to serve as governor of the Oregon territory, Lincoln joined the Republicans in 1852, and even received several votes for that party's vice-presidential nomination. Lincoln campaigned for Frémont, and in 1854, sought the Republican designation for the senatorship. Realizing that Lyman Trumbull had the nomination assured, Lincoln stepped aside gracefully, in such a way as to win the appreciation of the state's Republicans. Lincoln spoke for Trumbull and, when the Republicans swept Illinois in 1856, was in a strong position.

Lincoln traveled throughout the state, speaking before many groups and making himself better known. As a result, he became the leader not only of the state's Republican Party, but a national figure as well. Lincoln opposed the Kansas-Nebraska Act, and this led him into clashes with Douglas. Shortly after the Dred Scott decision was handed down, he spoke of what he believed to be moral fallacies in the majority decisions, and he came out against the further extension of slavery into the territories.

Was this enough for the increasingly radicalized Illinois Republicans? At the Springfield convention in June, Lincoln had to make certain that he was to the "left" of Wentworth, and at the same time formulate issues upon which he might challenge Douglas. With this in mind, he wrote a speech that, his law partner claimed, would electrify the audience and nation. "Lincoln, deliver that speech as read and it will make you president," said William Herndon.

> We are now far into the fifth year since a policy was initiated with the avowed object and confident promise of putting an end to slavery agitation. Under the operation of that policy, that agitation not only has not ceased, but has constantly augmented. In my opinion, it will not cease until a crisis shall have been reached and passed. "A house divided against itself cannot stand." I believe this government cannot endure permanently half slave and half free. I do not expect the Union to be dissolved—I do not expect the house to fall—but I do expect it will cease to be divided. It will become all one thing, or all the other. Either the opponents of slavery will arrest the further spread of it, and place it where the public mind shall rest in the belief that it is in the course of ultimate extinction; or its advocates will push it forward until it shall become alike lawful in all the States, old as well as new, North as well as South.

The speech was not delivered to make Lincoln president, but to win the Republican nomination against Wentworth and provide a jumping-off point for a campaign against Douglas. But it would serve to strengthen Lincoln's credentials among the more radical Republicans. In it he said the time for compromise had passed, and that Douglas' attempts to forestall a decision could no longer be accepted. The political descendant of Henry Clay, which was what Lincoln considered himself prior to the 1850s, was dead. Now Lincoln emerged as one who appeared closer to Sumner and the abolitionist Republicans than to the moderates, while Douglas had assumed Clay's mantle. What else could Lincoln have meant when he said, or at least strongly implied, that slavery should be placed "in the course of ultimate extinction"? The first step would be to limit it in the territories. Then, it would be ended, in time, in the rest of the country. This, at least, was the way the speech was received in the South, and as it was understood in the East. Four months later Seward, the leading radical Republican candidate for the presidency, would say, "It is in irrepressible conflict between opposing and enduring forces, and it means that the United States must and will, sooner or later, become either entirely a slaveholding nation or entirely a free-labor nation." To most who read both speeches, the two men seemed much alike.

But were they? Seward, Sumner, and Chase were men who had long spoken in such tones and with such words. Lincoln was a relative newcomer to the position. True, he had always opposed the extension of slavery into the territories, but never before had he spoken of the need to eliminate it from the nation. The speech would help Lincoln win the senatorial nomination, and in speaking before radical Republican audiences he would repeat its phrases and express sentiments which his hearers applauded. A month later, in Chicago, he would say:

> Let us discard all this quibbling about this man and the other man, this race and that race and the other race being inferior, and therefore they must be placed in an inferior position. Let us discard all these things, and unite as one people throughout this land, until we shall once more stand up declaring that all men are created equal.

This was the Lincoln whom, in the light of subsequent events, most Americans would remember. But in September, in an address before a proslavery audience, Lincoln would speak differently:

> I will say, then, that I am not, nor ever have been, in favor of bringing about in any way the social and political equality of the white and black races: that I am not, nor ever have been, in favor of making voters or jurors of negroes, nor of qualifying them to hold office, nor to intermarry with white people. . . .
>
> And inasmuch as they cannot so live, while they do remain together there must be the position of superior and inferior, and I as much as any other man am in favor of having the superior position assigned to the white race.

Like Douglas, Lincoln was walking a tightrope, though over a different abyss. In 1858 both men were setting their sights on 1860. Douglas wanted to win the presidency by taking votes from both North and South, and so emerge as a president of reconciliation, with the slave issue postponed indefinitely. Lincoln, the Republican, knew he could not hope to win any support at all from the South. If he did become president, it would be through northern and mid-western votes. But he wanted to assure the South he was no dangerous radical; like Douglas, he knew how to compromise. There would be no attempt to change the basic social structure of the South, the House Divided speech to the contrary notwithstanding. Slavery would not be permitted to extend into the territories. In time, perhaps, the institution would decline in the South. But like Douglas, he was willing to permit natural forces to do the work. On the surface, then, Lincoln had locked arms with Seward and Sumner. In terms of practical politics, however, he may have been closer to Douglas than was realized at the time.

Douglas understood this better than most. When he learned of Lincoln's nomination, he told Forney, "He is the strong man of his party—full of wit, facts, dates—and the best stump speaker, with his droll ways and dry jokes, in the West. He is as honest as he is shrewd, and if I beat him, my victory will be hardly won." During the campaign, the two men would attack each other with vigor and intelligence, each knowing the other's strengths and weaknesses. At times their language would be bitter, and lead to rumors that a duel was in the making. Douglas and Lincoln scoffed at such a notion, for they remained friendly throughout, as might be expected of two such seasoned politicians. "He and I are the best friends in the world," said Lincoln of his opponent, "and when we get together he would no more think of fighting me than of fighting his wife." And soon after the election, Douglas would write a letter to the president of Harvard, recommending Robert Lincoln as the son of his friend "with whom I have lately been canvassing the State of Illinois."

The campaign was exciting, important, and destined to become one of the most famous of its kind in the nation's history. Douglas embarked on a downstate speaking tour, with Lincoln following closely behind, answering his opponent's speeches as he went. Douglas' supporters charged that Lincoln couldn't draw crowds on his own and so had to rely upon those who came to see and hear the Senator. Then Lincoln's managers suggested a series of debates, seven in all, one in each of the counties not yet visited by the candidates. Douglas accepted the challenge, and the famous Lincoln-Douglas debates, held from August 21 to October 21, were on.

The Lincoln-Douglas debates were not really debates at all, but joint appearances of rival candidates seeking votes. Each man misrepresented the position of the other, with few attempts made to explore the basic constitutional arguments.

They tended either to expand or to moderate their positions in each meeting, to suit them to the audiences who came to hear. The two candidates would speak differently to audiences in northern Illinois than they would to those in the southern part of the state, and would ignore questions put to them by their opponent if the answer would prove embarrassing. Douglas portrayed Lincoln as a wild abolitionist, the leader of the radical Republicans, while Lincoln continued to picture Douglas as a captive of the South. Douglas charged that the mixing of the races would lead to intermarriage, and Lincoln denied it. Lincoln stated his belief that the broadening of democracy in America should lead to equal rights for all men when speaking in the northern part of Illinois, while Douglas responded, "I do not regard the Negro as my equal, and positively deny he is my brother, or any kin to me whatever." In southern Illinois Douglas asked his audience, "Do you desire to turn this beautiful State into a free negro colony, in order that when Missouri abolishes slavery she can send one hundred thousand emancipated slaves into Illinois, to become citizens and voters, on an equality with yourselves?" Lincoln counterattacked by saying that the Republican Party was not an abolitionist organization, and he no believer in that doctrine. "I have no purpose, either directly or indirectly, to interfere with the institution of slavery where it exists. I believe I have no lawful right to do so, and I have no inclination to do so. I have no purpose to introduce political and social equality between the white and black races." Having said this, however, Lincoln refused to go further. The black man might not be the equal of the white in terms of mental and moral facilities, he said. "But in the right to eat the bread, without the leave of anyone else, which his own hand earns, he is my equal, and the equal of Judge Douglas, and the equal of every living man."

What was Lincoln's true position on the slavery issue? Clearly he was opposed to slaveholders, as much because he wanted America to be a land dominated by free whites as anything else. But how far would he go to bring about an end to slavery? In 1858, at least, the answer was not clear.

Even more dangerous, however, and more paradoxical, appeared Douglas' defense of popular sovereignty and the Dred Scott decision. Earlier Douglas had skirted the issue by saying that he saw no problem in accepting both. Now Lincoln hammered away at the apparent inconsistency. In Freeport, a town in the most northern part of the state, Douglas appeared to come down on the side of popular sovereignty. No matter what the courts decided on the "abstract issue" of slavery, he said, "the right of the people to make a slave Territory or a free Territory is perfect and complete under the Nebraska bill," and he added his often stated belief that without supporting legislation, slavery could not enter some parts of the territories. Thus, free-staters could prevent slavery from entering their areas, while at the same time avowing support of the Dred Scott decision.

This was not the way it sounded in the South. There it appeared Douglas had supported popular sovereignty *against* the Dred Scott decision. Even as Douglas attempted to win votes in northern Illinois, he lost support in the slave South. The so-called Freeport Doctrine was not new to Douglas in the campaign, but Lincoln made it appear as though it were, with Douglas portrayed as a trimmer, a man of little substance, one who would do anything for votes. "You can fool all the people some of the time, and some of the people all of the time, but you cannot fool all the people all the time," Lincoln was said to have remarked regarding the Douglas stands.

Douglas and Lincoln, in their campaigns, attempted to draw the lines between their positions as sharply as possible, and in so doing, exaggerated their differences while softening their similarities. Actually, they were closer in some ways than appearance would allow. Both men were strong patriots, loving the Union above all. Lincoln and Douglas would rise to defend it against those who would disrupt the democratic experiment, whether they were abolitionists or southern fire-eaters. Both idealized the free white farmer, and neither considered the black man his biological equal. Douglas and Lincoln did not believe in racial equality, but both opposed the further expansion of slavery, although in different ways.

There was, however, a key difference between the candidates, one often hidden beneath the strategic and tactical statements but that surfaced from time to time during the debates. Douglas did not appear to see slavery as a moral question. During the debates and after he spoke of the institution as a political entity, to be resolved by political means. The white majority of any given area could decide the question, and Douglas would fight any attempt on the part of outsiders, be they from the North or South, to interfere with this right. Lincoln, on the other hand, clearly considered slavery morally wrong. In Galesburg he enunciated this sentiment strongly and eloquently:

> I do not think that Judge Douglas and whoever, like him, teaches that the negro has no share, humble though it may be, in the Declaration of Independence, is going back to the era of our liberty and independence and, in so far as in him lies, muzzling the cannon that thunders its annual joyous return; that he is

blowing out the moral lights around us, when he contends that whoever wants slaves has a right to hold them; that he is penetrating, so far as lies in his power, the human soul, and eradicating the light of reason and the love of liberty, when he is in every way possible preparing the public mind, by his vast influence, for making the institution of slavery perpetual and national.

Since in Illinois senators were chosen by the state legislature, the victory would go to the party that captured control of that body. The Democrats won, carrying all the southern and border counties but three, while the Republicans made a clean sweep of the northern counties. The vote showed that Illinois, as though a microcosm of the nation, was divided on sectional grounds. Thus Douglas won reelection by a legislative vote of 54 to 46. On the other hand, the Republican legislators polled 125,000 votes against the Democrat's 121,000 while pro-Buchanan Democrats took another 5,000. Lincoln had lost the election, but in the process had become a major force in the national Republican Party. Douglas had won, but the plantation South no longer considered him acceptable in 1860 because of the interpretation given the Freeport Doctrine. The sectional ties were further loosened by the election, and a sectional war seemed more probable.

The Republicans did well nationwide in 1858, gaining control of state houses in the North and sharply increasing their representation in Congress. At the same time, the party's mood was tending to become more radical, what with talk of Lincoln's House Divided and Seward's Irrepressible Conflict. And the South responded. Men who previously had been considered moderates were drifting toward the fire-eater camp. One of these, Jefferson Davis of Mississippi, replied to the North that should the Republicans win the 1860 election, he would favor secession.

By early 1859 there was no statesman of national stature capable of preventing the escalation of words, no individual who held the confidence of leaders both north and south of the Mason-Dixon line, and no program capable of winning the approval of both sections. To be sure, a vast majority of Americans still wanted peace. The abolitionists were still a small minority in the North while the fire-eaters did not have much in the way of solid southern support. But onlookers were increasingly confused, and took rhetoric for reality. To many southerners, Seward and Sumner *were* the North, and Lincoln intended to end slavery if and when elected. Many northerners believed the secessionists spoke for a united South. Normally moderate people in both sections were drawn to more extreme stances than they had ever held before, frightened by specters and stereotypes that had little connection with reality. Fear had replaced reason, and hate the desire to conciliate.

11 / JOHN BROWN OF OSAWATOMIE

"I AM JOHN BROWN OF OSAWATOMIE."

In this way, the most famous abolitionist to emerge from the Kansas struggle introduced himself to northern audiences in 1857 and 1858. Many came to hear what he had to say, but even more came out of curiosity. Most seemed impressed by Brown's arguments and by the man himself. Already he was a national figure of no little renown.

There were abolitionists who had condemned Brown for the Pottawatomie raid. At the time moderate abolitionists had been torn between their desire to end slavery on the one hand and their dedication to peace on the other. Such individuals might have belonged to one or several pacifist organizations as well as abolitionist societies. Slavery must be ended, they said, but without bloodshed and violence, and in a spirit of love. They would work and pray for it, but would not advocate violence. In time, the nation would see an end to human bondage. This they ardently believed, since God was good and man created in His image. In 1858, after a generation of talking, writing, and praying, it appeared the abolitionists hadn't accomplished very much.

Brown was gentle, even understanding, when speaking to individuals such as these. This surprised them, since he was known as a man of violence, one who thundered against his enemies and spoke with relish of the coming bloodbath. But Brown was a man of two faces, one kindly, the other angry. This fifty-eight-year-old radical, a man who had accomplished little before throwing himself wholeheartedly into the movement, seemed to scorn the comforts and ambitions of middle-class society. Along with many of his kind, the ones passed by as the nation grew richer and more powerful, Brown had submerged himself in a cause. It mattered little if he had failed. The cause was pure, and so transfigured him. The cause would succeed, even though he as an individual had failed. As a soldier in the good fight, he would share in that success. Brown could be understanding to others who found themselves in the same situation. He would be gentle to individuals whom he might convince of the cause's morality. But Brown was angry at those who rejected his appeals, and violent toward people who had come to conclusions different from his.

He told his audiences that slavery was an unmitigated evil. How could one come to terms with it? Even to admit the possibility of compromise was in itself an immoral act. Clearly the slaveholders were either morally blind or agents of Lucifer. In either case, they would not relinquish their slaves without a fight. Debate was a sham, a device to lull the weak

282

into submission. What was required was a confrontation, one in which good would meet evil and triumph.

Brown was an eloquent writer and speaker. His words were simple and direct, clear and without guile. Often he would exaggerate, speak of events that had never occurred, and twist the facts. This was not apparent to his northern audiences, who came to believe, not to doubt. In 1858 Brown appeared an Old Testament prophet, with flashing eyes and resounding voice. When he grew a beard the following year, his similarity to woodcuts in family Bibles would be even more pronounced.

Do you still reject violence? In 1858? Brown would ask his listeners. He could understand pacifism a decade earlier. Even in 1856 some might not have seen the coming storm clearly. But after Buchanan's election, the Dred Scott decision, the Lecompton constitution, and so much more of the same, could they still believe slavery would be ended peacefully? Either fight slavery and reject pacifism, or remain pacifists and leave the abolitionist movement, he said. There was no other choice. Could any person claiming to be a Christian have any doubt as to the correct path? Slavery must be crushed, he said, and soon. To wait any longer is a sin against God. We all agree on this. Since no other way remains, we must employ violence.

Most Americans who knew of John Brown in 1857–58 assumed him to be a long-time abolitionist. Actually, he had come late to political activism, and even later to violence. As a young man Brown had learned to hate slavery, but he had done nothing about it. Most of his time had been spent in his several business ventures and in raising a large family—seven children born of his first marriage, thirteen of the second. He had gone to Kansas in 1855 not to fight slaveholders, but to make a fresh start, this time in farming. Soon after, when he became embroiled in disputes with slaveholders and saw the violence erupting around him, Brown became an activist. Then he turned complete attention to the fight, and would remain in the struggle for the rest of his life.

During the two years following the Pottawatomie massacre Brown traveled between abolitionist centers in the East and Kansas, raising money, buying arms and supplies, and providing them to Free Soil forces. Most abolitionists viewed Kansas as the testing point between slave and free America. Brown felt otherwise. The admission of Kansas to the Union as a free state would be no great victory. The real battle was elsewhere, in the South. He would not rest until the heartland of the institution was smashed. Brown meant to strike at that heartland, and soon.

In early 1857, less than a year after Brown had become a national figure, he signed a contract with a Connecticut blacksmith to provide him with from five hundred to a thousand pikes, or long spears, at a dollar and a quarter apiece. Friends recall him talking of military strategy that year, especially guerrilla warfare, in which ill-trained but fanatic troops could hold off an army many times their number. Pikes for Kansas farmers, already wise in the use of firearms? Guerrilla warfare in Kansas, a place still sparsely occupied, with no army to fight? Later in the year Brown talked with close friends of organizing a cadre of volunteers, able to lead untrained troops in battle, and financed by money obtained from those who had backed his Kansas operations.

The spears were not for Kansas farmers, but for freed slaves, unaccustomed to firearms. The cadre would lead the slaves, and not in Kansas. "Our ultimate destination is Virginia," he told his close supporters. Kansas was only an arm of the slavocracy, outstretched to grasp the rest of the nation, but not dangerous in itself. Virginia was its heart. Let others flail at the arm. I will go for the heart.

Like most of Brown's plans, the campaign against Virginia was simple, based on hopes rather than knowledge, poorly planned, and audacious. To radical abolitionists untrained in military arts, whose knowledge of the slave South had been obtained secondhand and then through clouded ideological glasses, it was most appealing. Brown was convinced most of the slaves were eager for emancipation, and that given a chance they would rise up against their masters, slay them, and join in the fight to exterminate slavery throughout the nation. It was the kind of plan formulated by a man of ideas and words, not of action, and for all his reputation, Brown was an intellectual, not a man of action. His military forays in Kansas had never been very successful; Brown was far more effective at church meetings in Concord than in the field in Kansas. Even today, he is remembered more for his words than his deeds, more as a person who inspired men of action than for any action of his own.

But his idea was not completely outlandish. There had been many slave revolts in American history. The ones led by Denmark Vesey in 1822 and Nat Turner nine years later had struck fear in the hearts of slaveholders throughout the South. In the 1850s there was much talk and writing of a possible slave insurrection. The very fact that the plantation

South was concerned with the matter encouraged Brown. If those who knew the slaves best anticipated an uprising, could those who wished the slaves well not help them in bringing it about?

Once freed, the slaves would form their own nation, based on small farms, in the southern Appalachians, an area easily defended. Brown's cadre would retain power for only a short period before relinquishing it to the freedmen. Could the former slaves rule themselves? Brown had no doubts that they could. The slaves of Saint-Domingue had done as much a half century earlier, and although their government had been oppressive, it was no more so than that of the French whom they expelled. Brown even held a convention in 1858 to draft a provisional constitution for the new nation. It consisted of forty-eight articles, and in part was based on the United States Constitution. The preamble read:

> Whereas slavery, throughout its entire existence in the United States, is none other than a most barbarous, unprovoked, and unjustifiable war of one portion of its citizens upon another portion—the only conditions of which are perpetual imprisonment and hopeless servitude or absolute extermination—in utter disregard and violation of those eternal and self-evident truths set forth in our Declaration of Independence:
>
> Therefore we, citizens of the United States, and the oppressed people who, by a recent decision of the Supreme Court, are declared to have no rights which the white man is bound to respect, together with all other people degraded by the laws thereof, do, for the time being, ordain and establish for ourselves the following Provisional Constitution and Ordinances, the better to protect our persons, property, lives, and liberties, and to govern our actions.

Brown had no illusions that the plantation South would accept such a nation. There would be violence, especially when the freedmen called upon all slaves to join them in their struggle. By then, however, the former slaves would be skilled in the use of arms and this, matched with their indomitable will to remain free, would enable them to prevail. Such a war between former slaves and masters might be long, and many might die. Brown thought it better to have a generation of violence and death than a continuation of slavery.

In the spring of 1858 Brown met with Massachusetts and New York abolitionists to obtain backing for his plan. He found support, and secret committees were formed to help in his work. For years, even decades, the New England and New York abolitionists had spoken, often rashly, of the need for a civil war before the slaves could be freed. Later on, of course, they would temper their remarks with talk of the need for peace as well. Now Brown was taking them at their word. None volunteered to go south with Brown's army. But he would have their money, prayers, and good wishes.

During the next year Brown helped fugitive slaves escape to Canada and went to Kansas in the hope that the war there would escalate. He was disappointed with the way events were moving in Kansas and the nation. The Kansans, both slaveholders and Free Soilers, seemed tired of their struggle, and the fighting slowed to irregular forays by one side against the other, often more a sign of presence than a true test of wills, and seldom provoking retaliation. Kansas was a big place, and there seemed no reason to contest for the same plot of ground when more lay over the next rise in the land, free for the taking. The English compromise had delayed statehood for quite a while, and the Kansans appeared content to let the matter rest there.

Brown was dismayed to find the Free Soilers no longer welcomed him, and indeed considered his presence in the ter-

ritory an embarrassment and a threat to their safety. By early
1859 Kansas was far more important as a symbol in the East
and South than as a reality in the West. So much was this so
that Buchanan, grasping at straws perhaps, predicted that
within a year most northerners would accept the Dred Scott
decision.

Brown was also somewhat disappointed by the electoral
results in 1858. The Republicans had done quite well, but
political activity seemed to go underground after the election, with most Americans concerned with other problems.
In any case, Brown never considered political action the way
to end slavery. It would be vanquished by the sword, not the
word, and he had always been prepared to grasp the sword.

Increasingly his mind turned toward the Virginia plan.
He spoke of it often with his friends, turning aside their
objections, while the scope of the attack and its expected
results grew monthly. One of his associates later wrote, "He
replied that with a hundred men he could free Kansas and
Missouri too, and could march them to Washington and turn
the President and Cabinet out of doors." Brown was possessed
by the idea. "He seemed unable to think of anything else or
talk of anything else." Even his friends now felt Brown was
perhaps deranged. There was a name for it in the 1850s:
monomania.

The nation's business prospects were good in early 1859.
There were clear signs the depression was passing. Employment was up in New England's shoe, textile, and machine
tool shops. In Chicago Cyrus McCormick reported record
orders for his harvesters, reflecting an increased demand for
American grain, the result of warfare in northern Italy.

Demands for cotton were never greater, and the price of slaves, needed for the harvests of 1859 and 1860, also reached record levels.

Railroad construction boomed, not only in the East, but throughout the nation. Although the banking system still was unreformed and badly in need of reorganization, the institutions that had survived the 1857 panic were thriving. Oregon was admitted as the nation's thirty-third state, and soon after announced the discovery of gold. At the same time, a huge silver strike was reported in Nevada, at the Comstock Lode, and miners throughout the West rushed to the site, while San Francisco prepared to assume the role of major capital center for that part of the country. Gold had ushered in prosperity once before. Silver and gold, combined with strong demands for American products and harvests, would do the same a decade later. As though to cap this story of progress, Colonel Edward Drake dug the nation's first successful oil well in Titusville, Pennsylvania.

Prosperity brought more jobs to the eastern cities, even for members of the street gangs. The crime rate dropped in New York and elsewhere along the Atlantic seaboard. Instead of worrying about the next clash on the streets, Americans were amazed at the feats of Charles Blondin, a fifty-five-year-old French acrobat who on June 30 crossed Niagara Falls on a tightrope, and then repeated the feat blindfolded on Independence Day. The comedy hit from London *Our American Cousin*, by Tom Taylor, had come to America late in 1858, and toured the nation in 1859, filling houses wherever it went.

The political scene was calmer than it had been for years, although leaders of both parties realized the lull might be of short duration. Douglas hoped for the Democratic nomination in 1860, after which he would attempt to unify the two wings of his party and then go on to victory against his Republican opponent. There were many Republican hopefuls, and all were busily mending fences, especially with the moderates. There was little talk of ending slavery throughout the nation. Even Seward and Sumner talked mainly of the territories, while Lincoln went out of his way to play down some of his more extreme statements of 1858.

The elections of early October 1859 confirmed the tide of moderation rising through the land. As expected, the Buchanan Democrats did poorly in the North and Midwest, an indication the President was no longer trusted there. The Republicans benefited most from the swing away from Buchanan, but the party's most impressive victories came in areas where slavery either was not of key importance or where other issues were stressed. The Republican Party of 1856 had concentrated on slavery; two years later it campaigned for a transcontinental railroad, federal aid for internal improvements, and a higher tariff. In some ways, it seemed more a reincarnation of the Whigs than an outgrowth of the Free Soil and Liberty parties. The spirit of Henry Clay, not the reality of William Seward, was abroad in the North and Midwest in early October. The trend boded well for Republicans, and troubled Douglas. So long as he occupied the center of national politics, with Republicans on his left and the Buchananites on his right, he could hope for victory. Now the Republicans were moving toward the center, challenging him on his own grounds. Douglas realized his fight would be difficult in the North, and only slightly less so in his native Midwest.

Moderation was on the rise in the South too. A strong radical call for a renewal of the slave trade, made in 1858, had not captured the imagination of the voters. Instead, moderate Democrats and former Whigs and Know-Nothings were coming together in a new alliance, one dedicated to avoiding conflict. In Texas, forty-one-year-old John Reagan won reelection to Congress with ease. Reagan defended the plantation South. "But I will not advocate a destruction of our government as a matter of policy, or those revolutionary measures, based on crime, which look to such a result," he said. Like other moderate Democrats, he feared the radicals on both sides of the Mason-Dixon line would bring the nation to civil war, and he and others like him would do all in their power to prevent one from taking place. "It is time that we should all see where we are drifting, to what the times are tending, and determine whether we are ready for revolution, with all its attendant insecurities to life and property, and with all its hazards to civil and religious liberty."

The moderates defeated the fire-eaters in Texas, putting sixty-six-year-old Sam Houston in the governor's mansion. The combination of moderate Democrat–Whig–Know-Nothing forces proved even stronger in the border states. Sixty-two-year-old John Bell of Tennessee was reelected to the Senate on a platform that almost ignored sectional rivalries. Men like Houston and Bell, vestiges from the intensely Jacksonian past, refused to accept disunionist talk, and intended to oppose vigorously those who would destroy the Union in order either to save slavery in the West or to end it anywhere in the country. There were some young men such as Reagan in the moderate cause, but for the most part it consisted of men from this older generation.

The moderates also looked forward to 1860, when they hoped to present the nation with an alternative that would place the slavery issue in the background. They would not support Douglas, who even though a moderate himself had become compromised by involving himself deeply in the issues surrounding slavery. But they could present one of their number as an alternative to the Republicans and the Buchanan Democrats, a man of compromise in the Clay-Webster tradition.

As such plans were being formulated, however, other forces were at work that would make them almost irrelevant. Secretary of War John Floyd received notice of it in late August, when an unsigned letter crossed his desk:

> Cincinnati, August 20
>
> Sir: I have lately received information of a movement of so great importance that I feel it my duty to impart it to you without delay.
>
> I have discovered the existence of a secret association, having for its object the liberation of the slaves of the South by a general insurrection. The leader of the movement is *"Old John Brown,"* late of Kansas. He has been in Canada during the winter, drilling the negroes there, and they are only waiting his word to start for the South to assist the slaves. . . . They will pass down through Pennsylvania and Maryland, and enter Virginia at Harpers Ferry. . . . They have a large quantity of arms at their rendezvous, and are probably distributing them already.
>
> As I am not fully in their confidence, this is all the information I can give you. I dare not sign my name to this, but trust you will not disregard the warnings on that account.

But disregard it he did. A half year later it would be introduced at a hearing to show the federal government knew that Brown was planning his attack. Floyd explained that the letter contained some information he knew to be inaccurate. "Besides, I was satisfied in my own mind that a scheme of

Clean shaven all of his life, Brown grew a beard as a partial disguise just before the Harpers Ferry raid.

such wickedness and outrage could not be entertained by any citizen of the United States."

After disguising himself somewhat and growing a beard, John Brown, two of his sons, and a friend drifted into Harpers Ferry on July 3, 1859. It was a small village, known primarily for the federal armory at its center, where arms were manufactured and stored. Harpers Ferry was on the Potomac, eighty miles by railroad from Baltimore and sixty from Washington by turnpike. One could cross the Pennsylvania border into Maryland, and from there travel twenty miles and be in the center of the village. It was a logical place for the beginning of Brown's attempt to end slavery in America. From a base in the free state of Pennsylvania, he could move swiftly into Harpers Ferry, seize the arms there, and put out a rallying cry to the slaves in the area to join him. Then, with his army of freedmen, he might march southward, gathering supporters as he went. Or he could even take his band to the capital itself, and seize control of the government. Such, at least, were some of the ideas Brown was considering as he walked through Harpers Ferry, telling people he was a land speculator and cattle buyer, and in the end renting a small farmhouse on the Maryland side of the Potomac, five miles from the armory.

By September Brown was in Boston, visiting with abolitionist leaders there, telling them of his plans, and seeking their aid. He also alluded to the project at several public meetings, so that if his attack was to be a secret it was badly kept.

Thomas Wentworth Higginson, who had long advocated an invasion of the South for the very purpose of freeing the slaves, was enthusiastic. Frederick Douglass, the self-educated former runaway slave who was now a man of prominence in the abolitionist movement, gave Brown his blessing, though he thought Harpers Ferry a poor choice for the invasion. Ralph Waldo Emerson, Theodore Parker, and Henry Thoreau, Boston's leading intellectual luminaries, were impressed with the plan, although they did not know all the details, and helped raise money for its implementation. As they had done in the case of Kansas, they would send their money and good will with Brown to Virginia, but would not join Brown's band of volunteers on its mission. Higginson, the most fiery of the group, remained in Worcester. Parker went to England, and was soon joined there by Edwin Morton, another Brown supporter. Afterward, Frederick Douglass hurried to Canada. Later he would frankly admit, "I have always been more distinguished for running than fighting, and tried by the Harpers Ferry-insurrection test, I am most miserably deficient in courage."

There were twenty-one men in Brown's force besides himself, five of whom were former slaves. Three of his sons marched at Brown's side, along with veterans of the Kansas war. By mid-October they were ready for the attack, which came the night of October 16, a Sunday, when few would be abroad in the hills around Harpers Ferry.

All went smoothly at first. Brown seized the bridge across the Potomac, cut all telegraph wires leading into town, and then captured strategic points near the armory. While a small force occupied the armory, others set out to free slaves on nearby farms. They also took hostages, one of whom was Colonel Lewis W. Washington, a great-grandnephew of George Washington. Colonel Washington surrendered a sword given the General-President by Frederick the Great, handing it over to one of Brown's black recruits. When told of this, Brown was pleased, especially by the symbolism of the act.

"When I strike the bees will swarm," Brown had told Douglass. Now, as word of his attack spread through the countryside, he awaited the expected flood of slaves to come to the armory, take up pikes and rifles, and enlist in his army of freedmen. Then the forces of Armageddon would march southward, bringing freedom to the slaves and death and destruction to their former masters. But none came. Either the slaves had not learned of the act, or were afraid to join

Brown, or were not as eager for revolt as the abolitionists had been led to believe. Still, the first blood was shed soon after. The train from Wheeling to Baltimore pulled in at Harpers Ferry, and Brown's men blocked the track. Hayward Shepherd, a free black who was the station baggage master, went out to investigate, and was fatally wounded by one of Brown's men.

Confusion followed, and in the process word of the raid reached the Virginia and Maryland militias. By Monday afternoon President Buchanan had been informed of the action, which by then seemed a major uprising. Buchanan conferred with Secretary Floyd and some officers and decided to send a force to Harpers Ferry to crush the "rebellion." This operation would be headed by two of the officers at the meeting—

The capture of Brown's remaining forces in the engine house at Harpers Ferry (Frank Leslie's Illustrated Newspaper, *November 1859).*

NEW YORK PUBLIC LIBRARY

Brevet Colonel Robert E. Lee and Lieutenant J. E. B. Stuart.

Lee's force arrived at Harpers Ferry late that evening. By then newspapers in the North were featuring stories of the raid, calling it an "insurrection," while some accounts claimed full-scale black uprisings were taking place in Virginia and Maryland, and spreading throughout the South like wildfire. Southern newspapers were also alarmist, so that within a day citizens in Atlanta feared attacks that might come at any moment.

Later on there would be talk of "the battle of Harpers Ferry." But it was hardly that, rather a series of minor skirmishes. Early Tuesday morning Stuart entered the engine house where the remnant of Brown's force had been surrounded, and a brief scuffle ensued, in which several were killed. Lieutenant Israel Green, his light dress sword in hand, went after Brown, and plunged the weapon into his stomach. The point caught on a belt or buckle, and so Brown was only slightly wounded. Had Green's sword been a regulation sabre, his victim surely would have died.

The uprising had failed, scarcely a day and a half after it had begun. It was a minor incident as such things went, dramatic perhaps, but one that might have been all but forgotten in a matter of weeks had it not been publicized. The New York *Tribune* called it "the work of a madman" soon after. Southern newspapers reflected a widespread fear in the South for a few days, but then wrote of the attack as proof of the abolitionists' inability to organize a proper invasion, their general ineptitude, and the slaves' acceptance of their status. Even William Lloyd Garrison's *Liberator*, the most famous abolitionist journal, was embarrassed. Garrison called the attack "misguided, wild and apparently insane, though a disinter-

HARPER'S WEEKLY.
A JOURNAL OF CIVILIZATION.

Vol. III.—No. 151.]   NEW YORK, SATURDAY, NOVEMBER 19, 1859.   [Price Five Cents.

Entered according to Act of Congress, in the Year 1859, by Harper & Brothers, in the Clerk's office of the District Court for the Southern District of New York.

EFFECT OF JOHN BROWN'S INVASION AT THE SOUTH.

"MUCH OBLIGED TO DAR AR POSSUM WATTOMIE FOR DESE PIKES HE GIN US—DEY'S TURRIBLE HANDY TO DIG TATERS WID."

"WHAT'S DEM FOOL NIGGERS FRAID ON? I'D LIKE TER SEE SEE ONE O' DEM FOLKS ONDERTAKE TO CARRY ME OFF, I WOULD!"

A SOUTHERN PLANTER ARMING HIS SLAVES TO RESIST INVASION.

Harper's Weekly *reaction to Brown's invasion.*

ested and well-intentioned effort by insurrection," and
seemed content to let it go at that.

Brown was still alive, however, and the question now was
what to do with him. There were those who thought he
should be placed in a home for the insane. Colonel Lee
favored dismissing the attack as the work of a crackpot.
Already jokes regarding the fiasco were making the rounds in
New York and New Orleans, Chicago and St. Louis. Had
Brown been treated as Lee had suggested, he might have been
forgotten, appearing in history books as a curious footnote.
Instead, with the aid of Governor Henry Wise of Virginia,
Brown achieved immortality.

Ever since 1856, when he called the governors' conference
in Raleigh to prepare for the eventuality of a Frémont victory, Wise had lived in fear of a slave rebellion and northern
invasion. From time to time he would write letters to northern newspapers warning of a secession movement should the
abolitionists gain national power. As time went on, Wise's
conception of who was an abolitionist broadened, to include
Lincoln in 1858, and a year later, even Stephen Douglas.
Others might view the Harpers Ferry raid as a fiasco. Not
Wise, who took Brown at his word. To him, it seemed the
first shot in an abolitionist war against the South, one with a
goal of freeing the slaves and killing their masters. Brown's
monomania on the subject may have been matched by Wise's
in this respect. In a strange way, each man recognized in the
other a kindred spirit, though on the opposite side of the
issue. Later on Brown would express understanding and even
admiration of Wise. As for the Governor, he went to see
Brown and came away impressed:

They are themselves mistaken who take him to be a madman. He is a bundle of the best nerves I ever saw, cut and thrust and bleeding and in bonds. He is a man of clear head, of courage, fortitude and simple ingenuousness. He is cool, collected and indomitable and it is but just to say of him that he was humane to his prisoners as attested to me by Colonel Washington and Mr. Mills and he inspired me with great trust in his integrity as a man of truth. He is a fanatic, vain and garrulous, but firm, truthful and intelligent.

So it was that Brown would not be placed in an asylum for the insane. Rather, Wise would press for a trial, with one of the charges being treason. He had his way, and was encouraged in his actions by a growing sentiment in the South for a showdown of this kind. With this decision, Brown and Wise, the bizarre antagonists, prepared the way for the abolitionist's last act, the period of his great glory.

Brown was taken to Charlestown, where the trial commenced on October 25. It was conducted with great care, and in the course of the trial Brown had the services of five capable attorneys. Later on, he would praise his lawyers, and the judge and jury. "I feel entirely satisfied with the treatment I have received on my trial," he said. "Considering all the circumstances, it has been more generous than I expected."

Brown told the court he had intended to lead the freed slaves to Canada, that he had not wanted to see the slaves revolt and tried to prevent bloodshed, and that he had never encouraged people to follow his banner, but merely accepted volunteers. Later on, after the trial, he repeated these claims. None were true, as his letters and recollections of friends demonstrated, and some of his actions in Kansas and Harpers Ferry indicated. It may have been that John Brown recognized that he was being placed in a position where he might easily become a martyr for his cause, a symbol for others to follow after him. Or it could have been that he actually came to believe it.

In any case, Brown's words and actions after his capture, his apparent candor at the trial, impressed many in the North, even those who earlier had thought him a fool, knave, or fanatic. Now John Brown, formerly the violent man of abolitionism, was transformed into an almost saintly figure. In a way, he managed to reconcile violence with morality, and death with life. Abolitionists who earlier had hesitated, their love of peace conflicting with their desire to see an end to slavery, now came to believe violence was indeed necessary in order to end the institution. What had been a cold, hard crusade in the 1840s and most of the 1850s had, during the Brown trial and after, become a fiery, passionate, single-minded drive toward freedom. And no one could have done this but John Brown, a man who had failed in so much during his life, perhaps because he had always lacked the proper setting for his talents. He had finally found such a place, not at Osawatomie, or in the meeting halls of Boston, or at Harpers Ferry, but in the court in Charlestown. After hearing the verdict of guilty, Brown was asked if he had anything to say. In the first of his big moments before the bar of history, Brown spoke, in deep eloquence.

> This Court acknowledged ... the validity of the law of God. I see a book kissed, which I suppose to be the Bible, or at least the New Testament, which teaches me that all things whatsoever I would that men should do to me, I should do even to them. It teaches me, further, to remember them that are in bonds as bound with them. I endeavored to act up to that instruction. I say I am yet too young to understand that God is any respecter of persons. I believe that to have interfered as I have done, as I

302

have always freely admitted I have done, in behalf of His despised poor, I did no wrong, but right. Now, if it is deemed necessary that I should forfeit my life for the furtherance of the ends of justice, and mingle my blood further with the blood of my children and with the blood of millions in this slave country whose rights are disregarded by wicked, cruel, and unjust enactments, I say, let it be done.

Writing of the speech a century later, Robert Penn Warren said, "It was so thin that it should not have deceived a child, but it deceived a generation." Gone was the memory of the man who had vowed to bathe a nation in blood to free the slaves, and in its place was a picture of a martyr standing before his judges, a Christ come to judgment. The Lawrence *Republican* reprinted the speech, saying, "For sublimity and solemn appeal, it has not been excelled since Paul spoke before King Agrippa." Raymond of the *Times*, no friend of abolitionists and a man who earlier had condemned the Harpers Ferry raid, now wrote, "Every thoughtful, dispassionate person must recognize, whether in the North or South, in his demeanor, in the language and ideas of this stout, old fanatic, the stuff of which great heroes of mankind are made—simplicity, absolute faith in his own ideas, a religious earnestness of purpose and the great courage of a man consciously honest of will." The New York *Independent*, perhaps the most antiabolitionist newspaper in the city, recognized that the trial, speech, and verdict had transformed Brown into a variety of secular saint. "When John Brown is executed, it will be seen that he has done his work more effectively than if he had succeeded in running off a few hundred slaves." Prophetically, the editor wrote: "Not John Brown, but Slavery, will be gibbeted when he hangs upon the gallows. Slavery itself will receive the scorn and execration it has invoked for him."

Paradoxically, Brown had always hoped to be remembered as a man of deeds, and not of mere words. All of his deeds had failed; the Harpers Ferry scheme had been bungled. Now Brown's words redeemed the failure of his deeds.

Of course, he would hang for his actions. At the time it seemed the Passion Play was being enacted in Virginia, with Brown on his way to his cross. Once executed, he would be a symbol for abolitionism, more powerful than any it had had before, or for that matter possessed by any other reform movement in America from independence to that time. Yet the execution need not have taken place; the abolitionists still might have been denied their martyr. Since John Brown had been found guilty of crimes against Virginia, Governor Wise might have commuted the sentence. For a brief moment it appeared he would do just that.

Wise came to realize that he had been placed in a difficult situation, one in which he was acting as an agent for abolitionists, not their enemy. If Brown were adjudged insane, however, he need not be executed, and the abolitionists would be thwarted. Wise instructed a medical expert to examine the prisoner to see if he indeed was deranged. But before the examination could take place, he canceled the order. "Did I believe him insane, if I could even entertain a rational doubt of his perfect sanity, I would stay the execution even at this hour," he told a visitor shortly before the execution. "All Virginia should not prevent me. I would sooner sever this arm at the shoulder than permit his execution. But I have no such belief, no such doubt." It was as though the Governor was saying that Brown had done just what he might have done in a similar circumstance. The fanatic Wise understood the fanatic Brown, even to the end. If Brown was to play Christ, Wise was agreeable to assuming the role of Pilate.

"Old John Brown, the leader of the Harpers Ferry Insurrection, dies upon the gallows today, the victim of a mad fanaticism which would plunge the country into bloodshed for its own gratification, and which is unhappily too largely shared by many who, like John Brown, esteem all measures right and holy whereby their own peculiar ideas can be made dominant." So did James Gordon Bennett write in the December 2 issue of the New York *Herald*. Bennett hated Brown and his kind, and considered Wise a fool. "The event which takes place in Charlestown today is the gravest which has ever occurred since the organization of this government, being, as it is, the sacrifice of a victim to the practical inauguration of that widespread abolition sentiment which pervades a large extent of the country." Bennett was convinced the country was in a crisis moment, with a possible civil war erupting soon after the execution. Raymond echoed Bennett's words:

> It is idle to blink the fact that John Brown, who dies to-day as a criminal in Virginia, will be honored and lamented to-day as a martyr by thousands of men and women in the Northern States. This fact our Southern kinsmen have thought it best and wisest to force upon the world's attention. The situation was in their control; they have made of it what their wishes or their passions, or their sense of duty commanded. All that is left to be done in the matter now by Northern men who love their country and would see the rights of all its sections justly maintained, is to protest against the extravagant and inflammatory use which fanatical and reckless men at the North will now be swift to make of this decision and this deed in Virginia.

Raymond must have known that such hopes were in vain.

John Brown's hanging (Frank Leslie's Illustrated Newspaper, *December 1859*).

With Brown's death, a giant step on the road to war would have been taken.

John Brown knew this. On the way to the gallows the undertaker spoke with him, saying, "Mr. Brown, you seem to be the most cheerful man here today," to which the prisoner replied, "That is so, and I have good reason to be." Then to the gallows itself. The noose was arranged around his neck, and the jailer asked Brown if he was tired. "No, not tired, but don't keep me waiting longer than is necessary."

The trap was sprung. John Brown was dead. Colonel J. T. L. Preston of Virginia Military Institute shouted, "So perish all such enemies of Virginia! All such enemies of the Union! All foes of the human race." But Virginia had not killed a man; rather, the hangman had helped create the symbol and myth. Horace Greeley recognized this in writing of his death.

> Yes, John Brown dead is verily a power—like Samson in the falling temple of Dagon—like Ziska, dead, with his skin stretched over a drumhead, still routing the foes he bravely fought, while he lived. Time will doubtless make plain the object and effect of this sacrifice, and show the errors of Man overruled and made beneficent by the wisdom and loving justice of God. So let us be reverently grateful for the privilege of living in a world rendered noble by the daring of heroes, the suffering of martyrs—among whom let none doubt that History will accord an honoured niche to Old John Brown.

John Brown, with the aid of Governor Wise, had brought to an abrupt end the strong movement toward moderation so evident until the Harpers Ferry raid. "The present political crisis promises to divide the Republican Party of 1856," wrote George Templeton Strong on Christmas Day. "Its radicalism will become avowed Abolitionism. Conservative Republicans will have to organize independently." Douglas' goals for 1860 now seemed impossible of achieving success. The moderate politics of the South, so successful in October, was all but snuffed out at year's end. Radicals in the North and South were cheerful, the compromisers at a loss for a policy. This was the initial legacy of John Brown, who as expected was the subject of celebration in abolitionist circles, even among those who had refused to fight by his side at Harpers Ferry. Famed poet and abolitionist John Greenleaf Whittier, writing in the *Independent*, added his words to the praise that Christmas, as Christ and Brown were intertwined in the North:

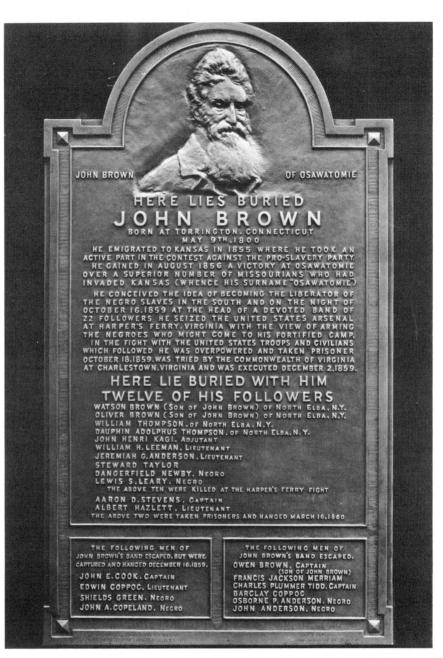

Memorial plaque at Brown's grave on his farm near Lake Placid, New York.

John Brown of Osawatomie
   Spake on his dying day,
I will not have to shrive my soul
   A priest in Slavery's pay.
But let some poor slave-mother
   Whom I have striven to free
With her children, from the gallow-stairs,
   Put up a prayer for me.

John Brown of Osawatomie,
   They led him out to die,
When lo, a poor slave-mother
   With her little child pressed nigh.
Then the bold, blue eyes grew tender,
   And the old hard face grew mild,
And he stopped between the jeering ranks,
   And kissed the negro's child.

The incident had never taken place. The raid had demonstrated, among other things, that the slaves would not rise up in response to the abolitionist's invasion of the South. Accounts of the time indicate his eyes were brown, not blue. Such details were of little interest in the inflamed atmosphere of December, 1859. And Whittier was interested in poetics, not hard, discernible facts. Even then, John Brown had passed from the world of history to that of legend.

CONCLUSION

DURING THE NEW YEAR'S SEASON OF 1850, HENRY CLAY went to visit Daniel Webster to enlist his aid in support of compromise. The aged New Englander agreed, and on March 7, in the Senate, delivered a three-hour speech on the subject, one that ranked with the great American orations. Webster himself considered it the most important of his life. He began:

> I wish to speak today, not as a Massachusetts man, nor as a Northern man, but as an American. . . . It is not to be denied that we live in the midst of strong agitations, and are surrounded by very considerable dangers to our institutions and government. The imprisoned winds are let loose. The East, the North, and the stormy South combine to throw the whole sea into commotion, to toss its billows to the skies, and disclose its profoundest depths. . . . I speak today for the preservation of the Union. "Hear me for my cause."

Webster went on to catalogue the injuries each section had done the other. Most were wrong, in part resulting from misunderstanding, the rest from fear and hate. All could be handled through calm discussion and, in the end, compromise. Talk of secession, emanating from men like Calhoun for the South and Seward for the North, was irresponsible. The Union would never be dissolved. In his stirring peroration, Webster shouted:

> Secession! Peaceable secession! Sir, your eyes and mine are never destined to see that miracle. The dismemberment of this vast country without convulsion! The breaking up of the fountains of the great deep without ruffling the surface! Who is so foolish ... as to expect to see any such thing? Sir, he who sees these States, now revolving in harmony around a common center, and expects to see them quit their places and fly off without convulsion, may look to the next moment to see the heavenly bodies rush from their spheres and jostle against each other in the realms of space, without causing the wreck of the universe! There can be no such thing as a peaceable secession.

Webster pleaded with his countrymen and colleagues. "Let us make our generation one of the strongest and brightest links in that golden chain which is destined, I fondly believe, to grapple the people of all the States to this Constitution for ages to come."

By New Year's season 1860, Webster and Clay were dead, as was Calhoun, while Seward was preparing for the elections of that year, which many predicted would be the last in the nation's history. In his speech Webster had asked the men of his generation to help bind the nation together. So they did, but Webster's generation was passing, while Seward's was on the rise.

Franklin Pierce, who had left the White House in 1857 to retire to a small law practice in Concord, New Hampshire, was one of the survivors. His attorney general, Caleb Cushing, who was preparing for a major role in the 1860 Democratic convention, went to visit Pierce that season, to bring him news of happenings in Washington. Cushing spoke of the coming crisis, and seemed to offer no hope of solution.

> We seem to be drifting into destruction before our eyes, in utter helplessness. The Administration is utterly depopularized; the President is embarrassed with insoluble questions; Congress is paralyzed by party spirit; and everybody seems to despair of any help from man, though many are looking vaguely for interposition from Providence.

Cushing noted that Buchanan was at a loss for ideas. In his annual message to Congress, delivered in December, he spoke of the need for mutual forbearance and calm, but offered no ideas as how to achieve such goals. Congressmen and senators were up in arms, with predictions of violent clashes on the floor being made by newspapermen and the senators themselves. There was talk of a southern confederacy should a Republican win the coming presidential election, or a northern one if, through some miracle, a Buchanan Democrat was elected. Cushing, who was destined to be the presiding officer at the 1860 Democratic convention, saw little hope for the Union, and he told his fears to Pierce.

The decade encapsulated by Webster's speech and Cushing's conversation was one in which the politics of compromise clashed with the crusading zeal of morality. As Lincoln had observed, if slavery was not a moral issue, then many compromises would be possible. If it was, then none could be had. At the beginning of the decade, the politicizers were many, the moralizers few. The situation was reversed by its end, and the spirit of John Brown roamed the land.

Politics and the morality of slavery were not the only concerns of most Americans in this period, however. Elsewhere there was great progress, and reason for feelings of confidence. Despite the panic of 1857, the nation's businesses were flourishing as Cushing spoke with Pierce. The railroad network, weak and incomplete in 1850, was strong and—for the times—remarkably efficient at the close of the decade. The factory system had established firm roots in the North, wheat was thriving in the West, and cotton was king in the South. New York, Chicago, and New Orleans were being transformed from regional cities to national metropolises, and even dreamed of world roles in the future, as commercial and perhaps industrial centers. The banking system was still weak and, as the 1857 panic indicated, in need of further reform. But the insurance industry was invigorated in the 1850s, in part due to the need to service the business sector, while credit services expanded and flourished, a certain sign of a healthy business climate. Finally, the nation demonstrated that some problems could be resolved, or at least be engaged, without civil war; the anti-Catholic campaign, vicious and heated though it had been, appeared on the wane by 1860.

Machines and morality were the twin themes of this decade. To put it another way, the nation underwent major changes in economics and politics in the 1850s. Insofar as the former was concerned, progress was great, and prospects for the future bright. In 1860, however, it appeared to informed observers that the benefits brought by the machine would be crushed by the clash triggered by the moral debates.

The potentials and problems of the 1850s were not new. Their origins could be discerned in the first joint stock companies organized to develop the New World, and the first slave ships to take their cargoes to America in the early seventeenth century. The twin themes of machines and morality would become sharply delineated in the 1850s, but a full realization of the machine and a resolution of the moral dilemma would not be achieved.

As Webster proclaimed in 1850, Americans share a common heritage and love of nation. At the same time, then and now, they are separated by moral issues involving matters of war and peace, social justice, and the environment. The American economy remains the strongest in the world and further progress seems inevitable. The promise of the machine has been fulfilled, at least for a large majority of Americans. Yet the moral problem remains.

There are always temptations to see parallels between the present and the past, to draw conclusions for today by reviewing the events of yesterday. Some may see the nation as being in the midst of a replay of the 1850s, with material prosperity ever growing, while moral conflicts disturb the peace, with an inevitable conflict in the wings. Certainly there are similarities, many of them striking, and behind many public figures of today we may see the pale shadows of Abraham Lincoln, Stephen Douglas, James Buchanan, John Brown, and James Gordon Bennett. There are differences too, however, not only in degree, but in kind. The nation is stronger now than it was then, and the people less divided on the issues. Perhaps history does not repeat itself. Rather, the past is prelude, from which we can draw lessons to prevent mistakes and miscalculations that unnerved our ancestors. Finally, we can see in the past alternatives. Not all would be acceptable today, but they did exist, and were meaningful for the people of the 1850s. To understand the positions of Brown, Douglas, Lincoln, and Wise is not necessarily to accept them. Understanding is, after all, only the first step toward coming to conclusions. So it is that to understand them is, perhaps, to begin to understand ourselves. This is a primary reason for exploring the 1850s, and were it the only one, it would be worthwhile.

SELECTED BIBLIOGRAPHY

ABELS, JULES. *Man on Fire: John Brown and the Cause of Liberty.* New York, 1971.

"AN AMERICAN." *The Sons of the Sires: A History of the Rise, Progress, and Destiny of the American Party.* Philadelphia, 1855.

BAILEY, HUGH C. *Hinton Rowan Helper: Abolitionist-Racist.* University, Alabama, 1965.

BEALS, CARLETON. *Brass-Knuckle Crusade: The Great Know-Nothing Conspiracy, 1820-1860.* New York, 1960.

BELCHER, WYATT W. *The Economic Rivalry Between St. Louis and Chicago, 1850-1880.* New York, 1968.

BENSON, ADOLPH B., ed. *America of the Fifties: Letters of Fredrika Bremer.* New York, 1924.

BIDWELL, PERCY W., and FALCONER, JOHN I. *History of Agriculture in the Northern United States, 1620-1860.* New York, 1941.

BOLLES, ALBERT S. *Industrial History of the United States.* New York, 1881.

BOWDEN, WITT. *The Industrial History of the United States.* New York, 1930.

BLEYER, WILLARD G. *Main Currents in the History of American Journalism.* New York, 1927.

BREWERTON, G. DOUGLAS. *The War in Kansas.* New York, 1856.

BROOKS, VAN WYCK. *The Times of Melville and Whitman.* New York, 1947.

BROWN, FRANCIS. *Raymond of the Times.* New York, 1951.

CATTON, WILLIAM and BRUCE. *Two Roads to Sumter.* New York, 1963.

CLARK, VICTOR S. *History of Manufactures in the United States. Vol. I., 1607-1860.* New York, 1929.

CLOUGH, SHEPARD B. *A Century of American Life Insurance: A History of the Mutual Life Insurance Company of New York, 1843-1943.* New York, 1946.

COLE, ARTHUR C. *The Irrepressible Conflict, 1850-1865.* New York, 1934.

COLE, ARTHUR H. *The American Wool Manufacture.* 2 vols. Cambridge, 1926.

CONSIDINE, BOB. *Man Against Fire: Fire Insurance—Protection from Disaster.* New York, 1955.

CORLISS, CARLTON J. *Main Line of Mid-America: The Story of the Illinois Central.* New York, 1950.

CROFFUT, WILLIAM. *An American Procession, 1855-1914.* New York, 1931.

DAVIS, ELMER. *History of the New York Times, 1851-1921.* New York, 1921.

DE BOW, J. D. B. *The Industrial Resources, Statistics, Etc. of the United States.* 4 vols. New York, 1854.

DEWEY, DAVIS R. *Financial History of the United States.* New York, 1936.

DODDS, JOHN W. *The Age of Paradox: A Biography of England, 1841-1851.* London, 1953.

DONALD, DAVID. *Charles Sumner and the Rights of Man.* New York, 1970.

DUFOUR, CHARLES L. *Ten Flags in the Wind: The Story of Louisiana.* New York, 1967.

DUMOND, DWIGHT L. *Antislavery: The Crusade for Freedom in America.* Ann Arbor, 1961.

EATON, CLEMENT. *The Growth of Southern Civilization, 1790-1860.* New York, 1961.

FISHER, MARVIN. *Workshops in the Wilderness: The European Response to American Industrialization, 1830-1860.* New York, 1967.

FORSYTH, DAVID P. *The Business Press in America, 1750-1865.* New York, 1964.

FOULKE, ROY A. *The Sinews of American Commerce.* New York, 1941.

GALL, HENRY R., and JORDAN, WILLIAM G. *One Hundred Years of Fire Insurance, Being a History of the Aetna Insurance Company, 1819-1919.* Hartford, 1919.

GATES, PAUL W. *The Farmer's Age: Agriculture, 1815-1860.* New York, 1960.

———. *The Illinois Central Railroad and Its Colonization Work.* Cambridge, Mass., 1934.

GRAMLING, OLIVER. *AP: The Story of News.* New York, 1940.

GRAY, LEWIS C. *History of Agriculture in the Southern United States to 1860.* 2 vols. Washington, 1933.

GREELEY, HORACE. *Recollections of a Busy Life.* New York, 1868.

GRIMSTEAD, DAVID, ed. *Notions of the Americans: 1820-1860.* New York, 1970.

HALE, WILLIAM H. *Horace Greeley: Voice of the People.* New York, 1950.

HAYES, DORSHA B. *Chicago: Crossroads of an American Enterprise.* New York, 1944.

HELPER, HINTON R. *The Impending Crisis of the South: How to Meet It.* New York, 1860.

HOGAN, WILLIAM T. *Economic History of the Iron and Steel Industry in the United States.* 5 vols. Lexington, Mass., 1971.

HOLBROOK, STEWART H. *Machines of Plenty: Pioneering in American Agriculture.* New York, 1955.

———. *The Story of American Railroads.* New York, 1947.

HUDSON, FREDERIC. *Journalism in the United States from 1690 to 1872.* New York, 1873.

HUTCHINSON, WILLIAM T. *Cyrus Hall McCormick.* 2 vols. New York, 1968 ed.

JAMES, MARQUIS. *Biography of a Business: Insurance Company of North America, 1792-1942.* New York, 1942.

———. *The Metropolitan Life: A Study in Business Growth.* New York, 1947.

JOHNSON, ALLEN. *Stephen A. Douglas: A Study in American Politics.* New York, 1970.

LEE, JAMES M. *History of American Journalism.* New York, 1917.

LEE, JOHN H. *The Origins and Progress of the American Party in Politics.* New York, 1855.

LESLEY, J. P. *The Iron Manufacturers Guide to the Furnaces, Forges, and Rolling Mills of the United States.* New York, 1859.

MANUFACTURERS MUTUAL FIRE INSURANCE CO. *The Factory Mutuals, 1835-1935.* Providence, R.I., 1935.

MATTHIESSEN, F. O. *American Renaissance: Art and Expression in the Age of Emerson and Whitman.* New York, 1941.

MAYER, GEORGE H. *The Republican Party, 1854-1966.* New York, 1967.

MC CORMICK, CYRUS. *The Century of the Reaper.* Boston, 1931.

MC CURDY, FRANCES L. *Stump, Bar, and Pulpit: Speechmaking on the Missouri Frontier.* Columbia, Mo., 1969.

MC GINTY, GARNIE W. *A History of Louisiana.* New York, 1949.

MERING, JOHN V. *The Whig Party in Missouri.* Columbia, Mo., 1967.

MONAGHAN, JAY. *Civil War on the Western Border, 1854-1865.* Boston, 1955.

MOTT, FRANK L. *American Journalism: A History, 1690-1960.* New York, 1962.

———. *A History of American Magazines, 1850-1865.* Cambridge, Mass., 1957.

NAVIN, THOMAS R. *The Whitin Machine Works Since 1831: A Textile Company in an Industrial Village.* Cambridge, 1950.

NEVINS, ALLAN, ed. *The Diary of George Templeton Strong. Vol. 2, The Turbulent Fifties.* New York, 1952.

———, ed. *The Diary of Philip Hone, 1828-1851.* Vol. 2. New York, 1936.

———. *The Emergence of Lincoln, 1857-1861.* 2 vols. New York, 1950.

———. *The Evening Post: A Century of Journalism.* New York, 1922.

———. *Ordeal of the Union, 1847-1857.* New York, 1947.

NICHOLS, ALICE. *Bleeding Kansas.* New York, 1954.

NICHOLS, ROY F. *The Disruption of American Democracy.* New York, 1947.

OVERTON, RICHARD C. *Burlington Route: A History of the Burlington Lines.* New York, 1965.

PATTEE, FRED L. *The Feminine Fifties.* New York, 1940.

PAYNE, GEORGE H. *History of Journalism in the United States.* New York, 1920.

PEVSNER, NIKOLAUS. *High Victorian Design: A Study of the Exhibits of 1851.* London, 1951.

PIERCE, BESSIE L. *A History of Chicago.* 2 vols. New York, 1940.

REDLICH, FRITZ. *The Molding of American Banking: Men and Ideas.* New York, 1968 ed.

REDPATH, JAMES. *The Public Life of Capt. John Brown.* New York, 1970 ed.

ROGIN, LEO. *The Introduction of Farm Machinery in Its Relation to the Productivity of Labor in the Agriculture of the United States During the Nineteenth Century.* Berkeley, 1931.

ROSEWATER, VICTOR. *History of Cooperative News-Gathering in the United States.* New York, 1930.

RUCHAMES, LOUIS, ed. *John Brown: The Making of a Revolutionary.* New York, 1969.

SKIPPER, OTIS C. *J. D. B. De Bow: Magazinist of the Old South.* Athens, Ga., 1958.

STONE, CANDACE. *Dana and the Sun.* New York, 1938.

STOWE, HARRIET BEECHER. *Uncle Tom's Cabin; or, Life Among the Lowly.* New York, 1956 ed.

TAYLOR, GEORGE R. *The Transportation Revolution, 1815-1860.* New York, 1951.

TEBBEL, JOHN. *The Compact History of the American Newspaper.* New York, 1963.

VAN DEUSEN, GLYNDON G. *William Henry Seward.* New York, 1967.

WELLS, DAMON. *Stephen Douglas: The Last Years, 1857-1861.* Austin, 1971.

WHITNEY, THOMAS R. *A Defence of the American Policy.* New York, 1856.

WHITRIDGE, ARNOLD. *No Compromise: The Story of the Fanatics Who Paved the Way to the Civil War.* New York, 1960.

INDEX